FREEING THE GOOSE IN THE BOTTLE

Books by Debra Jan Bibel

MILESTONES IN IMMUNOLOGY: A HISTORICAL EXPLORATION

FREEING THE GOOSE IN THE BOTTLE: DISCOVERING ZEN
THROUGH SCIENCE, UNDERSTANDING SCIENCE THROUGH ZEN

Mind, Buddha, and things are not different.
Lotus Sutra

Mind is not Buddha.
Zen Master Nan-ch'uan

FREEING THE GOOSE IN THE BOTTLE

Discovering Zen through Science, Understanding Science through Zen

DEBRA JAN BIBEL

Foreword by John Daido Loori Sensei

ELIE METCHNIKOFF MEMORIAL LIBRARY
OAKLAND, CALIFORNIA

Published by the Elie Metchnikoff Memorial Library
230 Orange Street, 6, Oakland, California 94610-4139

Library of Congress Catalog Card Number: 92-97036

Freeing the goose in the bottle:
    Discovering Zen through science, understanding science through Zen /
    Debra Jan Bibel; with a foreword by John Daido Loori

ISBN 0-9634067-0-1

Calligraphy, illustrations, and cover design by D. J. Bibel.

Cover character is *Zen*

FIRST EDITION
Printed in the United States of America

To Sara as she charts her own course.

DOUBT

CONTENTS

PREFACE

Where are the scholars whose only schoolroom is a banyan tree? What has become of the scientist more concerned with the impact that the work of others has on him than with the impact that his work has on others?

Melvin Cohn

With increasing frequency, for it is a sure sign of aging, I reflect on my many years of undergraduate and graduate training and take pity on the science students of today, who have it even worse. They must endure greater socioeconomic pressures of a rapid completion of the curriculum and fulfill the academic requirements of swallowing libraries of scientific knowledge and developing the related laboratory skills all for the reward of magical job-qualifying diplomas. Such a burden leaves little time for the budding scientist to explore other fields. This is unforunate because there is much more to science than its institutions, databases, and practices. Also, there is much more to life than science.

The educational system here in the United States and in much of the Western world has a long-standing significant flaw. In his astonishingly frank autobiography, François Jacob expressed it superbly, observing that his schooling suffered the persistent malady of compartmentalization:[1]

There was neither connection nor synthesis between the disciplines. To prepare for an undergraduate degree was like touring an archipelago where, on each island, an archpriest preached strictly for his own chapel. The idea never occurred to one of going beyond his boundaries, of showing us that the world is a whole, that life is a composite of many things. Each subject remained a closed system. It was up to the students to set about constructing their little universe and finding in it some coherence.

Most of my comrades and I were unable to find that uniting thread, and instead, during the turbulent but exciting period of social growth and cultural revolution, the decade circa 1964 to 1975, we deliberately cut our connections to tradition and dogma. Our holistic education came from the theater of the street, which occasionally spilled across the marked borders of the university. Over the ensuing years, the alternative perspective has served us well, giving us balance and direction. For the generation of today, this happy circumstance is absent.

Our psychedelic student experiences have colored our science. John Ziman, a sociologist of science, believes that[2]

> [S]cientists are free to choose from the set of scientifically tenable theories the one that accords best with their nonscientific preoccupations. Such preoccupations may be idio-syncratic and unself-conscious, but they are most likely to derive from the social context in which the research is carried out. Thus, any body of scientific knowledge may contain a significant component that is socially determined, and hence relative to the particular social group that has created this knowledge.

I plead guilty, since I interpret laboratory data, be it my own research or that of others, from the standpoint of holistic philosophy and process metaphysics.

Moreover, when I read someone's grand conclusions on nature, I gauge the insight from profound personal experiences. It was not always this way. Science behaves indifferently to its historical roots and its economic, political, psychological, and philosophical underpinnings. Like all my fellow students in immunology and medical microbiology who earned the doctorate in philosophy (Ph.D.), I regretably did not enroll in any course in philosophy, making a mockery of the words on the certificate and an affront to all the nature philosophers of the nineteenth century. It certainly would have helped my understanding of chemistry. However, the cloud of guilt I felt then was an isolated puff, and the urgency of vocation along with major breakthroughs in immunochemistry and infectious disease took me elsewhere.

The fundamental difficulty in recognizing the humanities within science and the sciences within social disciplines is the

Cartesian legacy of reductionism, the philosophical process of linking phenomena to singular causes. The isolation inherent in accepting the concept that parts dictate the behavior of the whole has justified compartmentalization. Years ago, it was easy, for example, to be blind to the relationship of a course in Middle Eastern studies and one in chemistry, and thus remain ignorant of the Golden Age of Islam during which classical Greek science and medicine were preserved and enlarged while Europe was lost in the Dark Ages. Even within the sciences, courses in zoology never linked phenomena back to the fundamental principles learned in physics classes. However, the times they were a-changin'. One of the outgrowths of the counterculture was the environmental movement and the blossoming of the holistic ecological sciences.

I have remained an academic hippie confronting reductionism in science through my investigations of the microbial ecology of human skin, a field I was obliged to enter and help develop on commencing active military service during the Vietnam War. My early experimental probes into the complex network of interactions among colonizing microorganisms, host-derived agents, and environmental physical and chemical factors began to fashion my new world view. Tentative connections to other fields were soon strengthened.

My graduate degree is in immunology, which most scholars and researchers regard as the science of self and nonself discrimination. Because of this philosophically rich interpretation, immunology stands out among the sciences; I have challenged this dualistic concept within the framework of history and broadly sketched an ecological and holistic alternative.[3] Two other dormant seeds of the 1960s, Eastern religiophilosophy and noetic science, germinated a decade later and have profoundly reinforced my scientific understandings. Peter Medawar described the varied approaches of scientists: 'Among scientists are collectors, classifiers and compulsive tidiers-up; many are detectives by temperament and many are explorers; some are artists and others artisans. There are poet-scientists and philosopher-scientists and even a few mystics.'[4] I freely admit that I am of the last cluster.

The writing of this book, therefore, fulfilled three personal needs. Primarily, it provided a belated opportunity to draw a philosophical thread — more like a guy line — through the various scientific and noetic disciplines. This perpective of phenomena, while comfortable and, I believe, plausible, must be considered as tentative; after all, thinking and its myriad concepts can never provide a complete description of nature. Moreover, how can skeletal words convey the flesh of even simple feelings? I fully expect to revise the perspective several times over the next decades as science provides new evidence and assuredly new problems and as my meditative and laboratory research practices further ripen.

Secondly, I have taken advantage of the freedom and style of popular science to develop some of the ideas in my earlier opus without being encumbered by the chains of pseudo objectivity, rigid formality, and lifelessness that characterize academic literature, including my own contributions. Because this book is a personal synthesis concerning the nature of self, this scientist will openly present her own views and experiences with the first person singular, I. Those who read scientific journals are aware that 'I' is ostracized from even one-author articles, as if the research were planned, carried out, and interpreted by itself!

Lest those defenders of the scientific method with arched eyebrows of indignation accuse me of nearly traitorous remarks, they should recognize that objectivity exists only in the automatic measurement, the recording, and the computation of data. While statistical analysis is objective, the choice of statistical tests—with its hazards—is often personal. Interpretation is clearly subjective, and the very design of an experiment is prejudicial by excluding many contributing agents of phenomena or by selecting behavior. What occurs isolated in the test tube is not always what is found in the natural entire system. An experiment designed to detect the wave-like behavior of matter will not permit its particle-like behavior, which is observed under different conditions. Furthermore, a particular world view will restrict test parameters and interpretations. The role of consciousness-mind and subconsciousness-mind in regulating or even in inducing phenomena is usually either ignored for simplicity or simply denied. Hence, the limits of science rest not in science but in the paradigm of reality by which it is conducted.

As for style, although one would never know it by the drab minimalism of scientific papers, designing, performing, and discussing experiments can be fun. The enjoyment that I feel in being a scientist can be and, in fact, needs to be conveyed by an open, less rigorous style. Finally, this book allows me to offer the readership, both public and peer, a penetrating East-West approach to personal growth and self-discovery. Along this unique path, the reader will encounter a challenging interpretation of various established and competing formative models, a scientific philosophy that rides the mystic curl of the breaking new wave, a philosophy that is ancient for some.

Because this book is directed chiefly at the nonprofessional and the generalist, one who is familiar with at least basic scientific terms, I have endeavored to select references that would be available in most public libraries. These include the journals *Science* and *Scientific American.* I prefer the short reviews and research news sections in *Science* for illustrating the spark and lively controversies of scientific investigations over the commissioned articles in *Scientific American,* written by researchers in particular fields who outline their key experimental methods and present their personal interpretations of the evidence.

I acknowledge the criticism and assistance of my brother, Bennett Bibel, whose lively, rigorous discussions about his multidisciplinary studies have served me over these many years as guideposts on my own journey. I thank Ed Morse for organizing through the Institute of Noetic Sciences an informal new paradigm inquiry group; the series of pleasurably animated exchanges helped glue together some of my very disjointed ideas. To Willis Harman, President of the Institute of Noetic Sciences, I offer my appreciation of being included in the Consciousness Research Circle. I further bow in gratitude to Korean Zen Master Seung Sahn, Kwan Um School of Zen and the folks of Empty Gate Zen Center, Berkeley, California, for providing the Eastern focus and framework of disciplined introspection and life direction for over ten years. I owe my small skill in Chinese calligraphy to the instruction and patience of Kazuaki Tanahashi. I am honored in having John Daido Loori Sensei, abbot of Zen

Mountain Monastery, Mount Tremper, New York, provide the Foreword with his insight as photographic artist and former research chemist. To Patti Weissman goes my regard for her talents in rooting out grammatical evils. No words can do justice to the love and respect I feel for my father, Philip Bibel, a guardian of the intellectual path of history, culture, and ethics, who continues to support my varied and challenging pursuits, and for my mother, Bassya Bibel, a master of energy and will, who brought drama and a sense of mystery to our lives.

FOREWORD

As we move towards the twenty-first century, it becomes increasingly clear that we have reached a critical point in the evolution of human history—a time that may decide the fate of both our species and our planet. On the one hand, we possess knowledge and capacities hardly dreamt of only decades ago, yet on the other hand, millions starve, our environment is polluted, the earth's natural resources are being plundered, and the specter of nuclear war continues to threaten our extinction. In spite of an immense databank of information regarding the intimate workings of everything from sub-atomic particles to the vast reaches of outer space, we have barely begun to scratch the surface of understanding human existence itself.

Our way of perceiving ourselves and the universe has remained virtually static throughout human history: a dualistic view based on the separation of self and other. As a result, all of our philosophy, art, science, medicine, ecology, theology, psychology, politics, sociology, ethics—every field of human endeavor—is also dualistic. From this perception of the universe certain consequences inevitably follow, as is evident throughout the globe. For the first time in human history all of the great potential disasters that we face are not the classical natural disasters of history: the plague, pestilence, earthquakes, and floods but rather the self-inflicted wounds of the human inhabitants of this planet. Our dualistic separation of science and spirituality has created potentially lethal consequences.

Only recently in the West have we become aware of the existence of an entirely different understanding of the nature of reality. The origins of the alternative world view begin in an ancient Buddhist text called *The Flower Garland Scripture,* which describes a universe in which everything interpenetrates everything else, in identity and causal interdependence; where everything needs everything else and there is not a single speck of dust that does not affect the whole. Here existence, described as the *Diamond Net of Indra*, is seen as a vast net that extends through out the entire universe—not only the three dimensions but in the fourth dimension of time as well. Each nodal point of this huge net contains a multi-faceted diamond which reflects every other diamond and, as such, 'contains' every other diamond in the net. The diamonds represent everything in the entire universe, past, present, and future: every particle, every atom, every thing, every form. Since the surface of each diamond reflects every other diamond, and since each and every diamond in the net is undergoing the same reflective process, every diamond, everything in the entire universe, contains every other thing.

This Diamond Net of Indra is not only an interesting philo-sophical viewpoint, it is also the direct and intimate experi-ence of hundreds of generations of Buddhist men and women, realized through personal practice and verification. Never-theless, for centuries this view of reality was regarded by most non-Buddhist practitioners as a quaint metaphor for a fanciful and barely comprehensible Buddhist belief system. Lacking a common framework for understanding the very basis of reality, science and spirituality seemed hopelessly divided. Then, in the latter part of the twentieth century, the discovery of laser light led to the development of a new method of perceiving and recording images: the *hologram*.

Holograms are created by using laser light to illuminate a subject, producing a photographic plate containing interfer-ence patterns. When laser light is projected back through this photographic plate, the result is a three dimensional image rather than the usual two dimensional image of a projected photograph. Viewing such holographic images is a marvelous experience, and a variety of types and sizes can be seen in museums throughout the world. What is even more remarkably is that fact that one can cut the entire photographic plate in half, project through only half of it, and still produce the entire image—no part of it is missing. Further, the half can be cut again into quarters and projected to produce the whole image, and so on down to the smallest fragments of the film. Each fragment, when laser light is passed through it, will project the totality of the original image. The image becomes progressively dimmer with each division, but all the information is still present.

Thus, 'holographic reality' can be recognized as much more than metaphor. Every part of a piece of holographic film literally contains all of the information of the totality, just as in the Diamond Net of Indra, each diamond, each thing in the universe, contains every other thing and is totally interpenetrated with it, mutually arising, mutually caused. You cannot affect the smallest part of the great net of existence without affecting every aspect of it.

Moreover, the discovery of holographic images is only one of a series of modern scientific advances that reveal the limitations of a dualistic and mechanistic world view. With the help of the sophisticated instrumentation of modern physics and chemistry, we have begun to observe the properties of the subatomic world, the world beyond the senses. As we have penetrated deeper into the nature of these phenomena, scientists have found that they have had to abandon more and more of their ordinary, classical understandings, images, and concepts. Paradoxes began to arise, and each time science went deeper into the paradoxes, more paradoxes resulted, producing an array of questions that were very much like Zen koans, those apparently paradoxical inquiries that baffle the ordinary, rational mind. A paradigm shift began to occur between the old static explanatory system of Western science and theology and the dynamic, process-oriented explanatory systems of modern science and Eastern philosophy and religion.

It is here that the two paradigms of religion and science merge. In my early years as a research scientist I found myself probing molecular structure and chemical reaction mechanisms, researching the origins of life. I was constantly searching for answers to the question of the nature of reality, indeed of existence itself. But these, too, are the questions that every religion must address. What is life? What is death? What is the self? What is God, truth, reality? Who am I? Yet neither classical science nor religion provided satisfactory answers. The mind was stuck, entangled in the web of dualities. The goose had grown and was unable to leave the bottle. Thus I found myself at a place that would have been inconceivable years earlier—taking the backward step, and beginning the quiet introspection of solitary sitting. I like many of my contemporaries, found myself ready to fully engage the process of 'freeing the goose in the bottle.' Doctor Bibel encourages all of us in this ongoing process. In this work she has fashioned an exciting tapestry that takes up the challenge of weaving together threads from the forefront of both modern science and religion. Drawing from her experience as scientist and Zen practitioner, she provides the reader with a virtual treasury of facts, information, and personal insight. Her imaginative lines of inquiry should nourish the new generation of twenty-first century scientists and theologians and perhaps heal the gaps that have separated these two traditions for much too long. As Zen master Dogen Zenji observed over 700 years ago, 'Those who regard the secular as separate from the sacred only understand that in the secular, nothing is sacred. What they have not as yet understood is that in sacredness, nothing is secular.'

August 14, 1992
Tremper Mountain, New York
John Daido Loori, M.R.O.
Abbot , Zen Mountain Monastery

Chapter 1

INTO THE ABYSS

Introduction/Overview

Man: Hello, my boy. And what is your dog's name?
Boy: I don't know. We call him Rover.

Stafford Beer

What are you? This is hardly a simple question. It is one of the great imponderables that has haunted sages and mystic explorers since the prehistorical beginnings of civilization. Arising with self-awareness and thought, it is a question that we all ask ourselves in the boiling crucible of adolescence, during the seemingly inevitable mid-life crisis, and throughout the reflective waning days of old age. It is an acutely significant enigma, a labyrinth obscured by painful shadows, faced by those with lethal diseases at the prime of their life. Indeed, it is the unexpectedness of the query, What?, rather than the Who? of Lewis Carroll's Wonderland caterpillar, that uncomfortably probes down beyond the superficial realm of conceptual phenomena. When asked this question, we become speechless and empty of thought. We then search for a peg on which to hang our opinions, but all are unsatisfyingly short. We are much more than the names our parents gave us, more than the biological cluster, *Homo sapiens*, into which taxonomists classify us.

We say that we are persons. However, as John Donne wisely observed in what has become an adage, no person is an is an island entire of itself. Is this sentiment self-contradictory? *Person* is a psychologically charged word. It is derived from the Etruscan term for the masks worn by characters in a drama that convey exaggerated emotions and social status. Such masks contained a built-in megaphone to project the particular character's voice. (In bold contrast and of philosophical significance, many of the masks used in Japanese Noh theater are emotionally neutral; character is derived from body movement and relationships with others on the stage. Spoken words are few, and they are mainly recited by a narrating chorus.) We are not singular in character; we play numerous roles everyday — loving parent, competitive worker, loyal friend — and our moods can rapidly change with each new situation. Sometimes we are warriors, sometimes we are priests, we can find ourselves as physicians, engineers, or creative artists, and occasionally we are merely rapt children. Even the most cursory self-investigation will offer the insight of the importance and the psychobiological merits of relationships and actions. Thus, the person is the manifested human. Each of us wears many masks; our personas are legion.

Donne was referring to our need for society, echoing Artistole's view that humans are by nature political creatures. Our internal, private aspect was the focus. Therefore, would not the synonym *individual* have been more appropriate? This general term, which can be applied to any form, living or inorganic, conveys—besides the limit of reduction— distinctness, completeness, and separation from similar things. We easily proclaim our individuality. We feel unique, self-contained, and apart. Reverend Donne's comment would then be nonsensical had he said that no individual is an isolated island. Or would it?

We are not static entities. We are not merely the unique biochemical arrangements of flesh and bone implicit in the stuff of genes, the unique sequences of DNA. We grow; we deteriorate. Perhaps you recently found a new facial wrinkle, gained or lost weight, or needed to alter your eyeglass prescription. If not stable in structure, neither are we unalterable or singular in mental patterns. Education, social experiences, and other forms of conditioning shape our self image; yet even here, such characteristics are ever changing. Are we the same individual we were ten years ago? Ten months ago? Ten seconds ago? We like to think that increased knowledge and wisdom compensates for the atrophy of body concomitant with aging. But the unstifled laughters and innocent, unguarded smiles of childhood soon leave us. We quickly forget the joy and magic of a seeded dandelion in the wind.

When we use the first person pronouns—I, me, and my—the reference is actually to ego and its crucial components of memory and projection. We feel and believe that we are individuals because of ego. By saying 'my arm aches', we separate ego from the physical world, the body, which becomes a possessed object. This split is reinforced when a limb is lost or a kidney is donated. We are no less a person or individual by the absence of the organ, nor are we more by having our organ in someone else's body or someone else's organ in ours. An even more absurd separation is implied when referring to one's mind: an upstart component claiming independence and superiority to the whole.

However, self and self-awareness are neither things nor constant or continual abstractions. The absorption of passively watching an exciting movie, of performing a creative act, or of sitting in deep meditation is not compatible with self constructs. Self-image is the result of intellectual activity. You need to think about yourself to create your self. Memory must be consulted to provide reference points, to draw the thread from childhood to the present moment. Without memory, there would be no ego, no thought, no coordinated muscular action, and no learning. Psychologists have long studied the origins, development, and structure—the separation—of ego and object as early as in infancy. Ego may be a mirage, but it has qualities. Ego can be stroked, bruised, and even inflated.

A classic incident attributed to Bodhidharma, the legendary Indian founder and First Patriarch of Chinese Zen, serves well here. The disciple Hui-k'o begged the master to pacify his troubled mind. The master replied, 'Bring me your mind so that I may pacify it.' Hui-k'o, taken aback, stated that he could not. 'There! I have pacified it,' laughed Bodhidharma.[1]

Hence, while the feeling or sense of individuality is real, self is a jovial illusion and sometimes a hazardous delusion of consciousness-mind. Still, you may protest, the street is full of clearly different human beings. Some are obese, some are slim. There are tall, old, brown-haired men as well as petite, young, blond women. In this amazing era of medical engineering, we are familiar with the immunological distinction of each person's tissues and the requirement of approximate matches for successful organ transplantation. Furthermore, we all differ in intelligence, in work and recreational interests, in musical and artistic talents, and in behavior. Surely, you may insist, such diverse people must be unique individuals, unique selves, even if their self image is discontinuous and always in revision.

Generally, such views would be correct, but only to the extent of common perception and only if you also ignore the following variety of exceptions, which will be discussed in the chapters to follow. Twins not only have nearly identical appearances, they think much alike, and seem to have some intersibling telepathic ability.[2] Autoimmune disease challenges the old view that the purpose of the immune response is to defend against foreign or aberrant matter, such as microorganisms and cancer cells.[3] Two psychologically anomalous groups, people with multiple personality disorder and those who are under hypnotic suggestion, have the extraordinary capacity to initiate or arrest the inflammatory aspects of the immune response and to regulate other physiological characteristics once thought to be involuntary.[4,5] To a varying extent, we all have these powers, latent but realizable with training in biofeedback or meditation. A profoundly significant development in science has been the recent colloboration of psychologists and medical laboratory scientists in such paradigm breaking investigations. Research has demonstrated the linkage of the endocrine, nervous, and immune systems with the intangible consciousness-mind and awareness-mind. Then there is the fabulous puzzle of the mother immunologically tolerating a fetus in her womb: two individuals exchanging metabolic molecules and occasional cells through adjacent blood vessels.[6]

Probing deep into the biology of humans, you would further discover that the human organism is not the singular independent object that you had assumed. The very term *organism* refers to a synergistic, holistic system of mutually dependent parts, some of which are organisms in their own right. Furthermore, governments and societies are also organisms of which we are components. Even our entire planet Earth (or Ocean, as science-fiction author Arthur C.

Clarke recommended) may function as an organism, according to the daring hypothesis proposed and developed by James Lovelock and Lynn Margulis.[7,8]

This brief introduction and overview may be inducing some uneasiness and doubts in your world view. I certainly hope so. It is my goal to stimulate. I will have failed if by the end of the book you have not reconsidered several cherished notions about self, the cosmos, and God, rejecting or adopting as you will some of the presented concepts. James Gleick's delightful and ingenious metaphor of frustration deserves to be applied to the quest for a definition or, at least, general understanding of the true self: 'It is like walking through a maze whose walls rearrange themselves with each step you take.'[9]

Whenever we read some passage from a religious or mystical philosopher trumpeting, 'You are the world' or some such grandiose conclusion, we smile utterly unconvinced. These are empty words, void of any teaching merit, hollow in compassion, lacking in foundation. In this age of science, we are, or should be, skeptics questioning authority whether it be politicians, physicians, priests, or scientists. We want all the facts so that we can reach our own conclusions, but some information is hidden from us by edict or by its complexity. There is also information we hide from ourselves. Even after recognizing our common inescapable cultural conditioning and subsequently fashioning a new world view, we must strive to incorporate it in our conduct, leading lives of wisdom, not merely of knowledge.

I should warn right from the start that no final answers will be or can be provided. This book will not open the locked cabinet of truth, but will offer some tools for you to fashion the key. The primary and Western approach will echo the Hindu method of perpetual elimination, *neti, neti* —not this, not that. If intellectual satisfaction is desired, the reader must seek it in the intrinsic pregnant silence separating the lines of text. The Eastern approach will then utilize that silence, the wellspring known to poets, artists, and occasionally scientists.

Indeed, is intellectual satisfaction truly possible? Scientists and philosophers are certain that their noble quests will never be fulfilled, that they will always have one more experiment, one more grand synthesis to complete. It is within religion, so clerics claim, that the emptiness or longing in the depths of our consciousness-mind, the driving force of questioning intellect, can at last find rest. However, it is the experiential and transcendent core of all religions that frees, not their tenets and practices. Even then, such rest is of enhanced satisfaction through attainments of larger truths; questions and doubts within the world of differentiation remain.

The phenomena but ultimate fiction of self and individuality is the focus of this book. However, instead of simply summarizing the often and well-described psychological and cognitive aspects, the major discussion will center on the quasi-objective realm of matter and physical nature. The more dramatic or exemplary scientific evidence from a wide variety of disciplines, including the latest results and concepts, will be surveyed. Indeed, through this worthy 'popular science' aspect of the book, the reader may acquire a feeling of the scientific enterprise. More important, the various findings will be integrated in the hope of demonstrating that we are not discrete objects but, rather, multi-tiered psychological, biological, and environmental systems of process both within and underlying four-dimensional space-time.

From this perspective, external and internal conditions and structures, including those of consciousness-mind, are operatively inseparable. The composition of each human being is much like a community or network, and the present state of this organism can not be isolated from its history (and also its future). The very notion of life and death is questioned. Also, the duality of matter and mind, cast aside as obsolete and false, is replaced with a hypothesis of identicalness through interpenetration and mutually dependent processes, as symbolized by the T'ai-chi T'u, 'The Diagram of the Supreme Ultimate', the dynamic circle of yin-yang. These notions are neither novel nor wholly unorthodox, yet they are vigorously resisted by many and ignored by most. Other scientific writers have already presented some of this information, with emphasis in their own specialty, and have reached similar conclusions.[10-12]

Are any ideas truly original? A body of experiments nearly always provide a foundation of exceptions and anomalies on which to construct the next hypothesis. This continuum was wisely appreciated by Francis Crews in his often paraphrased statement,[13]

A few of the results of my activities as a scientist have become embedded in the very texture of the science I tried to serve—this is the immortality that every scientist hopes for...I find great pleasure in the thought that those who stand on my shoulders will see much further than I did in my time. What more could any man want?

At times a modest modification of the experimental design within the reigning theory is called for, but at other times, when facing particularly awkward data, an experienced researcher may reach into the archives or across to different disciplines for less familiar information to inspire a new explanatory framework. Usually, this investigator awakening and nurturing the dormant seed some years, some centuries old, becomes associated with a ripe radical thought. Louis Pasteur expressed this before with a metaphor suitable for Halloween:[14]

Science is the graveyard of ideas. But some ideas that seem dead and buried may at one time or another rise up to life again more vital than ever.

All endeavors, not only science, can advance in this fashion. Each generation, it seems, must rediscover the essences for itself, and within its own context use the debris of the past to erect a new ediface of novel design. While science and technology never look back as they skim along the surface of phenomena, the humanities, finding that surface curved, take the circle or helix as their symbol.

We are in the midst of a profound cultural change in Western metaphysics and philosophy of science, popularly termed a paradigm shift after Thomas Kuhn's seminal proposal.[15,16] Although this development is virtually forced on us by experimental and theoretical science, Greek, Indian, and Chinese philosophers had long ago meditated and speculated on such holistic concepts. An anonymous scholar once wisely observed:

> In the East, look deep into your Self and discover Nature.
> In the West, look deep into Nature and discover your Self.

There are three ways of accommodating Western scientific knowledge systems with traditional structures and taxonomies derived from Eastern transpersonal experiences. The first is exemplified by B. Alan Wallace, who summarized the 'essential philosophical question' as whether 'scientific theories represent and make intelligible the natural world as it exists independent of human experience, or...they serve only as instruments for organizing and predicting natural phenomena that are part of our experience.'[17] Dissatisfied with the two choices, he attempts a central position in which the two systems of knowledge are equally valid and complementary but forever separate. This is intellectual surrender. The stand also tends to equate the transpersonal and deep meditative experiences with their descriptions. Unfortunately, while such attainments may be alike among peoples, the implications are only coarsely similar, varying in detail by particular social and religious backgrounds.

The second approach is for the mystic to bring scientific concepts into the interpretation of the experience. To a certain extent, the Asian religions did so at the time of their institutionalization, which means that from our present-day perspective their physical and biological sciences are crude and largely obsolete. However, their psychological systems are exceedingly advanced. Indeed, the various psychological training programs involving master guides, student autoexperimentation, and testing are superb examples of empirical science. Furthermore, we are now appreciating the merits of their metaphysics and medical intuitions.

In early human tribal society, the scientist-philosopher was also the priest and sometimes also the shaman-healer. With the evolution and expansion of civilization, the development of scientific tools and methods, and the accumulation of challenging scientific knowledge, the scientist-philosopher diverged from those practicing the religious and medical arts and often took an antagonistic position. Later, the physician-scientist arose to compete with the priest-healer. Scientists transformed their role from the development of useful models to the discovery of universal truths. If the mystic did not incorporate new scientific knowledge and philosophy, the scientist would ignore or ridicule the untestable and unobservable (never putting the onus on the temporary inadequacy of tools and methods). If the transcendent experience and the so-called paranormal had no place in science, the mystic had no reason to adopt scientific views of reality. Albert Einstein lamented this schism succinctly:[18]

Science without religion is lame,
religion without science is blind.

Now, at the threshold of a new century and through noetic science (*noetic* refers to mind), the priest, the scientist-philosopher, and the physician-scientist are striving for a reconciliation or synthesis, a 'reenchantment of science'.[19,20] Note that it is science that is opening to mysticism. Most religions have already accepted the sciences as institutions that discover, describe, utilize, and alter natural behavior. However, the underlying standard scientific philosophy is rejected as delusion. By the mid twentieth century, the mounting paradoxes, the weirdness of subatomic behavior, and the fusions of once parted scientific disciplines had impelled even the most practical researchers into philosophical thought, philosophies that bear strong resemblance to those of the mystic.[21,22] Today the world, increasingly more a global village, allows a dedicated student with either Western or Eastern training to follow both paths, seeking their union, or at least intersections.

Contact with radically different cultures typically effects the arts and philosophies of both social groups. Syntheses from East-West interactions have a long history. Neo-Platoists in 250 B.C.E. were influenced by Buddhist missionaries sent from India to the Greek domains in Syria, Cyrenaica (Libya), Macedonia, Epirus (Albania), and Egypt.[23] Last century, the vivid hues, solids, and outlines seen in imported Japanese prints triggered the artistic explorations and development of

Impressionalism in Europe; Vincent van Gogh paid homage to the Eastern eye by painting himself as a Buddhist monk.[24] Modern abstractionists found a compatible language in Buddhism and Vedanta, and the psychological concepts of Carl G. Jung owe much to Hindu thought.[25] The great theoretical and nuclear physicists, including Niels Bohr, Werner Heisenberg, and Erwin Schrödinger, were to a modest degree also familiar with Asian philosophy. The dialogue continues, especially in psychology and medical science.[26]

Is the goal of joining Eastern mysticism and Western science possible? Larry Dossey, a physician, warns 'not to homogenize science and religion, for nothing would be more disastrous. Rather, we must insist that science and religion stand side by side, respecting the domain of the other, and give up the incessant battle to usurp each other's territory.' [27] However, homogenization is the extreme case, which no one advocates and which is unworkable, anyway. Also, the separation should be restricted to the clearly incompatible institutions of science and religion, not the practice. In fact, segregation is not possible, since there is science in mystic practices and articles of faith in science. Dossey further observes, 'The differences between science and religion are just as important as any convergences that may exist, and must be maintained.'[27] I certainly agree here, but convergences there are!

Being such a long-term practitioner of both science and Zen Buddhism, I shall, in these discussions, be referring to both philosophical arts, the introspective experiment, and especially the more familiar external assay of the laboratory. There are many paths to the center, and science, as jñana yoga, is a perfectly good approach. Nature is the guru. But the scientist must also be an epistemologist, philosopher, and historian, going deep and wide to discover the general in the specific, the particular in the whole. Fritjof Capra, reknown for his most influential book, *Tao of Physics*, was asked at the end of a seminar whether he practiced meditation. He replied that he often sits six to eight hours a day. After waiting a moment for his young questioner to be duly impressed, he continued that he sits at the typewriter composing.

Anyone who, in the midst of writing, pauses to consider how words pop out, how thoughts and associations arise seemingly by magic, is practicing. Indeed, 100% concentration on a task is itself an effective noetic technique. Anyone who is dissatisfied by only *knowing*, anyone who has a gnawing distrust in concepts—even though or because it is one's stock and trade—and anyone who yearns deeply for the experience of true essence that supersedes thought has become a noetic explorer of the mystic ocean. Such a mythic hero searches behind the rites and tenets of religion and seeks the absolute foundation of phenomena and of corresponding scientific principles.

Whether meditations be the direct and powerful traditional, nearly ritualistic forms of mindfulness and zazen or the less effective, casual yet intense Western forms of athletic concentration and the creative arts, all sessions begin with a question. An early step in Zen training is the master's instillation of doubt (meaning here the wonder and thirst of inquiry) to a solvable problem that defies common rational thought. *Thus, philosophy is the retaining pin that penetrates and joins science and interpretative religion, and the transcendent experience is the origin and culmination of all three.*

Many of the more credible so-called New Age books superficially mention scientific evidence and concepts, often inappropriate quotations from distinguished or usually presenting broad summations and trying to impress the reader with extensive hodgepodge volleys of popular scientists. Directed toward the already converted, the scientific, information is reassuring. However, the skeptic is unconvinced by the shallow scientific aspects and, if a scholar, recognizes the philosophical conflicts among the quotations; at best, the ardor and scope of the posed psychological questions may be alluring.

Certain other books seem to be divided into two parts, with an initial sketch of novel science followed by a discourse on the equally structured categories and inferences of mind in, for instance, Tibetan Buddhism. These offerings perpetuate the schism.

Books of popular science with mystical bents are, of course, excellent in presenting scientific evidence, but the

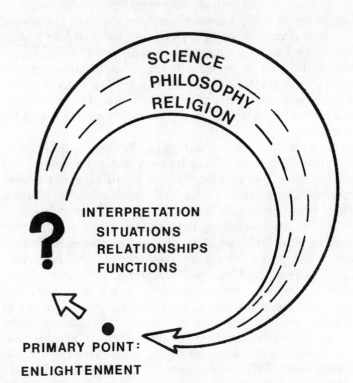

THE GRAND CIRCLE: Approaches united in the spiritual quest of individual and civilization.

mere quotations of the perennial philosophers do little to convey—no—induce an appreciation of the transcendent. Furthermore, these books center on a particular science, typically quantum physics. Theoretical physicists certainly ushered in the revolutionary new philosophy, but there is much happening in the other sciences, as well. This cascade is becoming more important, because it demonstrates the efficacy of the concepts beyond physics and heralds forthcoming changes in society and culture.

My approach to East-West harmonization is different. I am attempting a grand synthesis; my tactic is a pincer maneuver. This book covers the major sciencific disciplines: yes, physics, but also chemistry, cosmology, biochemistry, molecular biology, evolution and development, organismal biology, ecology, immunology, and psychoneuroscience. As in the common view of evolution of elementary matter to thinking biological organisms, each chapter will build on the previous. In addition to reviewing some fundamentals (even scientists can feel a little rusty), I will offer specific experimental results and their resonances across the entire scientific landscape in the hope that they will lead the reader to new philosophical insights.

Simultaneously, strategically placed questions, tales, haiku poetry, and Zen koans (kong-ans in Korean)—effective 1,000-year-old psychological tools—will in some manner relate to the particular scientific and philosophical topic. A Zen Master once warned that adding Buddhism to Zen is like putting legs on a snake. Zen, which is a synthesis of psycho-philosophical Indian Buddhism and practical nature-rooted Chinese Taoism, shies away from the named forms and structures given in sutras, and, indeed, eschews explanations whenever possible. Although a specific literature has long been accumulating, Zen itself and its attainment is, like love and nausea, far beyond verbal description and communication. It is the intellectual but nonscholastic wing of Buddhism. With its emphasis on action, epitomized by the phrase *Just do it!*, perhaps that form of expression known as Performance Art best approaches the Zen style.

The emphasis in Zen training is given to inducing in the confounded but still ardent student the direct and sudden understanding of what can not be explained. It is mysticism only to the extent that it breaks through the walls of conception and mystery we unconsciously construct as we become mature adults. Imagine the spontaneous, uninhibited, and often witty here-and-now mind of a young child having the wisdom, compassion, and life experience of its grandparent. Such an unusual combination is the manifested working mind of a great Zen Master. Sometimes the key that unlocks all barriers to the student's own attainment is the Master's skillful shout (tradtionally, *KATZ!*), sometimes it is the sight of the moon or a star, and often it is a turning word (an opportune meaningful phrase or comment).

Therefore, readers who squeeze these pincers of thinking and a-thinking could very well find themselves atop a 100-foot pole* with no way down, except by letting go, and in doing so, attain the relationships of self, others, and the universe. At the least, the reader will appreciate that 'mystic scientist' is not an oxymoron.

---

*By Buddhist tradition, *atop a 100 -foot pole* is the attainment of utter thoughtlessness-emptiness that encompasses equivalence and nondifferentiation. It is the awakening that explodes all the myriad dualities of phenomena — even life-and-death and defect-and-purity—as well as the separation of bird, cloud, and tree. However, this fearless oceanic wholeness, a magic sea of potentia, is a mud that entraps. Where the cosmos is process, it is stasis. Enlightenment is incomplete until put into action. The student must bring the wisdom of this attainment into the common world of forms by descending the spiritual mountain, by jumping off the pole.

DEFINITION

Definitions

I am fascinated with the poetic and artistic qualities of the Chinese language. While English, Latin, and especially German tend to be precise, detailed, and open, Chinese is contextual and deeply philosophical. It is unfixed. There is no set of rules for grammar. No isolated Chinese character or word denotes gender, number or case, voice, mood, tense, or person. For example, a phrase consisting of the characters for *horse*, *man*, and *lead* could refer to a man leading a horse as well as to the horse that had led the man; a single character composed of *man*, *horse*, and *permit* is the clever word meaning horseman. The Chinese say 'black horse' and do not and can not say 'the horse is black.' That would imply a static or permanent condition, which is contrary to their philosophies. Chinese is a concise language that supports and, indeed, requires a degree of intuition. It is a classic case for metalinguists.

Differences with Western languages go beyond syntax and root structures. European writing is done with a confining pen; East Asians use the less inhibited brush. Uniformity and precision is the mark of high quality in Western calligraphy; Chinese, Koreans, and Japanese value the controlled accident, the abstraction, and the dance of line. Thus, Chinese calligraphy, like that of Arabic, is a feast for the eyes; it is a window into the character of the scribe. Taken together, the language and writing also well represent a culture with an alternative view of time and space, individuality and society. There may be only one world science, but the scope and methods of inquiry as well as the philosophical foundations and interpretations are manifold. As noted above, throughout this book I shall be offering the Asian perspective to help break down the façades of traditional Western thought, so rigid in reductionism and materialism, that have kept us prisoners of illusion.

The Chinese expression for *definition* consists of two characters that may be translated as (1) decide, fix, or settle, and (2) connotation or meaning. It suggests a measure of freedom, contextual variation, and consensus. In contrast, *dictionary* in

Chinese is etymologically a rule or law of words or phrases. Whether the dictionary is English or Chinese, the terms *mind*, *awareness*, and *consciousness* are unfortunately ill-defined, inconsistent, and confused as synonymous, and we must reject their authority. Because everyone seems to have a different understanding of these words, and mine are as controversial, we should accept the option of modifying the meanings for the limited purpose of this book. Definitions are immediately required to maintain balance as we proceed up the steep rocky path.

Mind This inclusive term refers to behavior (altered attribute] through interactions of complementary or compatible patterns (forms). These patterns themselves are activities, rather than objects. The specific chemical reactions of molecules, consisting of atomic processes, is an example. In more complex systems, such informational processing includes sense, feeling, and thought. Minimally, mind is the relational process of pattern cognition, not limited to life, that establishes existence. Because a behavior is an abstract form and arises from such patterns, mind is essentially empty. It is not a thing.

Mind may also be taken as the undifferentiated transcendent reality, the inexpressible Tao. [The Chinese refer to mind as heart (core) or mystical essence.] The major categories or manifestations of mind follow below. Each encompasses several levels and functional forms.

Consciousness-mind Sequential thought conceptulization, self-awareness and observance of awareness not associated with self-identity, recognition, and volition take place at this level. Included here is subconsciousness-mind, which is analogical a-thinking without self-awareness, such as the spontaneous delayed retrieval of information 'on the tip of the tongue.' When speaking about mind, most people mean consciousness- mind. [In Chinese, consciousness is the thought from knowledge and recognition.]

Awareness-mind This is the nonconscious level where, in humans, emotion, sensory processes prior to perception, and pattern cognition occur. Physiological life support systems and muscular coordination are regulated here. It is the wellspring of creativity. It is the working memory. The base of this level, which is not ego restricted, is of the collective unconsciousness, a holistic and oceanic network of information exchange and storage that is the source of parapsychological phenomena. In lower orders of existence, it is also where primitive sense-like, environmental information-directed responses occur.

For example, you are driving your car and suddenly your heart pounds rapidly and you feel an adrenaline surge. You next notice in the rearview mirror a police car. In the first instance, you were aware through your senses of the black-and-white car, which unconsciously was perceived and then subconsciously was associated with potential trouble, a stored value-laden abstraction of consciousness-mind; in the second, you were conscious of the agent of your conditioned physiological reflex. [The Chinese characters in three synonymous phrases for *awareness* translate to acquiring knowledge, directed thought, and the way of wisdom.]

Matter-mind   A nondualist term indicating that from the cosmic to the subatomic level matter is not an object; matter is mind. [Although the Chinese recognize in matter or substance the attributes of both form and mind, the character for matter is a primitive referring to an ox, a massive live object.]

METAPHYSICAL SCHEME

Consciousness-mind

Awareness-mind

Matter-mind

Each lower level influences the higher, which in turn
influences the lower. Douglas Hofstadter described this self-
referral arrangement as a Strange Loop similar to the Möbius
strip, the twisted loop that has one edge and one side.[28]
These levels do not simply communicate nor do they interlock;
they are confluently united. The same sort of interpenetration exists among the orders of physical and biological
phenomena. The concept of generation or emergence of one
demarcated level from another is therefore false in operation
and, at best, tenuous in condition. For instance, most theo-
logicans and a few philosophers and scientists regard evolution of inorganic and biological organisms as directed by consciousness-mind, either external (God) or implicate through
self-organization.[12,29] Freeman Dyson observed, 'It would not
be surprising if it should turn out that the origin and destiny
of the energy in the universe cannot be completely
understood in isolation from the phenomena of life and consciousness.'[29] However, all these processes are only names for
different attributes of mind.

Several other definitions, which pertain to the perceived
physical world, should be given. Since they are commonly
used synonyms, I have attempted to differentiate them in
order to provide some clarity in these philosophical discussions.

Thing An indescribable or undescribed object, substance, or
entity. The result or purpose of activity. Derived from Old
English, once referring to an official assembly or legal meet-
ing. The Latin root of *real* means thing.

Object A discrete stable form that is tangible, that is solid
in consistency. Etymologically, that which is thrown forward.
For instance, a rock at the bottom of the ocean.

Substance The underlying essence that is tangible but shape-
less, such as the water of an ocean. Etymologically, that which
stands under.

Entity   An intangible thing that is distinct, with attributes, but is of diffused shape. Derived from Latin for *being* or *existing*. Examples are an ocean current or whirlpool.

What then is an ocean? We say that there are five oceans on Earth (the Atlantic, Pacific, Indian, Arctic, and Antarctic) but a glance at a globe will show otherwise. The divisions are arbitrary. There is only one ocean, indeed, one circulating system of water that flows also as vapor, clouds, and rain or ice in the atmosphere as well as creeks and rivers on land. Therefore, *ocean* is a convenient soft-edged geographic abstraction of consciousness-mind. Like his fellow astronauts and cosmonauts gazing at our kaleidoscopic planet from the envious perspective of an orbiting vehicle, Sultan Bin Salman al-Saud of Saudi Arabia recognized this unity: 'The first day or so we all pointed to our countries. The third or fourth day we were pointing to our continents. By the fifth day we were aware of only one Earth.'[31]

Chapter 2

THERE BE DRAGONS HERE

The quantum atom

A monk in the mist
I can see him
by his tinkling bell.
Meisetsu

Siddhartha Gautama (556-476), the Buddha, faced the large gathering of disciples who awaited his discourse and silently held up a flower. He saw that among the students only one understood—Mahakasyapa, who smiled. This wordless transmission of truths marked the origin of Zen. What did Mahakasyapa understand? What was transmitted?

One day during the T'ang dynasty a high official, Lu Keng, asked Zen Master Nan-Ch'uan (748-834) what Seng Chao (374- 414) meant in his statement that heaven and earth is of one and the same root as oneself and that all things are one with oneself. The Zen Master pointed to a nearby flower and answered, 'Ordinary people see this flower as if they were dreaming.' A thousand years later in England, William Blake, the mystic poet, wrote, 'If the doors of perception were cleansed, everything would be seen as it is, infinite.'

Today in Korea on a mountain path from Sudok-sa to Jeung-hae-sa is a pagoda in honor of a contemporary Zen Master, Mang Gong (1872-1946). The Chinese characters carved upon the pagoda read, 'The whole world is a single flower.' We need not be monks or poets to regard a flower or any other object with new eyes. To experience the entire eternal universe, to be a flower and let that flower be oneself, is the religious quest. However, a thorough scientific examination will also provide the insights to shape and predispose the perpective. After all, a scientist undergoes training that combines that of the priesthood and a medieval guild, with mentors, unique attitudes and practices in arcane languages, studies of myths and heroic predecessors, and rites of passage, which include an inquisition by guardians of the lore and the production of an adjudged original 'masterpiece'. Therefore, let us begin with the basis of the flower and all materials—elemental matter.

Without an iota of doubt, the most famous scientific equation is Albert Einstein's $E=mc^2$. It can even be found on T-shirts. Because of its unfair association with the atomic bomb, thanks to the art of the propagandist, and the exquisitely simple, easily remembered mathematical relationship, it is known to people who have no idea what the letters represent. (To avoid any embarrassment, the energy of matter is equal to its mass multiplied by the square of the speed of light.) We are well familiar with the splitting of the uranium atom and the chain reaction that, in weapons, leads to a destructive explosion of heat, light, wind, and radioactive particles and that, when controlled, can be harnessed for the generation of electrical power (along with hazardous radioactive waste).

At first glance, the equation seems to indicate that mass can be converted into energy. The same equation also informs us that energy can be transformed into mass. Be careful here. Matter does not contain energy as some alchemic elixir; matter in motion (mass) *is* energy. Therefore, as the disintegrating atom releases great amounts of energy as various forms of smaller matter, or mass, it is necessary to invest similar amounts of energy in the formation of diverse forms of matter. This requirement is achieved by colliding subatomic particles at extraordinarily high speeds in huge particle accelerators, which effectively increase their mass. These titanic devices, the technological descendents of what newspapers called atom smashers, are typically circular with circumference of several miles. An exception, the linear accelerator at Stanford University, is two miles long. Nuclear physics, the science of the ultimate tiny, is literally Big Science.

Werner Heisenberg, a nuclear physicist and discoverer of the quantum joker, the uncertainty principle, gave us a glimpse of the peculiarities of this phenomenon:[1]

The transmutation of energy into matter makes it possible that the fragments of elementary particles are again the same elementary particles.

This statement may seem nonsensical. Although the analogy is not exact, we can see some similarity in the biological example of a dividing energy-rich bacterium: The two daughter cells—barring mutation—are biologically alike and identical to the original cell.

In order to attain better understanding of how energy and mass can be equivalent in concept, let us briefly and somewhat simplistically consider the conventional atom. Atoms, of course, are the usually stable building blocks of the material world, although they generally consist of a nucleus of neutrons and positively charged protons and a blur of surrounding negatively charged electrons. The indivisible union of a set of quarks and gluons form the various nuclear particles, and the combination of different numbers of protons and neutrons yield the 103 kinds of atoms. The host of other particles that sometimes are mentioned in the occasional science feature of newspapers, such as neutrinos and positrons, are subatomic entities that are transformed and released with discrete energies and charges by experimental collisions of nuclear particles in accelerators or by astral and galaxial forces. Muons, for instance, are the chief cosmic rays. With their massive particle beam accelerators, nuclear physicists are true alchemists, able to transmutate elemental matter in their examination of the essences of material.

The transformation of matter may be explained in the following manner. Suppose that we equate energy with money, the representation of work, and consider the energy-work value of 25 cents, which is manifested as a coin in your pocket, to wit, a quarter. We collide with a merchant, to whom you owe 5 cents, and you give her the coin. This forces a transformation of our quarter into an abstraction of two dimes and one nickel without altering the total value. The energy-money value of 5 cents, the 'nickel', is kept by the merchant when giving you the manifestation of 20 cents, the two dimes that she conveniently had in her wallet.

If this analogy suggests that matter may not be a thing at all, but a mathematical construction, you are correct. This bizarre notion is not without precedent. The very idea of indivisible elementary particles with particular shapes, *atoms*, was conceived in classical Greece in the fourth century B.C.E. Rejecting Democritus' materialistic view of atoms as objects, the Pythagoreans, instead, regarded atoms as abstractions in the mathematics of their day, geometry.[2] Matter traditionally was of four kinds—fire, earth, air and water—and all materials reflected mosaics of these qualities. The indivisible elementary substances, the quarks of this new system, were two basic triangles, the 30° (half an equilateral triangle) and the 45° (half a square) which combined to form regular polygonal solids, the functional equivalent of nuclear particles. The tetrahedron was transformed into fire, the cube gave earth, the octohedron yielded air, and the icosahedron was associated with water. Today, higher mathematics and quantum mechanics describe atomic elementary units as probability wave functions. As Heisenberg observed, 'An atom is not an ordinary object.'[1] Although still taught to school children and used as a convenient metaphor in physical chemistry, the atom is also not the small scale solar system of orbiting bodies proposed in 1913.

The behavior of an electron in an atom can be described with precision and clarity only in the language of mathematics, particularly probability and statistics. One of the fundamental relationships of quantum physics is Heisenberg's uncertainty principle, whose simple mathematics show that locating an electron in the atom would prevent knowledge of its momentum or energy, and, conversely, the determination of its momentum would be at the sacrifice of locating it. What ensued was a description of probabilities, the odds, of where an electron might be at a certain energy. Each energy state would be associated with a different pattern of probability density — some areas are more likely than others — which is referred to as a probability wave. We have seen probability waves before in newspapers as the common, somewhat skewed bell-shaped distributions of, for instance, income versus age. Within specified confidence limits, one can estimate the most probable income any thirty year old will earn in twenty-five years, barring inflation.

Einstein, who never was comfortable with the apparent dependency of quantum phenomena on chance and random-ness, asserted that 'God does not throw dice.' To this, the theoretical physicist and cosmologist Stephen Hawking later observed, 'God not only plays dice. He also sometimes throws the dice where they can not be seen.'[3] The simile is appro-priate since mathematicians began their studies of probability and statistics through commissions from gamblers. While of divergent views, both Einstein and Hawkings, as most modern physicists, are neo-Pythagoreans with mathematically based religio-philosophies, which could be summarily expressed as 'God is a mathematician.'[4] Depending on whether we accept the Platonic view of preexisting eternal mathematical relation-ships, or the positivist modification that these relationships arise and evolve with the evolution of the cosmos—hence, the mathematics is discovered—or the opposite Aristotlean posi-tion that we create and develop them, mathematics may be either the universal language and, indeed, the language of the universe or a useful but empty cultural construction.[5,6]

The quandary of discovery versus conscious creation as the basis of reality can also be applied to any of our scientific principles.[8,9] Quantum theories as the *ad hoc* basis for a practical mechanics were not developed as descriptions of the stuff of reality, but of its *behavior*. Protons, neutrons, and so forth are the names given to specific patterns of behavior. However, after decades of successes in predicting and organ-izing phenomenona in physics, chemistry, biochemistry, and cosmology, these patterns culturally, if not scientifically, took on the interpretative mantle of reality as positivist objects or entities. They became particles.

The expression, quantum jump or quantum leap, has entered the popular idiom as a sudden advance to a higher understanding, complexity, or technology. Quantum jumps of electrons in the atom may occur both upward and downward in discrete levels of energy, the interger multiples of the fundamental quantum value based on Max Planck's photo-electric constant, which figures in Heisenberg's equation. The mechanical description is that an electron is of one energy

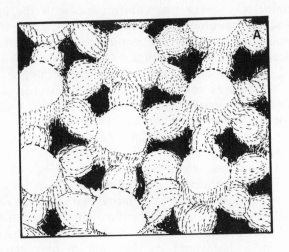

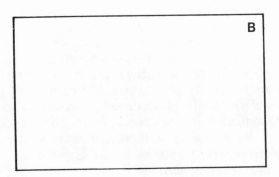

THE ATOM IS NOT AN OBJECT.
[A] Correlation from scanning electron microscopy: small iodine atoms and large platinum atoms.
[B] Diagram of an atom if time were stopped.

configuration and then—zap! It absorbs a photon, the unit of light, and immediately it is of a higher energy wave pattern; or it releases a photon and drops or decays, without any gradations, to a lower energy wave arrangement. It is like being in San Francisco and a moment later finding yourself in New York without crossing any territory. Remarkably, such quantum jumps have actually been detected.[10]

Both electrons and nuclear particles also have the amazing ability to materialize at comparatively distant sites from the atom as a means of overcoming energy barriers. This process of subterfuge is appropriately called tunneling, but through what do these particles tunnel? Quantum space is not continuous in our usual sense, and quantum particles are not our usual hard grains. Although the probability function is small, tunneling occurs sufficiently often to be important in chemical and biochemical reactions and of practical use in electronic technologies.

Treading on the quicksand of quantum weirdness, we seek the support of a safety line. Although the internal structure of the quantum atom is beyond the grasp of common experience, we still can hold a pinch of silver between our fingers. (Of course, the fingers are of atoms, too!) Perhaps the atom as a unit exists as a more familiar object. What does such an atom look like?

Using special microscopes, the atom appears in photographs as a fuzzy sphere.[11,12] With cinematography, the chosen atom, which is usually a heavy metal atom such as uranium or tungsten because of its larger size, seems to quiver and twinkle irregularly. Advances in technology would not likely improve resolution: In taking pictures of atoms, we actually record their attributes, their behaviors.

Because instruments themselves are composed of atoms, the problem is much like seeing your own eye; a reflective or transforming device, such as a mirror or photographic film, is needed to provide correlative images. Thus, the scanning electron microscope analyzes the scatter of reflected electrons with each incremental scan to produce one-to-one corresponding images on a television monitor.[13] Signal and noise, however, are overlapping probability distribution functions, making discernment of the atom as difficult as finding a polar bear in a snow storm. The new scanning-tunneling microscope can discern isolated elemental atoms, but the images of combined atoms, *molecules,* such as DNA chains, are smears.[14] The technique involves moving a charged microscopic metal tip across the molecular surface at a constant height, which is maintained by adjustments of electrical current. The hills and valleys of each incremental sweep yield the image on the cathode ray tube monitor.

A more significant difficulty in perceiving the structure of the atom is the constraints of our cognitive processes and instruments, which, in a manner of speaking, blur the particles in space-time. The operation of several familiar devices depends on similar effects. The phenomenon is more than the mechanical appearance of a disk produced by a rapidly rotating propeller. It is like film frames passing across the lens of a movie projector, or, in the television cathode tube, the cyclic stream of electrons entering the photon- emitting phosphor layer, systems which provide images of objects and the illusion of their movement. Indeed, it is impossible to freeze the action of an atom or to probe electrons with electrons, but even if we had the technology to observe such a static entity, we would see nothing at all!

In normal circumstances, electrons have no size; they are regarded as points of charged energy and of minute mass $1/1836$ of protons. However, since 1984, Hans Dehmelt and his colleagues at the University of Washington have maintained a single positron (an anti-electron), chilled at minus $270°$ C. (near Absolute Zero) and trapped alone in electric and magnetic fields.[15] Its vibrational behavior describes an atom, more accurately, a pseudoatom called geonium. The researchers extrapolated the radius of this electron, which they have nicknamed 'Priscilla' (see Chapter 4 footnote), as approximately 10^{-20} centimeter. In addition, mass is a relational characteristic of movement induced by a force or, as inertia, of its resistance to such movement. To stop the action of an atom would nullify time-dependent force, and with no force there is no mass. A sizeless particle without mass is emptiness, but as we shall later see, a void with potential.

Therefore, the spherical shape and solid, albeit diffused, exterior of the atom is an illusion. We can not directly see this

C

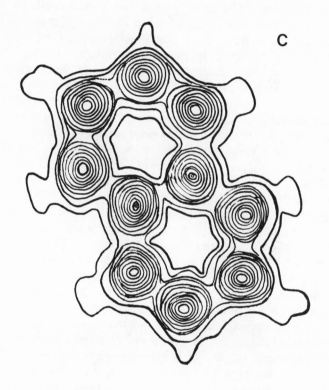

THE ATOM IS NOT AN OBJECT.
[C] Electron density map. The 10 carbons and 8 hydrogens
of naphthalene.

system of quantified energy, but we can see the patterns of its interactions with probes in the same way as scattering iron filings over a bar magnet manifests the electromagnetic field. The stuff of reality acts as if it were some moving shadow at the periphery of our vision that disappears when we turn toward it. Similarly, the way to see an object in the blackness of night is not to look directly at it—the central cells of the retina being dedicated to color vision in bright light.

Such detailed conceptions and descriptions of nature, of course, were unknown in the science of India and China 1,800 years ago, but the fundamental conclusions were already reached and recorded in Buddhist scriptures of this period. For instance, in the Diamond Sutra we find: Wheresoever are material characteristics there is impermanence and delusion If you view all characterstics as no-characteristics and non-appearance, this view is Buddha.[16]

Scientists continue to discover how changeable and dependent an atom really is. An experiment has elegantly demonstrated that probing atoms in the midst of a process leading to quantum jumping will inhibit the operation, as suggested by the folk saying, 'a watched pot never boils.'[17] Wayne Itano and his associates at the National Institute of Standards and Technology in Boulder, Colorado, encountered the effect when they captured some 5,000 beryllium ions in a magnetic trap. Nearly all the ions were in a low energy state. They next exposed the atoms to a particular radio-frequency field for precisely 0.256 second, which jumped them to a higher quantum energy. Itano's team verified this alteration by probing their targets with a laser pulse whose photon energy would not affect beryllium ions in the higher level but would induce those in the lower energy state to emit a photon. Now, if the researchers peeked at the ions during the test interval, they would reset the atoms' 'clock'. For instance, a probe after 0.128 second would result in only half the ions reaching the higher energy level; additional probing would reduce the yield such that 64 checks of the ions during the period would inhibit all but a few atoms from attaining the higher state. *Thus, any observation of an atom will alter its behavior.*

A further complication—I saved the worst for last—is that electrons, protons, and their ilk are, at times, particle-like, while, at other times, they behave as waves, depending on the experimental design and observing instrument, which may include consciousness-mind. Two famous thought experiments conceived as philosophically critical in investigating this paradox and the reality of quantum theory were realized as practical demonstrations. Their consciousness-mind-boggling results seem to justify the pessimistic conclusion that the absolute nature of matter, the quantum reality, will never be *known*.

In 1935, Einstein, in corroboration with Boris Podolsky and Nathan Rosen, outlined an experiment to challenge Niels Bohr's interpretation of quantum theory. Bohr, one of the principal architects of quantum mechanics, claimed it to be a complete theory of reality, one, however, that requires an observer. For Einstein, the universe existed external to mind and instrument; the universe was relativistic but nevertheless objective. David Bohm's later simplification of the experimental design from the complex determination of electron spin to the simple test of wave alignment of photons provided a practical means for actual experiments. These were accomplished in 1982 by John Clauser's team at the University of California, Berkeley and Alain Aspect's group at the University of Paris.[18]

In the first stage of the modified EPR experiment, as it became known, a certain decaying particle emits two photons in opposite directions, as a cook mightily cleaving an unheld carrot will send the pieces left and right. In each photon's path is a detector with a polarizing lens that can be adjusted in angle. Considered individually, a photon is of no particular polarized angle, and the chance of it passing through the detector with a given lens angle is 50/50. When the two photons are taken together, the same angle setting on both detectors will yield the same probability for both photons to pass through. This will occur no matter how far they have traveled away from each other or how long one measurement is made after the other, even ten light-years apart.

The hypothetical outcome implies that the two photons are not independent, and that setting the conditions on one automatically sets the same condition on the other. In essence, the photons are twins. Knowing that the speed of the photon is the universal constant and that no thing can travel faster, any divergent action-at-a-distance would be an affront to the classical order of space-time and cause-and-effect. In the original thought experiment, Einstein argued well that interactions were locally restricted and independent but that the two hypothetical electrons would be correlated and set from the outset; the measured spin direction of one particle would indicate the opposite spin direction of the second. In the modified proposal, the behavior of the photon twins to all polarization angles would be predetermined before the measurement. In quantum theory, photon behavior could be altered after its production. Who was correct, Einstein or Bohr?

John Stewart Bell considered what would happen if the two detectors had different angle settings. He calculated the probabilities for matches in polarization behavior based on the assumption of independent local interactions, and found them contrary to both quantum mechanics and experimental data. It was a two stage indirect proof by which shifting the orientation of one polarizing lens would alter the probability of passage of the given photon. The second photon would not be affected if independence was real. Next, changing the angle of the second lens in the opposite direction to arithmetically double the error rate of matches set the criterian for challenge. Quantum mechanics and subsequent experiments testing Bohm's and Bell's arrangements produced mismatches in excess of this threshold. Indeed, Aspect's experimental design had the bonus of changing the rules in the middle of the game by shifting the angle of the target polarizing lens while the photons were in flight. The experiment demonstrated that reality is not locally restricted and that the two photons and also the conditions for observation are united in some obscure fashion. *Matter is not discrete. Absolute independence is an illusion.*

The second experiment was even more magical. It was done with mirrors! A simple test system had displayed, in all its glory, quantum duality, the complementary behavior [not necessarily forms) of quantum particles and waves. The

INDEPENDENT OR DEPENDENT PHOTON TWIN?
PREDETERMINED OR UNFIXED ANGLE?

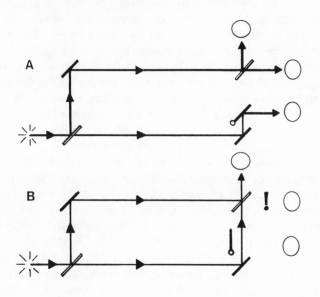

QUANTUM MAGIC.
[A] Single photon behaves as if an object particle.
[B] Single photon behaves as if a split wave with
self-interference and self-augmentation.

experiment was conceived by John Wheeler and realized in the laboratory of Caroll Alley at the University of Maryland.[19] A half-silvered mirror set at 45° in a light path will allow half the photon particles to pass while the remainder will be reflected. Half-silvered mirrors figure in spy novels, since what appears as a mirror to a person in a lit room is a window for another individual in an adjoining darkened room. When a single photon is involved, a detector directly behind the mirror has a 50% chance of recording a hit. We can bring the two possible light paths together, forming a rectangle, by placing regular full-silvered mirrors set at 45° along the path. We next introduce at the point of intersection, also at 45°, a second half-silvered mirror. Finally, a detector is placed behind the mirror in the path of transmission/reflection. This arrangement creates an interferometer.

From our experience of observing ripples in a pond, we know that the amplitude of intersecting waves can be increased or cancelled, depending on phase. Although we speak of light waves with frequencies or lengths, the photons are not physical ripples. Under certain circumstances a large series or a cluster of photons will behave *collectively* on a recording system, apparatus or retina-brain, as if they were waves. It is a statistical phenomenon. Single photons will hit or materialize on the target in no immediately apparent pattern. Thus, converging probability waves of photons will produce an interference pattern of light and dark bands. (You can see this for yourself, if you bring your thumbs very close together and, raising them to your eye, look through the slit.) Because only single photons are fired into the test system, multiple trials of various path lengths are required to produce the characteristic statistical pattern. *The merger of possible paths hence provides evidence that photons behave as waves.*

Let us introduce a movable full-silvered mirror that can be swung 45° into the light path just in front of the point of intersection. Two additional detectors are placed into the new branched paths. We now have one possible path that passes through the first half-silvered mirror and is reflected in zigzag fashion by two full mirrors into a detector; there is a 50% chance for a photon to follow this path. The second path begins with reflections by the half- and full-silvered mirrors and then transmission through the second half-silvered mirror to a detector; there is a 25% chance for a photon to traverse this path. The third possibility begins as the second path, but is reflected by the second half-silvered mirror into the last detector; a photon on this path also has a 25% chance of being recorded. *Thus, the prevention of path merging demonstrates the particle behavior of the photon.*

With a twinkle in her eye, the scientist-magician arranges the system of mirrors to detect wave behavior and fires a photon. Between the time it is reflected or transmitted through the half-silvered mirror and the moment of path recombination, she throws the switch of the movable mirror to block merger. The detector indicates particle. She fires another photon, waits for it to be transmitted through or reflected by the half-silvered mirror, and returns the movable mirror off the path just before the photon reaches a detector. Hocus-pocus, waves are focused.

Quantum interference is not limited to subparticles. Such experiments usually involve matter passing through a series of slits or gratings to produce a diffraction pattern. Several independent laboratories have now demonstrated that whole atoms, which have wavelengths 10,000 times shorter than visible light, also can produce an interference pattern.[20]

These experiments tumble the walls of common sense. The quantum entities do not follow any discrete path as would a marble in a groove. Even the famous curved, spiral, and starburst tracks in liquid hydrogen bubble chambers are, on close inspection, discontinuous and form a ragged line. These patterns are not of traveling particles, but of behaviors of serial interactions, like the wave that passes through a line of stopped cars when the signal light goes to green. Photons and other subatomic particles seem as if they reside outside space-time until recorded by some observing instrument or sensory organ, when the probability wave function collapses as a *system-directed behavior.*

Physicist P.C.W. Davies described Bohr's view of the atom as a 'fuzzy and nebulous world [that] sharpens into concrete reality when an observation is made. In the absence of an observation, the atom is a ghost.'[21] Davies later paraphrased Gilbert Ryle's *Ghost in the Machine* (a reference to the dualistic view of mind and matter) with 'the ghost in the atom', which is an unfortunate twist of the delightful and useful earlier perspective.[22] If the atom is ghostlike, then what are we, who are composed of atoms? The delayed-choice experiment clearly suggests that within the limits of underlying quantum reality and biology our consciousness-mind creates, not discovers, phenomena. *Our methods dictate, not merely permit, what can be found.*

This opinion should not be confused with idealism, which purports that everything we perceive in the universe is a fabrication of our consciousness-mind and that reality is but a thought. We do place our human stamp on reality; however, it is by the biological limitations unique to our species and by the openness and taboos of culture. Can we truly imagine the sonic, dark, floating, and viscous world view of whales and dolphins? Do we modern city folk have the same developed spectrum of perception and sensitivity as natives of the Borneo highlands? We creatures of consciousness-mind are sculptors of reality. This said, I nevertheless do regard the universe as mind per se, the inclusive mind of which human consciousness is a stitch in the fabric.

While the fundamental, absolute, or real nature of the amorphous quantum entities is vigorously debated, we should not ignore their equally important relationships and dynamics.[18,23] In these discussions one aspect is sometimes ignored or forgotten. The emptiness of the image of our earlier described hypothetical frozen atom is yet something. Heinz Pagels included himself when he wrote,[23]

Theoretical and experimental physicists are now studying nothing at all—the vacuum. But that nothingness contains all of being.

What he was referring to was the existence of the sea of evanescent particles that surround the atom as pesty gnats. These virtual entities, which arise from the void in tandem with atomic disturbances, are rapidly annihilated through interactions with the atom but primarily with themselves, since they include both matter and oppositely charged anti-matter. This emptiness may be considered as energy pregnant with form, and we already know form as energy manifested by interaction.[24] We now see that matter, emptiness, and energy are fundamentally the same. There is a name for this triumvirate: mind.

Interestingly, The Heart Sutra, which is daily recited in all branches of Buddhism, includes the analogous declaration:

> Form does not differ from emptiness, emptiness does not differ from form. That which is form is emptiness, that which is emptiness is form.

Scholars tell us that all of Buddhist philosophy may be distilled down to these few words.[25] That opinion goes too far, although the metaphysical equation *is* central. Structures and material patterns have no objective reality, and hence are empty concepts; yet, emptiness is itself an abstract form defined against illusive material forms. We shall be returning to both philosophical emptiness and physically potent emptiness often, especially with respect to discussions of Carl G. Jung's seminal concept of archetypes and the collective unconscious; of parapsychology; and of Rupert Sheldrake's provocative hypothesis of morphic resonance. The latter is a synthesis of Plato's eternal forms, Alfred North Whitehead's time-recapitulatory process metaphysics, and Conrad H. Waddington's clever mechanistic metaphor of chreodes (developmentally obliged paths).[26]

Most people, biologists included, are so comfortable in their experiences of common phenomena that they choose to shun the ultramicro world of the atom and its elementary particles. They assume that the weird quantum occurrences of the subatomic level do not affect biological organizations of matter. It is, at first glance, difficult to see how a jump in electron energy of a couple of atoms could alter heart activity or effect our choice of dinner menu. Conversely, these complex forms, although consisting of atoms, are deemed incapable of influencing constituent elementary matter. The ultra micro and micro/macro tiers are thus completely separated as if there were two disparate laws of nature; mind does not enter the equation.

This duality is a mistaken construct. Although there are unique properties of the subatomic world not shared with higher forms, the systems, nevertheless, interpenetrate. We have already learned how the perceptive observer can participate in determining quantum behavior. Often the effect of quantum matter in biology is detrimental. Cosmic rays continually crash through trees and humans with no apparent harm, but this conclusion is based on site sensitivity, pathology, and detection. Geiger counters are not the only detecting device. Astronauts in orbit have reported occasional flashes of light in their eyes; the source of this show was high energy cosmic rays colliding with atoms of the retina.[27] When the excited electrons decayed, they emitted photons. We also are well familiar with the mutagenic and carcinogenic capacities of radioisotopes and their particular emitted rays. Long wave ultra-violet light can be lethal to cells, and is routinely used to sterilize work areas in laboratories.

On the positive side, these mutagens may also be beneficial in adaptation and evolution. In addition, nuclear tunneling effects may be necessary for effective enzyme activity.[28] Indeed, quantum mechanisms have led to our understanding of chemistry and bonding of atoms. Quantum effects also influence the firing of nerve cells in the brain. Perhaps they do figure in our food selections!

The biological effects of positively charged ions in the atmosphere are most bothersome.[29,30] These ions are generated by pollution and by the notorious warm mountainous winds, such as the Santa Ana and the Foehn. Through the imbalances of serotonin and other neurologically active molecules in our brain, positive ions are responsible for foul moods and lowering of resistance to infectious disease. In contrast, negative ions, associated with falling water, provide refreshment and clarity of consciouness-mind. This explains why a shower, be it from cloud or faucet, cleans and invigorates. The physical nature of ions will be described in the next chapter.

Modern technology is very much the application of quantum mechanics. Radios, computers, diagnostic X-ray photographs, scanning-tunneling electron microscopes, and the laser reading of bar codes on our groceries are dependent on these strange doings. We even tell time by them. Mechanical drives in clocks, such as springs, vary in force and are prone to fatigue; electricity is subject to voltage fluctuations. What was needed was a device without gradations in force, a quantum characteristic, and governed by consistent oscillations, which could be derived from the internally regulated decay of excited energy states of electrons or other elementary particles. Because of its unique, invariable resonance frequency when stimulated by a particular radio electromagnetic field, the cesium atom has been employed in atomic clocks, the most precise measurement of time available.

Of course, troublesome quantum effects also occur. Who has not encountered the occasional untoward results of glitches, blips, misreadings, and other nuisances in electronics probably associated with quantum effects and chaos in atomic behavior.[31,32] Solar flares, which through ionization bring us the awesome light show of the *aurora borealis* and *aurora australis*, are especially disruptive to electronic communications. As technology continues the trend to miniaturization—making inevitable the bionic human, a union of biomembrane and computer chip—quantum randomness will need to be addressed as both friend and foe.[33]

To summarize, whether we view protons, mesons, and photons as particle-waves or as ghost-like energy vortexes arising and maintained by a hidden order described in the mathematics of chaos (much like the whirling red spot of Jupiter) they and atoms are in fact activities, not objects. The physical and chemical behaviors of atoms include interactions of the atom and the surrounding sea of no-thing-ness from which effervescent ephemeral entities arise. This paradoxical essence of patterned emptiness, of mutual dependence and interpenetration, seems to connect the particles holistically such that their behavior is induced by information shared faster than the speed of light. Information in this instance is not a datum, nor an impulse, but true to its etymology, a conformational alteration of the whole that affects all constitutent relationships.

This last point may be visualized by a frictionless teeter-totter in precise balance. The slightest weight put on one end will immediately perturb the status of the system driving the other end upward. The two ends are local features, connected in a higher order of form, that influence each other's behavior. Although useful, such a mechanical illustration, of course, is not exactly analogous; it involves an impulse traveling along adjacent matter. However, it is difficult to provide a better example when we do not know what matrix or higher system unites the diverging subatomic particles in the previously described investigation actualizing the EPR thought experiment

More important to our philosophical discussion is the fact that the entire conceptual universe is a house of cards erected on a cloud. At this bottom level of matter, we find only dynamic patterns of process and relationships of entities of energy, some of which are dimensionless and massless. It is a Wonderland of paradox, weirdness, and absurdity. It is the ground of illusion from which we build our sensory memories and develop our abstract thoughts. And yet the ediface of whispers holds as strongly as one of Buckminster Fuller's extraordinarily efficient geodesic domes and spheres.[34]

Can anything be said here about individuality and self? All atoms of the same energy are identical as are all elementary particles of the same class. For instance, the carbon atom, whose total mass normally is about 12 because of its six neutrons and six protons, may less frequently consist of one or two additional neutrons, giving carbon a mass of 13 and 14, respectively. Carbon 14 is unstable and radioactive. Its unique half-life (statistically, the time half the particles decay) has been used to determine the age of biological specimens that had incorporated it. Different atoms of a given atomic or proton number (carbon is 6) are called isotopes. Thus, to be more specific, all isotopes of the same energy are alike.

Furthermore, protons of an oxygen atom are no different than protons of carbon, and they are interchangeable. The old so-called elementary particles are transmutable, an attribute that challenges the concept of indivisibilty, unity, and independence. Under certain circumstances, for example, these said protons can transform into neutrons, emitting and then reabsorbing pions, and then return to protons. Because all such particles are of the same stuff—energy—pattern discernment among them is at the most primitive level, such as the balance of charge of electron and proton (in antimatter, positron and antiproton). There is no individuality, no permanence, and indeed no-thing at the subatomic level. With a nod to Alan Watts, popular teacher of Asian philosophy, should we not then regard atoms as verbs rather than nouns?

Yet the atom is a system, an organization of behaviors. Confronting the novel science of quantum physics in 1926, Whitehead wrote:[35]

Science is taking on a new aspect which is neither purely physical nor purely biological. It is becoming the study of organisms. Biology is the study of the larger organisms; whereas physics is the study of the smaller organisms.

The atom is the simplest and smallest organism, almost borderline, since transcending synergy is not strong. Because the general chemical behavior of an atom can be predicted from its parts, Dmitri Mendeleev was able to construct the first practical periodic table of the elements, and modern nuclear physicists were then able to predict the class characteristics of synthetic short-lived radioactive atoms created by high-energy accelerators. Still, the various attributes of protons, neutrons, and electrons when considered together can not describe the unique properties of atoms. It is the arrangement, motion, and interactions of these sub-particles that make the atom. But are the parts really separate? Are there parts at all? Waves at the shoreline vary in size and force and propel the surfboard toward land, but they are not independent of the ocean and rising seabed.

We have begun a difficult journey with a difficult subject. A Zen student also faces hardships and hurdles in the pursuit of enlightenment. A monk of the Japanese Rinzai or Korean Chogye sect particularly faces the *gateless-gates* of koans. These are numerous historical cases of Zen insights that must be grasped not by linear and literal thinking, for they could only be regarded as nonsense, but by subconscious a-thinking, by which they are metasensible.

One such barrier concerns the monk Te Shan Hsuan-chien (780-865), a young and proud philosophy student who sought to challenge the upstart advocates of Zen training.[36,37] However, it was his understanding of Buddhism that was continually challenged and found deficient.

One day his meanderings took him hungrily to a teahouse. After the old woman proprietor learned that he was a sutra scholar, she declared that she would give him *tien-shin*, a kind of snack whose name means 'mind-refreshment', provided he answer a question based on his expertise of a particular sutra.* Te Shan agreed. 'In the Diamond Sutra,' she reminded him, 'past mind, present mind, and future mind are unattainable. Which mind do you want to refresh?' (Wise old women frequently play pivotal roles in Zen stories.) Te Shan, in his confusion was at a loss for words, and he left still hungry.

Later he studied under Zen Master Lung T'an. In one visit to the master, the afternoon conversation continued until well past dusk. Lung T'an finally said, 'Night has arrived. You should retire to your quarters.' After respectfully bowing, Te Shan went outside but returned immediately, telling the Master that it was utterly dark. Lung T'an lit a candle and presented it to the monk. As Te Shan was about to take it, the master suddenly blew the flame out. Instantly, Te Shan was enlightened.

Can you penetrate this koan, which relates to our discussion of physics? How would you answer the old woman? How would you demonstrate — not explain — your understanding of Te Shan's insight?

From this brief overview we can appreciate how most of the physicists who developed the relativistic quantum perspectives came to regard in awe nature's extraordinarily complex intrinsic structures and behaviors that go well beyond the common world of our limited senses. Weirdness has become the norm in physics to such an extent that theoretical proposals sometimes have been challenged for not being sufficiently strange.

Mysticism among these pioneer nuclear scientists was intellectually based in philosophy, although also doubtlessly strongly felt.[38] None apparently had a significant transpersonal experience, and none agreed that physics furnished the proofs or disproofs of any religious interpretation or that it established the reality of transcendence. Many vehemently

The Chinese expression for atom is composed of two characters. One means seed, offspring, or fruit; the second refers to source or start; a graveyard; and a vast field. As diverse in denotations, the metaphors of these characters taken together give a splendid poetic portrait of the quantum atom. Selecting a set of these meanings, we thus can regard the atom as the seed of the source.

ATOM

Bibel'92

opposed and ridiculed any attempt to unite physics with religion, considering the two domains as incompatible as oil in water. However, their understanding of the very different Indian and Chinese psycho-philosophies was superficial, and Zen was entirely foreign. Also, physics in isolation from the psychological and noetic sciences may be flawed or deficient. Still, their scientific pursuits did provide one clear, unanimous realization, a perception that made these scientists philosophical mystics: Science does not study reality but its shadows, a powerful metaphor originating with Plato. Thus, scientific investigation catapulted them *almost* to the top of the 100-foot pole, which is as much as any scholarly religious study can accomplish.* There they remained, failing to climb higher, but they led the way for the modern noetic scientist, who may not be satisfied with pole-sitting and shadowboxing.

---

* Western societies tend to blur and blend Eastern philosophies, although they are as distinct and historically antagonistic as Roman Catholicism and Islam and consist of numerous orders, sects, and schools. Eastern approaches may be lumped only as to their being psychological, holistic, and nature dominant, in contrast to Western dualistic theologies where humans are regarded apart from nature. Because this book emphasizes Zen and Hua-Yen teachings, I should note that while Zen is Zen worldwide, the practice and tradition is not monolithic. This sect arose in China, where it was known as *ch'an* (transliteration of the Sanskrit *dhyana*, referring to meditation). In Korea it is called *Son*; in Japan and in the West it is *Zen*. Vietnamese Zen is influenced by the Theravada traditions of Thailand and Burma; Chinese Zen is strongly fashioned by Taoism; Japanese Zen has a measure of Shinto; and American and European Zen is still evolving under individualism. Styles mainly differ in whether enlightment is achieved suddenly and completely, as in the Japanese Rinzai (Chinese Lin-chi) schools; gradually through cultivation, as in the Japanese Soto (Ts'ao-tung) schools; or through sudden partial enlightment and gradual cultivation, as in the Korean Chogye schools. While Zen no longer thrives in China, the influence of Chinese Zen calligraphy, poetry, and art persists among Zennists everywhere.

Chapter 3

AND 'MID THESE DANCING ROCKS

Chemistry

We used to think that if we knew one, we knew two, because one and one are two. We are finding that we must learn a great deal more about 'and'.

Sir Arthur Eddington

If atoms, which implies everything else, are phantoms, what prevented the thunder fingers of Vladimir Horowitz from going through the keys of his piano? This is not a silly question, considering that when the fingers struck the keys, electrons 'jumped' from the atoms of each structure to the other, and atoms themselves were exchanged, physically merging musician and instrument if but for a moment. Any discussion of the union or coalescence of atoms concerns chemistry and molecules, and it is here that pattern comparison and complementary relationships become paramount in the processes of matter-mind. This chapter will focus on the three basic types of molecular bonding that convert shadows into objects and clouds into constellations: ionic, covalent, and polar.

The examination of the origin and activity of elemental patterns at first will be fairly technical and distant. The excitement of a game can occur only after the rules have been learned. We must lay a proper foundation because our regarding atoms and molecules as examples of mind and organismal behavior is a radical departure from classical chemical understanding. Not once was mind mentioned in my six courses of undergraduate chemistry. Although the instruction was twenty-five years ago, the absence of such philosophical thinking still holds true.

What insights can we gain from the Chinese, who have had an ancient tradition of alchemy? Considering first the word molecule, which is conveyed in a two character phrase, we find the character for role (function) or component joined with the previously noted character for seed, fruit, or offspring. At times, a third character, meaning minute, hidden, or subtle, serves as a qualifier. Chemistry is understood broadly; the two-character phrase refers respectively to learning, studying, or imitating and to changing or influencing. Thus, it could apply equally to social science as to material science. Westerners validate this scope when they speak of the chemistry between lovers, an interaction, I should add, that is said to involve harmonious vibrations.

With the advent of quantum mechanics, chemists found a testable explanation for the capacity and restriction of particular sets of atoms, the classical elements, to form compounds. The pioneer and dean of this field was Linus Pauling, who after undergoing his basic training in quantum theory at the foot of the masters, Max Born, Werner Heisenberg, and Niels Bohr, went on to an astonishing series of accomplishments in determining the structure of molecules and crystals.[1] In April 1931, Pauling published the first of his model-shattering essays, The *Nature of the Chemical Bond*. Chemistry has never been the same since, nor has biochemistry, for Pauling shortly afterwards investigated the structures of the amino acids, ascertained that sickle cell anemia was a defect (specifically a substitution of one amino acid in the protein of hemoglobin) and discovered the first order helical structure of proteins—and might have discovered the specific helical arrangement of DNA had external social circumstances been different.

The mechanism of chemical bonding between two atoms involves the interactions of respective electrons and their energy states. While the language, a vestige of earlier models, implies a micro solar system, a very peculiar one to be sure, we should remember that the following model is a contrivance to give convenient concreteness to a mathematical abstraction. 'Do I contradict myself? Very well then I contradict myself. I am large, I contain multitudes,' so wrote the mystic poet Walt Whitman.

Bibel 92

CHEMISTRY

In an atom, the possible positions of electrons of a given energy are spread within unique *probability patterns*, which are called shells and subshells. Each atom is composed of a series of overlapping concentric shells of quantum-limited heights, according to the number of protons in the nucleus. The size and energy of the orbital, the shape and orientation of the orbital, and the spin of the electrons are all quantum dependent. (How can a one-dimensional point spin? Why not? Mathematics is the ultimate fantasyland. If electrons behave as if they are objects with angular momentum, then explore the relationship. Some physicists are now seriously considering nine-dimensional space.) Because one revolution of the electron is 1/2 a quantum unit, a complete rotation to its starting point requires a 720° turn! (Similarly, tracing a finger along the side of a Möbius loop, we find that two circuits are needed to return to the point of origin.) Because no two electrons can have the same set of quantum values, each shell is restricted in the number of electrons it can support. For example, the zinc atom in free gaseous state has 30 electrons within four major shells. Calculating outward from the nucleus, the electrons are distributed as 2/2-6/2-6-10/2.

As the numerical series suggest, a vacancy in the outermost shell might be filled by an electron from an adjacent atom, particularly when it is alone without the energy support of shell sharers. There is a tendency, expressed as an energy potential, for completing the shell by gaining or losing electrons. Atoms that have already completed shells are chemically inert gases, such as argon and neon. Sodium, however, has only one of the two electrons allowed in its highest energy shell, while chlorine has five of the six permitted sites occupied. Loss of the electron by sodium and a gain of the electron by chlorine would be mutually advantageous. The process by which this takes place is termed *ionization*, and the altered atoms with deficient or surplus electrons to balance the nuclear protons are called *ions*

Metals are those atoms, like silver, copper, and mercury, that are converted to net positively charged ions. Ions vary in binding capacity, or valance, depending on the number of donated electrons, such that one magnesium ion, with valence (+2), will couple with two chlorine ions, each with valence

(-). The electrostatic attraction of oppositely charged ions provide the crystals of salts, such as the example, $MgCl_2$. Because the ionic bonds in salts are moderately strong, such crystals are hard and brittle.

These relationships of charges provide a mechanism for pattern testing and discrimination among atoms. Under most circumstances only the electrical opposites—and of these, only those ions that alone or with like partners have valences that allow reciprocity—will form the ionic union. Although wholly determined by quantum mechanics, this selective process is a major step in making the atom a space occupying object with character. Here we see how mutual interpenetration, even if spatially disjoined, can physically exist and how the interaction mutually defines the partners. However, ions are still phantoms, albeit with sticky clothes.

The discussion has been focused until now on the interactions of two and occasionally more independent atoms. Some metallic ions associate with negative ions that themselves are a strongly linked combination of atoms, such as the phosphate group of one phosphorus and four oxygen atoms with valence of (-3). This powerful union is more than an alliance; it is a federation. It is the *covalent* bond.

How do atoms with reciprocal gaps in electron shell potential share their electrons without separating? It would take a strange traffic control officer to keep order as the electrons weave around the two nuclei. Since quantum theory is strange, there is no problem. *The probability wave functions are distorted to accommodate the joint venture. They become a molecular, rather than an atomic function.* The inner shells are balanced by orbitals in bonding (merged) and antibonding (mutually repulsed) modes, and the outer, unbalanced highest shell of electrons overlaps the nuclei to form the covalent bond. The sharing is equal with two like atoms such as nitrogen, which as a gaseous molecule comprises about 79% of the atmosphere. However, when the two atoms are different, there is a tendency to share unequally, the larger atom being dominant. This produces an ionic influence on the bond. Covalent bonding is the principal form of atomic coupling in biological and 'organic' molecules.

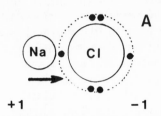

A

+1   −1

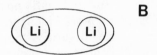

B

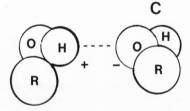

C

THE MIND OF STICKY GHOSTS.
A. Ionic bonding with transfer of electrons.
B. Covalent bonding with sharing of electrons.
C. Polar bonding from aymmetrical charge distribution and attraction at a distance.

Thus far in this nearly standard overview we have dealt with atoms as if they existed only in Flatland. There is, however, one particular atom whose covalent bonds with adjacent atoms are of such number and angle that it forces the three-dimensional perspective. This is the carbon atom, which has a valence of four. One of the primary keys to life, it essentially defines organic chemistry. Methane, for instance, consists of a single carbon atom surrounded by four hydrogen atoms in a tetrahedral arrangement. Strings of methane units form the familiar fuel hydrocarbons, butane and propane; the circle of six units describes the benzene ring. Branched chains also occur. Substitute a hydrogen with covalently bonded oxygen and hydrogen (the hydroxyl group) to attain an alcohol. If you take two alcohol molecules and remove the complete hydroxyl group of one and split off the hydrogen of the other hydroxyl group, hence the removal of water (dehydration), you will have produced an ether. And so forth and so on.

Most covalent bonds between atoms are single, but carbon and oxygen often form double covalent bonds. These help define acids, esters, aldehydes, and ketones. Double bonding between carbons is also common, and when speaking of unsaturated fats, we refer to this form of bonding. The two carbons of acetylene are held together by three covalent bonds. Graphite and mica are crystals with two dimensional or planar covalent bonds, which give them a soft and slippery texture; a three-dimensional covalent bonded crystal would be extremely strong, which indeed is the significant characteristic of diamond.

There are now some 4,500,000 kinds of chemicals, with an average composition of 43 atoms.[2] About 96% contain carbon. Thousands of new chemicals, mostly synthethic, continue to be added to the registry each week. Sample quantities of most, after being characterized, listed, and patented, are stored on the shelf and soon forgotten.

A significant contributor to the properties of water, including its solvent power, is the third type of chemical union, the *polar* or *hydrogen* bond. This weak connection, for it occurs at a distance, is also important among the biologically active molecules of proteins and nucleic acids and in the organization of some crystals. The first requirement is, as indicated, an acidic hydrogen atom with partial positive charge. This form exists in the hydroxyl group and in covalently bonded nitrogen and hydrogen. The partner is a basic, electron-rich atom, which typically is the oxygen in water, alcohols, and ethers, or it is the nitrogen in amines. Hydrogen bonding depends not on the higher energy electrons of oxygen, which are already occupied in covalent bonds, but on the nonbinding electrons of the lower shell. The charge distribution extends toward the hydrogen atom. This polar bond is in essence a localized electrostatic affinity.

Lone atoms when combined into molecules thus take on new and varied properties, although we should not forget that these federated atoms are still of the quantum realm, their energy being interger quantitized. A molecule may simultaneously involve ionic, hydrogen, and covalent bonding in a dance of charge distributions. The simple pseudo sphere of atoms becomes in the smallest molecules bumpy sausages, some bent at an angle. Rough-edged polygons and rings can also form. Most of the large biological molecules, which will be discussed at length later, are helical, and these may be secondarily contorted in supercoiled ropes, pleated sheets, and unique globular arrays. *Energy patterns take on concreteness as shape, and shape becomes a critical determinant of interaction.* The limited variety of forms encountered in atoms is exploded 10,000-fold when examining molecules, and this greater degree of freedom opens the door wide to creativity and organization.

Except for their intrinsic vibrations, we do not normally think of atoms as flexible. Molecules are. They even vibrate like springs through their bonds. Single covalent bonds permit rotation about the axis of the bond, but double covalent bonds provide rigidity. Long chain molecules are snake-like, with curves, coils, and folds. Bond angles are also adjustable to accommodate particular atoms as well as to meet environmental change.

The water molecule in liquid phase, for instance, has a bond angle of 104.5°, but in ice, to achieve maximal strength of hydrogen bonding, it is about 109.5°. The wider angle makes ice less dense than the liquid phase and thereby permits icebergs to float out to sea. Water molecules of ice cluster as tetrahedral sets of four hydrogens around each oxygen atom. Two hydrogens are the covalently bonded constituents of the given water molecule, and the two remaining polar-bonded hydrogens are of two neighboring molecules. Within a small mass of ice the hydrogen atoms are in line between the oxygen atoms; six tetrahedral groups along a plane form a hexagon. The classic six-pointed snowflake, which in any of its kaleidoscopic patterns is a familiar, joyful motif of winter and Christmas, is merely an extension of the core arrangement of hydrogen bonds.

The wondrous geometric variety of other crystals is also characteristic of the deep symmetries of bonds and planar alignments of the particular molecule. We prize many crystals of minerals for their rarity and beauty, but the light reenforcing properties of the synthetic ruby and the more efficient garnet have made them essential to the now ubiquitous laser technology, which repairs damaged retinas, interprets the digital codes on compact disks of music or data, and produces the extraordinary illusion of three dimensions in holograms. Crystals may grow and replicate through 'seeds' in a supersaturated 'mother' liquor; but despite the language, they do not reproduce.

Perhaps the most important feature of molecules is not their multifarious structures as such, but their diverse functions through structure. Reviewing the atom, we recall that isolated atoms are treated as limited entities of energy in which change occurs through subtraction or addition of energy as distinct units of mass and charge. This is largely a passive process of quantum fluctuations. When an atom is destroyed, only the configuration is lost; the essence, energy, is merely repackaged. Generally, atoms are either inert vapors or dead ores.* Molecules, however, are active agents of change.

*Two caveats: Atoms, especially when they are in crystalline array, are responsive to external electromagnetic influences; the palladium atom is known to serve as a catalyst, but it acts on molecular hydrogen and oxygen gas, and thus is defined by the higher order of molecules.

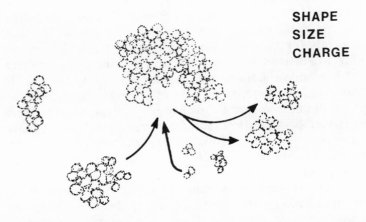

PATTERN RECOGNITION

SHAPE
SIZE
CHARGE

THE MOLECULE-ORGANISM

The moderate flexibility of globular enzymes, immuno-globulins, and cell membrane receptors is central in the regulation of biological processes.[3] *Taken together, molecular shape, size, and architecture create cognizant organisms.* The mouth of this creature is the cleft formed by juxtaposed atomic groups on one or several conjoined folded chains, and like a mouth, the atomic groups can converge. To carry the analogy further, some of the atomic groups lining the opening serve as senses and teeth. The shape and charge characteristics of the cleft limit and define the target substrate, for it must be complementary.

Daniel Koshland, Jr., at the University of California, Berkeley, has pointed out the significance of flexible receptors in regulating biological responses.[4] Focusing on enzymes, he described how some enzymes may not be in an active mode until an inducing regulatory molecule, such as a hormone, binds it at a distant location from the cleft; like a row of falling dominos, the realignment of the enzyme brings the cleft into a ready state for the substrate. Another form of regulator, the inhibitor, distorts the cleft into an inactive configuration. Variation in times for receptor realignment from nanoseconds and milliseconds to minutes would itself be an effective regulatory process. This is our first hint of the network activity that characterizes biological systems.

Biological receptors and enzymes are organized matter of awareness-mind. Cognition involves how well the external molecule fills the groove, hole, or pocket. With respect to enzymes, fit and flexibility must be optimal to permit proper entrance and binding of the substrate, its catalytic cleavage through polarization of covalent bonds, and the release of products. The pharmaceutical industry is now developing new drugs designed to accommodate such clefts or, conversely, to provide them.[5,6]

A complementary relationship such as this, so necessary for the formation of complex materials and for life, has been described as lock-and-key and glove-and-hand. Specificity (closeness and exclusiveness of match) and avidity (net strength of noncovalent bonds) are its attributes. Emil Fischer in 1894 first suggested the importance of complementarity in the splitting of sugars by enzymes, but it was through the works of Paul Ehrlich and later of Karl Landsteiner, who readily accepted the concept in their pioneering immuno-chemical studies of antibodies, that the metaphor became real as molecular configuration. Again, I must emphasize that, with few exceptions, interacting molecules are not entirely complementary; only the shape of particular areas of each molecule are involved. In addition, the two molecules may have both cavities and protrusions, such that they resemble two interlocking pieces of a larger jigsaw puzzle.

Complementarity goes beyond opposites in shape as a general principle. Taoism, for instance, centers on the origin and dynamic qualities of the opposites, as two excerpts from Lao Tzu's Tao Te Ching clearly demonstrate:

When everyone distinguishes beauty as beauty, there arises ugliness. When everyone deems good as good, evil is created. Therefore, existence and nonexistence mutually develop; difficult and easy are mutually realized in action; long and short are mutually contrasted; high and low arise together in establishing position.

Mold clay into a vessel; it is the space within that makes it useful. Cut out a door and windows for a room; it is the holes that make it useful. Therefore, profit comes from what exists; usefulness arises from what is not there.

Let us now consider two well-characterized molecules known to interact. We have determined the atom sequence, the angles of all their covalent bonds, and the probable zones of electron location and effective electromagnetic field density. In other words, we know more or less what the molecules look like. On our computer monitor, which depicts both molecular configurations, we observe the respective regions that come together. Upon designating the receptor, we simultaneously distinguish its complementary partner; they arise and act together as one. From the perspective of bio-chemical evolution, it is highly unlikely that the separate genes for both molecular regions came into existence together to meet the ideal. Instead, one molecule may have already been available; a mutation or other novel event may have then altered the genes of a second molecule, which, when synthesized, would have the fortuitous property of linking with some region of the first molecule. A survival advantage would support its retention in the next generation; alternatively, it could be detrimental to the point of being lethal and thereby eliminated.

As in the second Taoist example, *the very form and function of the molecules can only be described by the space around them.* The interrelationship is not like the Platonic sculptor recognizing as a template ideal a statue in a block of marble, nor like Chuang Tzu's wood carver intuitively finding a bell stand implicit within a particular tree, both of which are abstract projections of form within form. Like their atom components, *molecules are activities* and, hence, they are simultaneously and interdependently form and formlessness.

> Ghost buildings emerge
> through gray mists of a gray dawn—
> a pause in the rain.

Zen Masters warn us not to be dependent on such conceptual dualities. The relationships are useful in training, but they are also a trap. A philosophical monk, understanding the danger, asked Master Feng-Hsueh (896-973) how he could transcend the differentiation inherent in speech and the oneness found in silence. The Master replied with a quotation from a well-known poem, 'How fondly I remember Chiang-nan in March: partridges chirping among the fragrant flowers.'[7] The Master opened his mouth with words about birds and flowers, certainly different phenomena. How then was he free of the dichotomy? If you were the Master, how would you answer? Although you think or feel that you know, do not answer with an explanation. Such words would be lifeless and empty, and you would be like the philosophical monk in the above koan. KATZ! Now, answer!

Science, however, is a domain of words, although it, too, requires demonstrations. Its conduct usually follows deductive reasoning, but occasionally induction occurs, shaking apart complacency. For instance, trees, lungs, and snowflakes are extremely different forms, but they share a common feature:

bifurcations that seem to occur at random points. As science diverges into increasingly complicated fields, there grows a need for simple uniting principles of order. Chaos theory and fractal geometry are so exciting because they seem to offer a hitherto hidden mathematical order, the rules of the game, that is present in complex unpredictable phenomena across-the-board—from the branching shape of plants to the fluctuation of animal populations in an ecosystem, from heart and brainwave rhythms to the variability of planetary orbits, from turbulence in fluids to weather patterns.[8,9] What this means is that *absolute randomness is an illusion*, as, for example, the seemingly haphazard sequence, ...415926536..., is actually generated by the calculation of pi. Furthermore, the new tool is the mathematics of confronting an equation through approximation and iteration rather than solving it. Thus, Heraclitean process instead of stasis may be the better approach to understanding existence.

Such a broad perspective is felt among mathematicians:.

> No longer just the study of number and space, mathematical science has become the science of patterns, with theory built on relations among patterns and on applications derived from the fit between pattern and observation. Patterns suggest other patterns, often yielding patterns of patterns.

So wrote Lynn Arthur Steen, chair of the Conference Board of the Mathematical Sciences, in 1988.[10] To some extent, the ancient Greeks, for whom science, mathematics, and philosophy were still overtly and dependently intermeshed, knew this relationship as indicated by their word *idea*, which means pattern.

The most perplexing problem today in the morphological study of molecules is the mechanism or agencies through which molecules assume a particular shape. This is apparent in attempting to predict the form of crystals of complex organic molecules. The growing of crystals by astronauts in orbit, free of the distortive gravity-induced effects of convection, has the secondary purpose of providing clues to this puzzle. The primary objective is to produce large, uniform crystals suitable for X-ray crystallographic studies of their molecular arrangement.[11]

While the unresolved development of crystals into particular forms spurs curiosity, discovery of the determinants of molecular shape in protein folding would be for medicine an acutely significant advance. Proteins, of which the often mentioned enzymes are a variety, consist of one or more chains of amino acids, which are of 20 major types. Two such amino acids contain a sulfur group; the juxtaposition and subsequent covalent bonding of two such sulfur groups in most proteins help form and stabilize chain folding, but the confining bonds alone do not force a particular arrangement among the numerous possibilities.

In his obligatory lecture given in 1972 upon receiving the Nobel Prize for Chemistry, Christian Anfinsen described a prevalent thermodynamic hypothesis by which proteins under physiological environmental conditions take the shape directed by the lowest free energy of the entire system.[12] We already noted this idea in the shape of ice crystals. Anfinsen found that among some proteins, including enzymes, an enzyme was required to accelerate the process of folding from 24 hours to the proper 2 minutes. The reduction of disulfide bonds in an enzyme, he pointed out, unravels or denatures it, eliminating biological activity, but subsequent oxidation restores both the bonds and the activity. Direction for folding through amino acid sequence and maximal thermodynamic stability has become the accepted principle, as presented, for example, in two lauded textbooks of biochemistry.[13,14]

For a long while, the follow-up work of Alfinsen as described in the lecture was strangely ignored, probably because the explanation for conformation would not be tidy. If the chain is reduced and then shortened at either end or even chopped into two or three fragments and allowed to refold or recombine, activity returns with very similar physical properties as the unaltered molecule. Thus, something is amiss, and *amino acid sequence alone can not be responsible for configuration.*

One particular enzyme that breaks apart DNA consists of 149 amino acids without any disulfide bridges nor any sulfhydryl groups. The number of possible spatial arrangements approaches 10^{149}. Clearly, trial-and-error in achieving the optimal confiaguaration is inconceivable. There is no known enzyme to help fold this enzyme, and the contribution of any other molecular structure can be eliminated through the isolated synthesis of the enzyme from constituent amino acids, much like stringing beads into a necklace. Despite their flexibility, the great majority of these molecules in solution are of one configuration, which occurs in mere minutes. Anfinsen edited the chain with cleavages and deletions. Despite this dissection, some 10% of the molecule fragments aggregated in such a fashion that activity was restored. Anfinsen spoke of 'geometric sense' and 'structural memory', and observed that 'biological function appears to be more a correlate of macromolecular geometry than of chemical detail.'[12] He concluded that only the geometry and specific internal amino acids along the active cleft need to be conserved to provide proper function.

It was a good hypothesis. Experiments have now demonstrated that up to half the amino acids in a protein, particularly those on the periphery of combining sites or buried, may be substituted without affecting general structure or activity.[15] This tolerance explains why functionally analogous proteins from different species, which differ in sequence, remain active when placed in foreign tissues.

A further proposal was that, like the seeding of a small nucleus for growing crystals, the chain folds upon a nucleation site or at least along some restricted 'pathways'. This idea is now regarded as each folded structure itself, with the assistance of metal ions, mediates the folding of the next group of amino acids.[16] Each moment, the molecular structure sets new functional conditions for self-folding. It is almost like pulling oneself up by the bootstraps. Anfinsen's original reductionistic explanation was a good approximation, but it clearly lacked something that the dynamic whole provided.[17]

There is a curious phenomena of crystallization that occasionally occurs much to the amusement and bewilderment of chemists. Some chemicals that are synthesized for the first time seem to resist crystallization. Attempt after attempt fails even when performed independently by several laboratories. Then when at last crystals are produced in one vessel, it becomes increasingly easy to repeat the feat. In fact, spontaneous crystallization may then occur in previously sealed containers. Such a course of events has happened with glycerine and with ethylene diamine tartrate mono-hydrate.[18,19] The physical mechanisms by which geometric forms of crystals and globular proteins are selected and develop have thus far defied discovery. The difficulty may lie in not considering emptiness as part and parcel of form.

Hawk glides the sky
along hidden thermal paths
watchfully silent.

Anfinsen used the same metaphoric language as the biologist C.H. Waddington. In advancing the concept of morphogenetic fields, Waddington formulated the topographical description of development or change called chreodes, derived from the Greek for obliged path.[20] As hills, saddles, branching valleys, gullies, and other features in a descending landscape would direct the path of a frictionless ball, so would the combination of genes and undescribed nongenetic hereditary agencies cause the *sequential* formation of particular structures and patterns. Such a terrain would include regulation by including alternate but merging paths. Also, the steepness of the terrain would provide quantitative control. There was no metaphysic behind this model.

The philosophies of Hua-Yen Buddhism and Alfred North Whitehead, while differing in several fundamental ways, would have supplied the Anfinsen structural memory or the Waddington relief map. Hua-Yen is derived from mystical experience operating psychologically at the level of sub-consciousness-mind; Whitehead process philosophy is solely an intellectual development, which mainly concerns the physical realm.[21-23] Both, however, are holographic in regarding each momentary event as arising from the influence of every other event in the universe and, thereby, is not localized, but is spread throughout.[24]

We have become familiar with holograms and their astonishing look-around three-dimensional images of objects. The holographic plate itself appears blandly as an arrangement of intersecting concentric circles, which is formed by the interference of object-reflected and incidental laser light. The plate has an interesting property. If it is broken, any piece, when projected by laser, will yield an image of the entire reflected scene. As each jewel in Indra's net reflects each other, each event contains and pervades every other. Whitehead summarized the relationship as *everything is everywhere at all times.*

The Hua-Yen perspective has an atom, a person, and a thing as simultaneously noumenon and phenomenon, object and subject, and cause and effect..[22,25] All phenomena are interdependent and interrelated through origin, manifestion, and activity. Hence, what we regard as one atom pervades the universe and the universe is this one atom. In addition to interpenetrative structure is mutual influence, such that each event or thing — i.e., activity — affects simultaneously every other event or thing. While the manifold or whole consists of and is influenced by these separate yet integral parts, these parts in turn consist of and are influenced by the whole. What then becomes of identity? Merged, both part and whole are empty and insubstantial. We find no *whole,* no *parts,* indeed, no boundaries. Yet, if we identify a flower with the soil, cloud, sun, and even a distant galaxy or the entire universe, we lose sight of the flower; when, in turn, we identify the soil, cloud, sun and so forth with the flower, we manifest the flower and submerge all else. All of these principals are qualitative.

With respect to sequential causality, the Hua-Yen interpretation evaporates time. The Hua-Yen Sutra includes the statements that 'In the past there is the future, and in the future, the present...The infinite kalpas [in Hindu mythology, cyclic periods of universal creation and destruction equaling 8,640,000,000 solar years] are but one moment, and that moment is the infinite kalpas...Realizing this, one knows the incalculable kalpas are but one moment, and that moment is no moment.' [22] Time, therefore, does not exist of itself, but comes into being by interactions of forms. Some critics have focused on the interpenetration of past, present, and future, while ignoring the last crucial point that time is formless and empty.[21] Also the existence of future events as potentia or projections rather than unalterable facts has not been considered. No such confusion is found with Whitehead. He clearly advocated only cumulative penetration of past in the present, declaring that 'The many become one and are increased by one,' and that the endurance of physical forms is 'the process of continuously inheriting a certain identity of character transmitted throughout a historic route of events.'[21]

The fate of a protein completing synthesis and commencing folding, according to these schemes, depends on the simultaneous and continual influences of the arrangement of already existing molecules of its kind and the recapitulation intrinsic to each moment. Using the creode model, every other copy of the molecule superimposes its form and canalizing landscape as a template.

Rupert Sheldrake summarized his hypothesis of morphic resonance as follows:[26]

The persistence of material forms depends on a continuously repeated actualization of the system under the influence of its morphogenetic field; at the same time the morphogenetic field is continuously re-created by morphic resonance from similar past forms. The forms which are most similar and which will consequently have the greatest effect will be those of the system itself in the immediate past.

He calls for unique hierarchial fields for every form, and describes the fields as probability structures that depend on statistical distribution of previous similar forms, hence vibrations and resonances.

This metaphysical concept is a feedback loop of auto-resonance. The activities leading to a particular form are directed through probabilities of paths; in turn, the completed form influences and reinforces the probability functions. Perhaps it would be advantageous to relate this arrangement to our own experiences. The system strongly resembles *karma*, a strictly psychological term meaning 'action' in Sanskrit. Lama Anagarika Govinda explains karma in reference to volition:[27]

In other words, only where there is intention, i.e., consciously motivated exertion, can we speak of karmic action, and only such action has character-forming consequences, determining our inclination and thus our future actions and reactions. Character is nothing but the tendency of our will, formed by repeated actions....Karma [is] the law of movement in the direction of least resistance, i.e., of the frequently trodden and therefore easier path.

I describe karma as mental momentum. In physics, momentum is the product of mass and its velocity. An object with greater momentum will make the greater dent, impulse, or impact on a second object. Momentum also relates to impetus, or strength of maintaining direction and velocity against surrounding influences. In psychological terms, karmic momentum is proportional to the importance or meaningfulness of a situation wherein a decision must be made (the path divides) augmented by the quality of deed (such as efficacy, confidence, precision, or potency). For example, going to the movies over watching television would have little effect or karmic influence on oneself, the community, and surroundings; helping a friend or especially a stranger in need has great impact on oneself, other people, and society. In other words, minor decisions and commitments make little impression on the psychological landscape, and require numerous repeats to produce a significant groove to force a change of habit; the more difficult path of decision-making in important circumstances is made smoother and more level with fewer repeats.

Therefore, by the concept of morphogenetic fields, a major change in form produced by mutation or other force outside hereditary control will significantly shift the probability limits for morphological variation. A small number of approximate repeats, changing the frequency of auto-resonance, leads to macro-evolution. Minor alterations of developed forms yield micro-evolution.

This philosophical digression is included in order to open the frontiers of etiology. From what we have learned about the quantum atom, we can not avoid nonlocal action. There is something deep in phenomena that science must confront and include, even if it has the stain of parapsychology and philosophy. I have personally validated the Hua-Yen experience, but this psychological attainment, limited to one individual's self-exploration, can not serve as evidence in the manifested world of objects. However appealing and plausible the holistic and organismic concepts may be, it is too early to subscribe to their reality. Many experiments designed to test these frameworks need to be performed. Physicist Nick Herbert points to possible work in his field. His description of phase entanglement of quantum probability waves bears remarkable resemblance to the above philosophies:[28]

> Since there is nothing that is not ultimately a quantum system..., then it links all systems that have once interacted at some time in the past...into a single waveform whose remotest parts are joined in a manner unmediated, unmitigated, and immediate. The mechanism for this instant connectedness is not some invisible field that stretches from one part to the next, but the fact that a bit of each part's 'being' is lodged in the other.

This interpenetrative action has a strong impact on the question of individuality. It makes it a false concept, an illusion. As this book proceeds, we shall find the principles of interpenetration, feed-back loops between orders, and resonance in whichever organization we inspect.

From the flawed common macroscopic perspective, the sorts of molecules are myriad and virtually endless in composition and arrangement; however, the individual molecules of a kind are exactly alike, excluding the instances where a constituent atom differs profoundly in energy, as in isotopes. Even with this exception in structure, the interactive activities of particular molecule types do not vary. Whether oxygen gas contains oxygen 12, 13, or even 14 is irrelevant; these assorted isotopes all allow respiration and keep us alive. Atoms within molecules are interchangeable, and portions of molecules are broken off and then combined with other molecules or molecule fragments. Indeed, whole molecules are combined into new forms. This obligatory choreography of transforming shapes is described as chemical reactions, although the term *interactions* would be more appropriate. Therefore, individual molecules are individuals because reduction to atoms would eliminate all their properties and activities. However, individuality here is not synonymous with unit uniqueness.

We have earlier sought in vain the 'real' shape of atoms. By the slight increase in scale, the larger molecules can be satisfactorily resolved by the several forms of electron microscopy.[29,30] The uncertain positions of electrons in atoms and the resulting electronic blurs seem less important in giving us a sense of the molecule. Our impression is strong that a molecule is a discrete object within space, but this idea is false. Electron-density maps of molecules, which resemble the irregular contour lines of geological survey maps, give us a more realistic image.[31] Molecules are still nebulous, but these ghosts have a skeleton.

The complexity and variety of probability waves in molecules, thanks to regional flexibility and rigidity, raise the limit of possible actions far above those of atoms. At the molecular levels of matter-mind (inorganic ions and crystals) and awareness-mind (proteins, DNA, RNA), cognition of patterns does not only occur, it is essential.

Going back to the question posed at the beginning of this section, we still need to address the apparent solidity of fingers and pianos. The answer is simply that the atoms push back. There are forces of repulsion as well as attraction. Particles of the same charge or electromagnetic polarity repel each other, as we learn by playing with a set of magnets. The closer the positive poles of two bar magnets are brought together, the stronger the force of repulsion is. If the repulsive forces of two atoms are overcome, fusion can occur with the ejection of vast amounts of energy as heat. In the hydrogen bomb, the already powerful force of a surrounding nuclear fission reaction compresses hydrogen atoms into the inert gas helium. Why hydrogen? The hydrogen atom consists of but one proton. The bringing together of atoms with greater numbers of protons would compound the energy requirements. As we shall see in the next chapter, nature also takes the easier path.

Chapter 4

2,000 LIGHT-YEARS FROM HOME

Astronomy/Cosmology

West of these out to seas colder than
   the Hebrides
I must go
Where the fleet of stars is anchored
   and the young
Star captains glow.
                              James Elroy Flecker

As a medical microbiologist, I casually toss around figures of millions to billions when describing populations of bacteria in broth. These are calculated numbers, only mathematical expressions derived from serial ten-fold dilutions. We learn to correlate such figures with a density pattern, such as the cloudiness of broth in a test tube or the concentration of microbial dots and dashes seen through a microscope. Since a billion colonies would completely cover the agar surface in a Petri dish, and for certain other technical reasons, I select for counting only those dishes containing fewer than 300 colonies, as estimated from previous experience.

I have not personally experienced *billion*. I do not believe that anyone truly has this capacity. Considering that feelings are the stuff of experience, can a person marching in a large political demonstration distinguish a crowd of 10,000 participants from one of 100,000? Even from a distant vantage point, crowd estimates are notoriously inaccurate. Many state lotteries have winning odds of about 1 in 10,000,000, which might seem reasonable for an investment until you attempt to count to but 10,000. The national debt of the United States has far surpassed one trillion dollars—$1,000,000,000,000—a totally incomprehensible number.

The very small is no improvement. It is worse. Spherical bacteria have a diameter of approximately 0.000001 meter, or 1/1,000 millimeter. The AIDS virus is one-tenth the size, 0.0001 millimeter. An atom is approximately 0.0000001 millimeter. Here we are comparing microscopic and ultra-microscopic objects with a macroscopic or sensory standard, and we suffer the incompatibility. After all, these materials were invisible and unknown until the invention of the light and electron microscopes.

Our assimilation of temporal relationships are likewise fraught with numerical and psychological obstacles. The duration of certain synthesized radioisotopes is measured in minute fractions of a second, while the sequoia survives for thousands of years. What is an hour in the life of such a tree? What is a century to a butterfly? Now consider ten thousand years. You are that butterfly.

Despite the aid of computers, working with and discussing very large or infinitesimally small numbers is exceedingly impractical. Mental numbness sets in within moments, immediately followed by the erroneous addition or subtraction of ciphers, or simple incomprehension. Scientific notation, therefore, was instituted as a remedy. This is the use of exponents or powers of 10, such that 10^6 is 1 followed by six zeros, i.e., one million. Another contrivance to maintain effective communication is the coining of terms of equivalence. The *kilo* in kilometer means 1,000 (10^3); the *nano* in nanosecond is 0.000000001 (10^{-9}). A *jiffy* is 10^{-43} second; a *googol* is 10^{100}.

We are now ready to shift our focus from the ultra small of the atom and molecule to the ultra large, the cosmos. We have learned that the universal constant is the speed of light; no thing can go faster, although in-form-ation (a result of perturbing a common matrix) apparently does. Einstein's theories of relativity concern this peculiar relationship of time-space. The photon thus defines the universe and is eternal in the sense of being outside of time. The speed of light is 300,000 kilometers per second, and if you were to travel one year at this speed, you would have traversed 9.5 x 10^{12} kilometers, or 6 trillion miles. In describing size and distances in cosmic terms, the light-year is the standard unit of measurement. Our galaxy, the Milky Way, has a diameter of 100,000 light-years, a figure certainly easier to express and grasp than the equivalent 6×10^{17} miles. The closest star, Alpha in the southern constellation Centaurus, is a mere (!) 4 light-years away.

Cosmologists are astrophysicists and philosophers who examine the universe and venture guesses — sometimes validated—on its development and structure. Of course, the origin and destruction of the universe is also the concern of the clergy. Indeed, priests and astronomers were once one and the same. Each culture, each religion, each epoch has a myth concerning the origin of Earth and moon, the stars, the planets, and the celestial visitors, meteors and comets.

The Judeo-Christian and Islamic traditions envision an external God, who, having created the cosmos, promises to destroy it in due course, usually, according to the biblical prophets, in disgust. Inquiries on what God did before creating the universe were not appreciated by the clerical authorities; few thinkers were satisfied by their descriptions of an anthropomorphic God outside the confines of time, space, and action. The date for the creation of the world was calculated, according to a literal intrepretation of the Bible, by a seventeenth-century English theologian and metaphysician, Isaac Newton, who, of course, is better known as a scientist and mathematician. Newton wrote that God created the universe in 3988 B.C.E. Another theologican, Bishop James Ussher, made it a little earlier, 4004 B.C.E.

A linear cosmology of beginning and end is common to the Near East, but other parts of the world fashion their myths and philosophies from the observed cycles of nature: day and night; the shadow of the moon; the seasons; birth, death, and regeneration. The Hindu cosmos is one of periodic creation and destruction with no beginning and no end. Each cycle is a day and night of Brahma (equivalent to 8.64×10^9 solar years) who lives 108 cosmic years.* And each Brahma is one dream episode of sleeping Vishnu. Furthermore, as presented

---

*The numbers 864, 432, and 108, which figure in the time cycles of diverse cultures, may stem from the 86,400 beats in 24 hours of a relaxed human pulse of 60 beats per minute.[1]

in a medieval Hindu story, countless separate universes may exist simultaneously.[1] When asked about such matters, Buddha remained silent, since the speculation is idle and irrelevant to the moment, place, and circumstance. Moreover, his silence was a demonstration that in true emptiness there is no time, let alone the concept of time. Buddhists, however, generally maintain a cyclic cosmological system.

For the Chinese, whether Confucian or Taoist, the universe arises and dissolves into chaos by its own nature. The neo-Confucianists of the eleventh century declared that each cycle of construction and dissolution lasts 129,600 solar years.[2] Within each great cycle were said to nest the various cycles of material forms from heavenly orbiting orbs to the pulses of the body all intermeshed as some vast clockwork. The metaphoric timepiece, however, was elastic to the extent that the occasional disharmonies of humans could be corrected. Also, the alchemist could hasten certain processes.

While the followers of Kung-Fu Tzu were content in bureaucratic bliss with the intricacies of organization and order, the Taoists were cautious with the principle, preferring the ideal of simplicity over complexity, playful independence over regulation. Chuang Tzu, in characteristic humor, related a story in which the ruler of the Southern Sea, Shu (Hasty), and the ruler of the Northern Sea, Hu (Careless), met at times in the land of the ruler Hun-tun (Chaos), who entertained them well. To repay his kindness, the two sea lords deliberated, and observing that all creatures have seven orifices for seeing, eating, hearing, and breathing, decided to bore an opening in their host each day. On the seventh day Hun-tun died.[3]

The Greeks myths also begin with formless Chaos, but see the benefit of order arising from its midst with the help of Eros (Love) and Gaia (Goddess of Earth). The subsequent world of matter was regarded as a living organism, indeed, a god.[4] Anaximander believed that our world was one of the innumerable that arose as eddies or bubbles, through rotary action, in the uniform medium of aspatial and atemporal Boundlessness. Anaximenes, who followed, suggested that the chaotic stuff was vapor, which, when rarefied, was thrown centrifugally to the periphery to form the stars and, when condensed, was drawn to the center of the vortex to congeal into our home planet. He further proposed that instead of existing apart in space, the various worlds were separated by time, one following the other. Other Ionians put the world cycle at 72,000 solar years. The Pythagoreans, as noted earlier, superimposed a most orderly world of geometric forms, an organism of interacting ideals or models.

In contrast to these metaphysical conjectures, astronomy is a science based on observation and analysis, using the tools of physics and mathematics, rather than on manipulative experimentation. Its concepts, nevertheless, require testable predictions for validation. Of course, nature provides the time and place of the required phenomena. A modern scientific cosmology, which replaces the model of a static universe and echoes in some parts the ancient speculative philosophies, is arising.

Evidence for the model includes two main exhibits. The first was introduced in 1929 by Edwin Hubble, who earlier had discovered that the then called 'spiral nebulae', including Andromeda, were not in our 'universe', but, in fact, were exceedingly distant and seemingly independent organizations of stars, now known as galaxies. This realization meant that our star system and the Milky Way were part of a galaxy, too. Our once cozy universe now suddenly became a small island among other islands in a seemingly cold endless ocean.

How did Hubble compartmentalize and expand the universe? All elements and molecules vibrate, and each type absorbs or, on heating, emits light at specific frequencies related to their quantum energy and bond resonance. We know that sunlight, when passed through a prism, is diffracted into a rainbow-like spectrum; however, some frequencies are absent. These missing spectral lines are related to the composition of the sun, which includes only a few types of atoms and molecules, chiefly hydrogen and helium. Different star types have their own characteristic spectra. Outstanding intensities of certain frequencies indicate higher proportions of particular molecules, while general differences in luminosity in spectra from similar sources are correlated with distance. Determining the spectra of molecules in randomly chosen galaxies, Hubble observed the shifting of the characteristic patterns of spectral lines to lower frequencies (toward the red) relative to stars of our own Milky Way.[5]

The displacement of light frequencies was not entirely novel. Physicists were well acquainted with the Doppler effect, in which the degree of pitch fluctuation depends on the speed of the traveling object, as exemplified by the familiar sound of an approaching, then passing train or other noisy vehicle. Hubble found the extent of red-shifting to be directly proportional to the distance of the observed galaxy. Hence, the furthermost galaxies are the earliest and the fastest. Andromeda, the closest spiral galaxy, has a minor red shift, equivalent in distance to about 1.5 million light-years. This ubiquitous lowering of frequency strongly suggested that all the galaxies are receding from each other.

A common origin was thus deduced, but was this well-spring in or outside of space? Is there an expanding edge of matter in emptiness? Einstein pointed out that matter describes space and that space itself was expanding. Furthermore, a mass curves surrounding space.[6] Accordingly, near the sun, unquestionably a massive object, the straight-line path of light from a distant star should bend relative to an observer on Earth, 93 million miles away. This displacement was substantiated by comparing photographs of such a star taken at night and during a total solar eclipse in an opposite season.[7,8] Similarly, the orbital path of one body around another is not curved but straight, space being distorted. As the craters of the moon are nested, all the various cosmic masses are displacements within displacements of space-time.

As dramatic as the red shift was in offering a new cosmology, science demands corroborative evidence from a different perspective or method. Substantiation was also necessary because Fred Hoyle and other astronomers championed a view that the universe, while dynamic and expanding, is in a steady state whereby matter is being formed everywhere at a rate that offsets dilution.[9] This radical alternative would collapse if, diffused in the skies, one could detect the predicted residual thermal radiation from the single explosive event, disdainly nicknamed the Big Bang by Hoyle. Because of red-shifting, the heat would be found in the microwave range of the electromagnetic spectrum. In 1964 at Bell Laboratories, two scientists working in satellite communications, Arno Penzias and Robert Wilson, serendipitously discovered such background noise in whichever region of space they pointed their antenna.[9,10] The subsequently calculated temperature of the intergalactic universe was approximately -270° Celsius, 2.7° above Absolute Zero Kelvin. This confirmation also established that any attempt to find the center of the universe in a galaxy map would be futile. Every point is its center. *You are the center of the universe.* (Do not encourage an egotist with this information!)

However, the uniformity of backgound radiation itself presented a problem. If the Big Bang was homogenous in every way, what led to the formation of galaxies? Today, thirty years later, a dedicated satellite, the Cosmic Background Explorer, has provided data showing the background not be to uniform, but spotchy with temperature variation of only 0.00003 degree![10] Any trace of steady-state theories among cosmologists vanished.

The universe, it seems, arose from a point in mythic, metaphysical Chaos. Whether there will be a Big Crunch, when gravity reverses expansion, or a Big Freeze, when the still dispersing star matter of an expanding universe is extinguished from lack of heat energy, is yet unknown. The reversal depends on a sufficient total mass of the universe and the mutual attractive force of gravity. These data are incomplete, and speculation on the nature, let alone existence, of the missing mass, called *dark matter,* fills the pages of scientific journals.[11,12] For instance, neutrinos, of which the universe abounds, may not be massless, as thought, or the mass could be occluded in black holes. Another candidate for dark matter is the long sought brown dwarfs, gaseous substars, whose numbers may be well beyond expectations.[13] New, poorly characterized and highly speculative particles, axions and photinos, and other massive entities have been proposed: names and forms awaiting reality. Therefore, the question of linear versus cyclic cosmology remains open. As a biologist, I place my bets on a cyclic or helical process.

Stephen W. Hawking, a theoretical physicist at Cambridge University, has recently offered a new option.[14] He suspects that the organismic Universe [my usage] buds like yeast, that there are multiple, nay, an infinity of coexisting and inter-connecting universes each developed through its own Big Bang. Where did our universe come from? From a bleb of another universe. Where will our universe go when it contracts? Into another universe. The size of each joint would be 10^{-33} centimeters and the time of the *wormhole* opening would be 10^{-43} second, a jiffy, which is of the same order as quantum fluctuations.

In less eruptive, normal circumstances—when there is not a compact universal mass awaiting an exit—wormholes at every point between adjacent universes would allow electrons and other particles to transfer domains and interact with particles there. The appearance of emerging particles in a given universe would be the previously mentioned virtual particles, appearing suddenly from the substrate like a trap-door spider. The novel larger size Hawking Universe is a self-contained, closed, compartmentalized system subject neither to creation nor to destruction. Matter is squished about through minute orifices as the air in a balloon is manipulated by a clown constructing animal shapes.

This odd, intriguing, consciouness-mind-boggling proposal shows how quantum nuclear physics intermeshes with developmental astrophysics; how the largest form arises from the smallest, how the smallest emanates from the largest. Of course, all of these cosmological schemes are speculation built upon multiple brick tiers of conception with quantum theory being the mortar. Considering the long history of evolving ideas, will the mortar endure the pressure of model accom-modation and the erosive forces of forthcoming data? Will we be like haiku master Masaoka Shiki (1865-1902)?

Looking back,
the man I passed
is lost in the mist.

To seek individuality and uniqueness among the starry organizations, we need to scrutinize the visible objects of our own small universe. Insights from old China are of little help. There is no traditional Chinese character or phrase for galaxy, since their distinction from nebulae was not established until 1923. However, the dense belt of stars, the Milky Way, was differentiated. Two phrases have been used to describe this heavenly feature, sadly unknown to most modern urban dwellers who view the night sky through the gauze of electric lights and air pollution. The characters are literally translated as 'silver stream' and 'river of the sky'. Of course, *star* is a primitive character, being composed of the radicals for sun and life, alive, or to come forth. *Universe* or *cosmos* is expressed as a phrase meaning eternal space. *Eternal* is time without beginning or end. *Space* here is allied with house, roof, or abode, an association understood by Robert Lewis Stevenson when he wrote, 'The untented Kosmos my abode, I pass, a wilful stranger.'

Time and space of our present cosmos came into existence some 10 to 15 billion years ago, depending on the choice of standards.[15] Extrapolation to source or zero point from present day instrument readings is inherently risky. As the conventional scenario goes, in the beginning there was light, photon energy, an explosive flash well approximated by the detonation of our comparatively insignificant nuclear weapons. Here, the scientific and religious image is one. 'Shedding blinding brilliance; overspreading—boundless, beautiful—all spaces with His all-regarding faces; So He showed! If there should rise suddenly within the skies sunburst of a thousand suns flooding earth with beams undeemed-of, then might be that Holy One's majesty and radiance dreamed of!' is the metaphoric description in the Bhagavad-Gita.[16] Out of nothing-ness, emerging and inflating from a peculiar point—the singularity, where mathematics fail in a deluge of infinities —expanding at the speed of light (for it consisted of just that, along with pi mesons, muons, neutrinos/antineutrinos, and electrons/positrons) the extraordinarily dense bubble was the cosmic photon torpedo.

But the glorious universe in its entirety was then only a half light-year wide. Early within the very first second, the temperature was sufficiently cooled—10^{10} degrees Kelvin—to produce an unorganized plasma of the above particles plus the heavier protons/antiprotons and neutrons.[9] This level was still too hot for a nucleus to hold. Further expansion and cooling

COSMOS

to 10^9 degrees Kelvin led to a homogeneous ocean of nuclei of hydrogen and helium with smaller amounts of lithium and beryllium. After a million years or so, at temperatures of 10^3 Kelvin, nuclei would be joined by electrons to form atoms. Soon after this point the universe faced the force of gravity and the cumulative influence of nonpredictive chaos, as described by nonlinear mathematics.[17,18]

One of the great unknowns of cosmology is why our universe is almost all matter rather than a more even balance of matter and antimatter. On coming together, matter and antimatter destroy each other. Somehow selective asymmetric processes have permitted the universe to exist by eliminating or transporting away one of the sets of charged particles. Perhaps there is an antimatter universe a wormhole away.

Slightly denser areas within the uniform growth of our newborn cosmos led to fracturing zones. As described by Hawking, most of these regions were given a rotative pull by gravity.[9] The concentrating, slowly swirling zones of matter, which were the mother of galaxy clusters, were further subjected to shearing forces. The rotation of the newly separated clouds accelerated as their mass condensed into smaller forms, the spiral galaxies, in the same centripetal manner as an ice skater, performing a pirouette, increases the rate of spin by drawing in her arms. Our mature Milky Way completes a revolution in 10^8 years. The irregular and elliptical galaxies probably originated from areas with little or no rotation. Smaller eddies and the mutual gravitation of atoms in all these protogalaxies increased the temperature of the gas, begetting the fusion furnaces of stars. Cycles of expansion and compression in some hot young stars generated carbon, oxygen, iron, and other heavier atoms in their core, which after star death by supernova explosion, condensed as molecular compounds into the comparatively frigid planets.

In 1989, a colossal rotating cloud of hydrogen was discovered 65 million light-years away near the constellation Virgo.[19] The entity is ten times the size of our Milky Way with one-tenth its mass and is spinning at one revolution per 10^9 years. Astronomers have interpreted the phenomenon as an embryonic galaxy developing in our backyard. If this is so, then our dependence on extrapolative hindsight on this phase of cosmic evolution is giving way to direct observation. Inapparent mass in the form of diffused intergalactic clouds indicate that the our yet young universe may indeed have the potential for ultimate collapse.

The formation of stars and planets is not a one-time activity. Generations of stars are recycled from gaseous discharges and the remnants of supernovas. Within our own spiral galaxy are gaseous clouds, nebulae, that are the nurseries of stars. Molecular hydrogen, the major component of this vapor, is accompanied by smaller proportions of heavier elements, such as calcium, potassium, iron, and titanium; of molecules like carbon monoxide and cyanide; and of various dusts. Indeed, dust permeates the galaxy, obscuring observation of stars on the opposite side of the swirling disk. The density of nebular gas is about 1 atom per cubic centimeter. Stars begin to condense in eddies where surface densities of atoms are greater than 10^{20} per square centimeter. The sun, born 5×10^9 years ago, is at least a second generation star with 2% carbon and other heavy atoms.

This cosmological drama is broadly presented, for the details are widely contested. Scientific evidence, nonetheless, is plentiful for the main features. For instance, astronomers, strangely, are witnesses to events that took place eons earlier. Cosmic distances are so great that the light of such happenings reach us after considerable delay. Thus, when they look through their optical and radio telescopes at areas outside our Milky Way, these galaxy explorers look back in time. J. Anthony Tyson, Patrick Seitzer, and their associates at Bell Laboratories and the Space Telescope Science Institute, having photographed the limit of the visible universe, offer us a view of the cosmos some two billion years after the Big Bang.[20,21]

Recognizing that red-shifting of the furthermost galaxies would take the relative spectra into the invisible infra red, if such galaxies existed, these investigators limited their observation to the visible spectrum. They focused their telescope on 12 different regions of the sky apparently clear of any object. Each area would cover only 2% of the full moon. They made 6-hour exposures of these sites at three wavelengths, and utilized a special detector that could register single photons. More than 25,000 densely packed 'blue fuzzies' were counted on each image, which can be extrapolated to 20 billion such objects in the entire sky. (This veritable blanket helps instill a feeling of the size of a billion.) They interpreted each spot as a galaxy, and equated the blueness to the red-shifting of the ultraviolet radiation characteristic of newborn stars. These colorful objects, hence, are the young condensing galaxies, whose development proceeds over 1 to 6 billion years.

A simple demonstration of what these researchers have accomplished may be achieved by marking thousands of dots on a large, well-inflated balloon, representing the present universe, and then releasing its air; the dots and their neighbors on the now small flattened toy, representing the early cosmos, become compacted, approaching confluence. This is exactly the reverse of the standard teaching aid presented in most popular and academic books for illustrating the Big Bang theory.

Another striking observation of the large scale universe is the distribution pattern of the galaxies. Consider the analogy of a photograph appearing in a newspaper. Looking very closely at the figure, you will see an array of dots and shadings that seem to be part of an abstract design. Holding the paper at normal distance, the dots blend to produce a higher order image. They same effect occurs in forming recognizable images on a television screen. At first, the discovery of galaxy clusters led one to conclude that the supposed smooth homogenous universe is instead homogeneously lumpy and of no particular order. Indeed, astronomers have observed a rare rogue galaxy, veering off the radial vector to collide with another galaxy in hellish interaction.

This idea of randomness has been overthrown. Valerie de Lapparent, Margaret Geller, and John Huchra of the Harvard-Smithsonian Center for Astrophysics plotted 5,000 galaxies in three thin sections of the sky, each 6° thick, 117° wide, and 900 light-years deep.[10,22] Their maps, like the example of the newspaper photograph, clearly show a foamy pattern of empty bubbles and galaxy-studded filaments. The circular forms increase in size with time/distance. Since map slices are adjacent, the major filament that extends across the entire sector of each map suggests a perpendicular sheet, which the

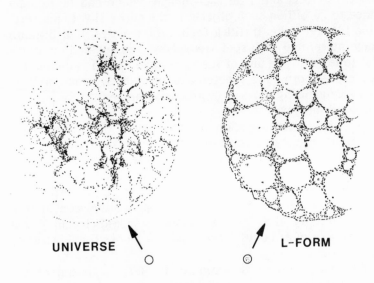

UNIVERSE   L-FORM

TWO VACUOLATED ORGANISMS:
Our universe of galaxies (limit of detection) expanding
from the particle bubble; L-form bacterial large body
growing from an elementary body.

researchers call the 'Great Wall'. This feature contains more
than half the galaxies. Nature often repeats a theme at different levels of order. Rather than reaffirming the simple physical example of aggregated soap bubbles, I see the arrangement
as a biological structure. This froth resembles the internal
vacuolar structure of L-form bacterial *large bodies* and of
macrophage white cells situated in lung tissue.[23,24] L-form
large bodies can arise from *elementary bodies*, which are far
smaller and lack vacuoles. Perhaps there is an equivalence in
the structure of the universe of the chaos-directed surface-
volume trigger of biological invagination and vacuolation.
Does the universe also have an equivalent of cytoplasm and a
microfilament and microtubular cytoskeletal network?[25,26]
Apparently it does.

One of the first features recognized on microscopically observing a plant or animal cell is a streaming of internal granules and vacuoles. In yet another instance of seredipity, a group of astronomers* in a purely technical survey of a 3×10^8 light-year segment of the skies, designed to improve the calibration of distances to elliptical galaxies, noted that a number of galaxy superclusters were moving irregularly.[11] While up to a thousand galaxies compose a cluster, a super-cluster may encompass 10^5 galaxies over 10^8 light-years. Their velocity measurements indicated that some superclusters move in opposite direction of their neighbors, some hundreds of kilometers per second. Furthermore, from their calculations

---

*Colleagues of this group of astronomers soon nicknamed the agitators 'The Seven Samurai'. Another collection of scientists advocating superstring theory, a Theory of Everything, to unite into a common order the four fundamental forces (strong and weak nuclear forces, electromagnetism, and gravity) was dubbed the 'Princeton String Quartet'. Particle physicists, conceptualizing the behavioral components of protons, neutrons, and other entities, coined the terms *quark* (borrowed from James Joyce) and their six classes, called *flavors*, which include the *up, down, strange, charmed, top* and *bottom* (or *truth* and *beauty*). Indicating their additive and subtractive properties, each flavor includes three *colors: red, green,* and *blue. Gluons,* which connect the quarks, are also of three colors. Various combinations characterize each elementary particle. (The failure to discover quark top has placed this model in jeopardy.) Some astronomers postulated dark matter as being composed of 'weakly interacting massive particles' or WIMPs. Such wit and whimsy are rarely found in the biomedical sciences; in my own field, there is only the old mechanistic concept of an antibody generator of diversity (GOD) and an antiviral agent, *interferon.* A team of sociologists and psychologists should investigate this! Do physicists have more fun, or do they especially require comical relief and a touch of humanity from their heady work of arid, distant mathematical abstraction? Or are they naturally jocular? Whatever the reason, my biological colleagues should take their example and lighten up!

they determined that the galaxies are hardly moving relative to our Milky Way, which moves at 600 kilometers per second against the cosmic background radiation. Most of these galaxies, including our own, formed more or less a plane or plate that seems to be attracted to another region of space. And our Virgo supercluster is not alone. Superclusters in Perseus, Hydra-Centaurus, and Pavo-Indus are streaming at 700 kilometers per second toward a mysterious *Great Attractor*, which may be a more distant and massive collection.

This cosmic plate tectonic has been confirmed by independent teams measuring the velocities of spiral galaxies in the same areas.[27] In fact, galaxies on the back side of the hypothetical Great Attractor are falling inwards, establishing the existence of some fantastically large mass. Curiously, the mass of the Great Attractor approximates the mass that Geller and Huchra have inferred for the observed portion of the Great Wall.[22] Lastly, other Wall-like concentrations seem to be spaced periodically in intervals of some 400 million light-years. *More and more the universe appears to be a great fluid and elastic organism of undulations, whirls, and resonances.*

Thus, in review, we have stars, galaxies, galaxy groups, galaxy clusters, galaxy superclusters, and now probably galaxy plates. Moreover, if Hawking is right, we will need to add universes within the Universe. Hierarchial orders of the very large should not come as a surprise; as below, so above (and as above, so below) is the Hermetic dictum. Or in the words of the great satirist Jonathan Swift,

> So, naturalists observe, a flea
> Hath smaller fleas that on him prey;
> And these have smaller still to bite
> 'em;
> And so proceed ad infinitum.

However, we should keep in our consciousness-mind that these organizations are not independent, but interpenetrate as a vast inseparable system. The smallest flea is the largest; this great flea is still the lowest. As the nutritional process of biting, not differing flea size, is the essense of Swift's hierarchy, *the transformation of energy, not the varied quantities of mass, is the cosmic principle.*

What is the stuff of plates? What is this mesh? No one knows. However, some cosmologists believe that dark matter may be involved. This hypothetical material is not minor by any means; it would need to compose 90% of the mass of the universe! Cosmic strings, a universal scale version of micro-tubules, the flexible endoskeleton of cells, is a recent proposal.[11] Said to be 10^{-30} centimeter thick—or should I say thin?—and having an extraordinary mass of 10^{22} grams per centimeter, these ultra tense strands and loops of energy supposedly stretch across the universe in a sparse network. In the newborn expanding universe, through the attractive action of gravity, their mass would leave dense regions of atoms and dark matter in the form of flat sheets and elongated ellipses, hence, the seeds of galaxies and clusters.

All of this is conjecture, of course, but what is evident is that *galaxies are united in tiers of social groups, and collectively interact. The cosmic level of matter-mind is the relational behavior of these patterns of galaxial units, a process dependent on mass and gravity and seen by us as velocity and direction.*

Gravity poses a problem in physics. We all know what it does, but we can only surmise what it actually is. Gravity even exists between atoms, although compared to the electromagnetic effects, which are 10^{42} fold greater, its force is obviously insignificant. However, when the objects are as massive as moons, planets, and stars, let alone galaxies, the cumulative force of gravity dominants. While it acts over immense distances, the force falls off exponentially (the inverse square law). A broad quantum model of gravity includes the exchange of virtual (*as if*) massless entities between the bodies, called *gravitons*, in the manner that virtual photons act as communicative agents between electrons and protons. Also, perturbations of space by massive bodies would induce gravity waves. Thus far, no one has detected any such wave, although some marvels of metallurgy have been utilized. As mentioned earlier, gravity is also responsible for shaping space in the form of an optical lens. The light from a celestial object hidden behind a massive body may be focused, from our perspective, 'around' the near object to appear as twins on both sides.[6]

Although there exist billions of galaxies in the universe, each composed of some 10^{11} stars, it is reasonable to assume that, like legendary snowflakes, no two are exactly alike. (In reality, patterns are limited and duplicates are inevitable; indeed, one such set of snowflakes has been experimentally demonstrated). However, unlike snowflakes and galaxies, whose respective myriad sundry shapes are indirectly related to a common composition and activity, stellar forms are distinct composites of atoms and molecules. *Stars and their parent forms, galaxies are the first organizations of matter that, as units, are structurally unique.*

We should not be lured by the notion of singular static forms to proclaim these cosmic assemblies as independent and true individuals. Differences of even a hundred galaxial stars or a billion steller atoms are functionally trivial. Process is paramount, and the workings and interactive properties of certain galaxies and stars are sufficiently similar to be organized into classes. There is an unusual feature about these cosmic relationships, one that deserves to be emphasized for contrasting with our impression of chemical and biological processes: the parts are issued from the whole. *The uniform, undifferentiated universe built downward.*

Optically, galaxies are elliptical, globular, completely irregular, or classically and elegantly spiral, a hurricane of hot matter. Their shape and size vary, their heat and light vary, and their stellar and interstellar components likewise vary . Recorded by instruments sensitive to radio microwaves, X-rays, and ultraviolet and infra red light, these patterns are even more specific and differ considerably from the optical forms. In fact, parabolic radio antennas have received powerful signals from the edge of the observable universe of unknown objects associated with some elliptical galaxies. These quasi-stellar radio sources, *quasars*, while relatively small in size—10^8 miles in diameter—are themselves of a mass sufficient to rival a small galaxy of 10^8 stars. We should also note that galaxies have extensive magnetic fields, but we will never be able to send probes into them.

Again optically, stars may be blue, white, yellow, red giants, white and brown dwarfs, and neutron pulsars, and differ in atomic composition, mass, size, density, pressure, temperature, and so forth. Yet, like galaxies, something basic connects them into an interactive system: gravity. Double stars, one orbiting the other, are common. Furthermore, steller ionic winds exert force outward, demonstrated by the tail of comets, and across intergalactic space cosmic rays and other elementary particles bombard surrounding systems.

A star is an organism, born of dust, that grows and decays and dies with either a bang or a whimper, perhaps to be regenerated from its ashes as a glorious phoenix. It is self-regulatory and oscillates with superimposed rhythms, such as, in our sun, the 11-year cycle of sunspots and the 10-minute cycle of corona extension. A star is also a massive aggregate of molecules and atoms. Since these tiny forms of matter-mind are ghostlike blurs, how should we regard stars? Entities or objects? The answer depends on the star and its stage of life. Because we are fortunate witnesses to an exemplary and extraordinary cosmic event, it would be advantageous to summarize Supernova 1987A.[28,29]

When a massive star runs out of thermonuclear fuel, the pressure of autogravity is no longer balanced by the outward pressure of heat and the core of the star collapses. The rapid heat-generating compression follows quickly by a brilliant explosion called a *supernova*. This phenomenon is hardly rare, being part of the normal life cycle of stars. Perhaps every 40 years one star in our galaxy undergoes the supernova stage, although intersteller dust usually blocks our view. Since the time astronomers began to record their observations, fewer than 650 supernovae have been listed. Most appear through the telescope in far distant galaxies, but within the last 1,000 years five have been visible to the naked eye, the next to last occurring in 1604. There is a small irregular satellite galaxy in our own backyard, if you consider 160,000 light-years close. This is the Large Magellanic Cloud. On 23 February 1987, a star in this system went supernova and Ian Shelton at the Las Campanas Observatory in Chile sounded the tocsin. Astronomers rushed to the southern hemisphere. Telescopes and orbiting scientific satellites were trained on the target.

Supernovae are always exciting events, but this one was special. It was the first supernova whose progenitor was characterized and the first from which neutrinos, cast off from the newly transformed neutron star, were detected. For 10 seconds at the start of the explosion these neutrinos were the solely emitted radiation; another hour passed before the shock wave from the exploding core ruptured the surface of the star. At the time, deep in the earth in both Japan and the United States were arrays of photon detectors designed to record any proton decay, a yet unobserved theoretical event. Thus, by serendipity (Hello again, mythic Sri Lankan princes!), the neutrinos crashing through Earth from the opposite side set off photons in these detectors; the recorded patterns, which gave the angle of origin, and the time of the simultaneous event confirmed the discovery.

The previous form of the star, which arose 10 million years ago, was atypically a massive blue, 25 fold the diameter of our sun and 60,000 times brighter. Most of its radiation occurred as ultraviolet light. Originally, when the hydrogen of its core was converted almost completely to helium, it contracted while the surface layers expanded to nearly 100 million miles in diameter. The heat of the dense core rose to 170 million degrees Kelvin, sufficient to produce fusion, this time leading to carbon and oxygen. The now red giant continued to fuse hydrogen for a million years, losing mass by unknown causes but probably through steller winds. Again, a helium core developed, surrounding the heavy atom center. The red giant became a rare blue giant. Again, contraction took place, which through carbon fusion temperatures of 700 million degrees K., yielded neon, sodium, and magnesium. Soon the density reached 10 million grams per cubic centimeter and the temperature surpassed 1.5 billion degrees K. In mere years, neon was transformed, and then oxygen was converted to silicon and sulfur. In but a few days, at a temperature of 3.5 billion degrees K. and a density of 100 million grams per cubic centimeter, iron was formed. In less than a second at one-fourth the speed of light, the central core shrank to a 50-mile diameter sphere, leaving the outer layers without support. The inner density of 10^{14} grams per cubic centimeter forced the nuclei to repulse each other. The core thus rebounded. It smashed into the collapsing outer layers. The shock wave ensued. EXPLOSION!

An interesting demonstration can illustrate the force dynamics. Take a common large plastic beach ball and place upon it a tennis ball. Drop the two together, ensuring that the tennis ball remains in contact with the soft beach ball. On reaching the ground, the beach ball bounces a short distance but the tennis ball absorbs the energy to rebound well beyond the release height.

What does a supernova leave behind? Depending on mass, a *white dwarf*, a *neutron star*, or the fabled *black hole* may develop. Below a certain threshold, the star condenses to a highly dense dwarf with a radius of some thousands of miles. Neutron stars are far smaller—a radius of only 10 miles—and some 10^4 times as dense—millions of tons per cubic inch. Some neutron stars rotate exeedingly fast; 100 to 1,000 times per second is typical. If the magnetic field strength, rotation rate, and surrounding matter are of particular conditions, a radio pulse is given off on each cycle, hence the term *pulsar*. If the mass of a supernova is even greater, the residual star contracts to such a degree that gravity pulls photons back. The black hole is black because light can not escape, not because it is empty. Furthermore, a *singularity*, that point orifice to the unknown, may occur in the midst of a massive black hole. Our galaxy, as recent observations suggest, includes an enormous black hole in its center, drawing surrounding matter into its infinities and mysteries.

In 1930, mathematician, physicist, and astronomer, Sir James Jeans, entitled his most successful book (incidentally, a fine example of Art Deco) *The Mysterious Universe*, in which he permitted himself some philosophical speculation.[5] Jeans was a neo-Pythagorean. Beginning the lecture with Plato's simile of our ability only to perceive shadows on the cave wall and not the truth behind them, and having 'considered with disfavour the possibility of the universe having been planned by a biologist or an engineer', he concluded that 'the Great Architect of the Universe now begins to appear as a pure mathematician.' Mathematics, Jeans reminded us, 'can never tell us what a thing is, but only how it behaves; it can only specify an object through its properties.' With all events of the universe reduced to mathematical abstraction, Jeans was 'almost compelled' to picture the universe as 'a world of pure thought'. (I should note that throughout his exposition he mushed *thought* and *mind* and it is difficult to grasp whether he refers to consciousness-mind, creative ideation, mental activity in general, or mind per se.) For him, the dualism of mind and matter disappears 'not through matter becoming in any way more shadowy or insubstantial than heretofore, or through mind becoming resolved into a function of the working of matter, but through substantial matter resolving itself into a creation and manifestation of mind'—a mathematically thinking or operating mind. Mind becomes 'the creator and governor of the realm of matter. . .the mind in which the atoms out of which our individual minds have grown exist as thoughts.'

Except for the principle of mathematics, Buddhist literature expresses similar conclusions. The Lankavatara Sutra declares that 'mind is beyond all philosophical views; it is apart from discrimination; it is not attainable, nor is it ever born. There is nothing but mind. . . .Apart from the mind nothing whatsoever exists.'[30] In the Hua-Yen Sutra we read, 'You should view the nature of the whole universe as being created by mind alone.'[31] However, we should not let ourselves be attached to words, since what constitutes mind for the Buddha and for James Jeans may not be identical.

I wonder whether Jeans could have grasped the following: A scholarly monk asked Zen Master Chao-Chou Ts'ung-Shen (778-897), 'You once said that when the universe is destroyed, its essential nature (Buddha-nature) will not be extinguished. What is this essence?'

The Master replied, 'The four elements and the five components.

The monk immediately attacked, These are precisely what will be destroyed. What resists destruction?'

Master Chao-Chou answered, 'The four elements and the five components.'[32] There is great wisdom here, if you can attain the four elements and the five components. KATZ!

Chapter 5

SHADOWS IN THE FLAME

Evolution/Life

We ought to dance with rapture that we should be alive and in the flesh, and part of the living, incarnate cosmos. I am part of the sun as my eye is part of me. That I am part of the earth my feet know perfectly, and my blood is part of the sea.

D.H. Lawrence

Among what astronomer Carl Sagan calls 'star stuff', created by fusions of fusions, ejected in a violent astral fit of lethal starvation, and chemically reacted in a cloudy celestial retort, are simple but reactive nitrogen- and carbon-based molecules. Our human scale, so inadequate, prevents us from appreciating this relative soup of matter and the eon-long periods during which it simmers. Throughout our brief intellectual history, we had thought space to be an absolute vacuum. We now know that space, at least intersteller space, is populated by inorganic molecules and simple biochemical precursers. Found also within many meteorites, free of earthly contaminants and shielded from degenerative radiations, are fatty acids, long chain hydrocarbons, porphyrins, and the beads of the protein necklace, amino acids.[1,2] 'I believe a leaf of grass is no less than the journeywork of the stars,' intuited Walt Whitman.

There is no barrier above our planet; atmospheric hydrogen molecules, rising to ever increasing elevations, occasionally float off the fingers of Earth gravity, while space flotsam is gathered up in our yearly circuit of the sun. Comet Halley and its ilk have been described as 'dirty snowballs' for their motley coating of dust, partially shed during their own sweep around the windy sun. Since common heavy bacteria and fungi have been detected 75 kilometers above Earth in the mesosphere, could not smaller and lighter microbes, the viruses and viroids, protected by mineral dusts, reach even higher elevations into and maybe through the ionosphere?[3]

Stimulated by such aerobiological studies and the concerns of NASA about the possibility of extraterrestial life on the moon, Michael Crichton wrote in 1969 a highly successful science fiction novel based on the premise that an Earth-orbiting spacecraft brought back a deadly microbe, the 'Andromeda strain.'[4] Taking a page from Crichton several years later, the astronomer Fred Hoyle, assisted by Chandra Wickramasinghe, crashed into the domains of medical science with the wild speculation that certain epidemic infectious diseases originate from space.[5] However, they also had a somewhat less fantastic, even plausible notion based on the mentioned evidence derived from primordial meteorites as old as the solar system. Conveniently placing the first biological actor offstage, they hypothesized that life did not originate on Earth, but was carried to it by comets or other cosmic messengers or traders.[5,6] (In 1980, Luis Alvarez and associates proposed that the crash of a comet or asteroid was reponsible for the demise of the dinosaurs: the comet giveth, the comet taketh away?)

Perhaps. Or perhaps the seeding mechanism was more like biological pump-priming, a prerequisite to initiate the already existing latent or incomplete biological processes. And then again, perhaps the elementary stuff and concomitant processes of biology were here all along, developing with the formation of the planet, indeed, any planet of similar form and circumstance. Life, thereby, would not be unique to Earth.

Do we have any evidence for this last, almost traditional possibility? The moon likely was ejected from Earth in its early molten stage through a collision with a planetoid. The rocks brought home by our lunar astronauts were devoid of any organic matter, but there is no reason why such material should survive billions of years on any orb lacking protective atmosphere, biochemically hospitable niches, and an active geology. The only life form found on the moon was a stowaway bacterium from Earth inside a Surveyor spacecraft.[7]

Our biochemical exploration of Mars was limited to surface scratches, and the results, while demonstrating the absence of organic soil, certainly no living microorganisms, did indicate some peculiar oxidative chemistry.[8,9] There are those who believe, James Lovelock withstanding, that microorganisms survive in oases on otherwise barren Mars, as in the recent discovery of the extraordinary highly defined and circumscribed ecosystems of sulfur bacteria, giant tube worms, clams, blind crabs, and other strange marine life around thermal vents on the deepest, darkest points of the desert ocean floor.[10,11] Before declaring Mars 'dead', we need to sample more carefully in better chosen sites, such as near the polar ice caps, in deeper layers, in protected pockets, or in sedimentary rocks of some ancient river or sea. Like Lovelock, I doubt that microbes currently dwell there, but I suspect that at one time they did. A future biological investigation of Mars should at least find the remnants of complex organic matter.[12]

Life on Earth is truly ancient, appearing far earlier than even the most imaginative biologist dared speculate. While the planet is 4.5 billion years old, the fossils of probable anaerobic, methane-producing archaebacteria were formed 3.5 billion years ago in Australian and South African sedimentary rocks.[13] Life arising in a billion years from the spheroid condensation of hot gaseous stellar debris hence implies that biology began in some hundreds of millions of years, a mere sneeze from the astronomical perspective. Surely, since Mars had a similar early geological history, there must be an analogous biological record. Martian paleontology may well become a future science.

The general features of this question remind me of my research in skin microbiology. I suppose that any scientist well versed in her or his particular specialty will always find applicable associations. We must not forget that the various disciplines of science are artificial branches; all knowledge is linked vertically and horizontally. Wisdom, however, does not have such dimensions.

A young man asked Zen Master Hsuan-sha Shih-pei (835-908), 'I have come seeking the Truth. Where can I begin Zen?' The Master responded with his own question, 'Can you hear the murmuring mountain stream?' 'Yes, I can hear it.'

'Enter Zen from there!'[14] (Warning: this is a koan that works wondrously on many levels, well beyond the appropriate and relevant literal meaning. For instance, what would the master answer had the student replied that he could not hear the stream?)

A cursory inspection of the cutaneous ecological model may be helpful to this discussion. Suppose that a disease notoriously associated with a certain bacterium is spreading through a population. In earlier days, the cause was said to be a miasma, an atmospheric influence. After Louis Pasteur began to talk about *diseases* of beer and wine and established that living ferments, germs, are found in the air, Joseph Lister, already a respected surgeon, took to spraying the operating field with a mist of antiseptic phenol. He later found antiseptic dressings to be more effective for the patient. It was also healthier for the surgeon! Soon pathogenic microorganisms were found in water and sometimes in food. There was also the ancient idea of fomites—the clothing, bedding, carpets, and other belongings of patients—thought to be the chief reservoir of disease; the burning of homes and possessions of the stricken dead was the drastic expediency. Another font of germs, later demonstrated by American pioneer microbe hunter Theobald Smith, was the indirect path of a vector, such as mosquito, louse, or flea, which transmits certain microorganisms from one host to another. Our particular bacterium, however, is not carried by vectors nor is it commonly found in the air or surface environment. Nevertheless, it is easily detected in the infected patient. What is the source of this germ? How does the patient acquire it? How is the disease spread?

Again, before Pasteur met the challenge, microorganisms were said to be spontaneously generated from organic debris or decay, a concept that, when limited to the prototype level, is accepted by all evolutionists.[15] Pasteur was wise enough never to deny that such an event could occur; Charles Darwin himself recognized in 1871, in the midst of the debate, that any prebiotic chemical form 'at the present day. . .would be instantly devoured or absorbed, which would not have been the case before living creatures were formed.'[15] Pasteur, instead, simply attacked the evidence in favor of spontaneous generation (growth in boiled and sealed hay infusions) with contrary evidence from his own research (no growth in boiled but air-exposed urine). Actually, the results, not the interpretations, of both sides were experimentally correct, and had Pasteur used the same culture media as his opponents, he either would have discovered the culprits, boiling-resistant spores, or would have found his career stalled in disgrace.[16] Thus, the acceptance of the germ theory of disease was foremost the subscription that life begets life.

Pasteur's German rival, Robert Koch, proposed a simple but daring radical solution to the clinical origin of insidious microbes: the pathogenic microorganism resides within and on the body without harm to its benefactor. Healthy people are the reservoir! Both normal flora and disease-inducing bacteria and fungi may spread with no adverse effects from person to person, as from mother and attending medical personnel to newborn baby. Furthermore, because ecology is defined by dynamic processes, the patient may have carried the microorganism benignly for long periods before stress or some insult upset the dynamic environmental-physiological balance. In the new ecological perspective, the distinction between pathogenic and saprophytic is somewhat archaic; all microorganisms are opportunistic but differ in their capacity to colonize, invade, and damage tissues and to trigger inflammatory responses.

I will say much more about infectious disease and immunity later. The main point of this aside is that while skin microorganisms do indeed move from host to host via loose or wafting rafts of skin squames, *microbial survival on the new host and the induction of infections are linked to the alteration of the environment*—the surface, where other microorganisms may already quietly reside, or the internal, where they have been traumatically introduced into exposed susceptible tissue. Similarly, while life could spontaneously arise from some primordial clay, or come to Earth by some interplanetary, intersteller vector, it could also have been acquired during the birth of the planet from the nebular womb.

The origin of life is one of the great scientific mysteries, as death is the ancient medical enigma. This book is leading to a philosophical, some would say mystical solution that attacks these related problems at their weakest points: memory, conceptualization and definition, and social conditioning. However, before tackling that knot, we need first to consider the primary molecular forms of life matter-mind and awareness-mind, as well as what we call biological organisms. It is time we return to biochemical structures and functions.

The common denominator, the necessary constituent shared by all biological classes from virus to us humans, is a chain of nucleic acids, not any particular sequence of the four kinds of purine and pyrimidine bases, just the helix, double or single stranded, of deoxyribonucleic acid (DNA) or, in some viruses, ribonucleic acid (RNA), which makes up the chromosome. This is the genetic material.

Take care not to equate genetics with heredity. The genes encoded in DNA and RNA are static and symbolic forms, and are associated with the biochemical building blocks and the sequential timing and duration of their synthesis and assembly. *Genes are hereditary units of physical form.*

More encompassing, heredity involves process, such as recombination (found between paternal and maternal chromosomes during cell division); programmed randomization (as in the assembly of sections of certain complex proteins); and selective expression of genes (for example, the sex-induced methylation of DNA).[17,18] In addition, heredity may possibly include nontangible agencies: morphogenetic fields, environmentally stimulated and organism-directed specific mutations, and topographical relationships.[19,20] The importance of these highly technical activities will later be discussed in detail. I should add that heredity likely involves the transmission of some mental aspects, from talents in music, art, and mathematics to behavior and character, and may incorporate the hypothetical but plausible Jungian collective unconscious.[21]

No gene or set of genes obliged me to become a scientist (a drive established at age eight) or my uncle to choose art, although the long familial history is dominated by both woodcrafts and philosophical scholarship. Therefore, the chains of nucleic acids only provide the tools, the toolshed, and a means of management in the development and activity of a biological organism. The memory and patterns of cellular and organismal shape and function lie elsewhere in unfolding processes. An experienced adult and a youth, each assembling a full-rigged plastic model clipper from equivalent kits, will produce ships differing significantly in quality despite the instruction sheet.

Imagine three flasks containing DNA or RNA. The first holds strands of the DNA chromosome purified from disrupted bacteria. The second bottle is filled with DNA synthesized in the test tube by linking one sort of nucleic acid to another to code for the production of a repeating polypeptide chain of three amino acids. The last flask encloses crystals of intact poliovirus, which consists of a superhelix of RNA within a shell of protein units. Which of these containers hold living organisms? Science, too, has koans!

Macfarlane Burnet issued in 1945 his series of lectures entitled *Virus as Organism*.[22] Viruses do not grow in size or have a metabolism, yet they reproduce, mutate, usually induce mischief in their host, and under certain circumstances act as a vector by transferring host nucleic acid to another host. Microbiologists study viruses as microorganisms, clinicians respect viruses as infectious agents, and molecular biologists, whom I prefer to call molecular geneticists and engineers, depend on viruses as ultra small syringes. However, the viruses in the vessel are as active and alive as the sugar in your kitchen cabinet. These viruses are not dormant, not asleep. They are dead chemical complexes. Otherwise, we would have created life in the second flask, and, in the instance of the bacterial DNA, a component would be the whole. (For the sake of argument, I am assuming here the ordinary perspective of positivism and empiricism.)

Let us go one step further. Suppose that we remove the protein shell of the virus, which occurs naturally when it infects a cell. Is this naked chromosome still a virus? Some plant viruses, the viroids, are just that. However, if you say that it is, do the chromosomes of a human cell define that individual? If so, then each time you eat a meal, brush your teeth, or cut your finger you are destroying thousands of cells and murdering thousands of humans, clones of yourself. For much the same reason, the fertilized human egg, a single cell, is not a human.

Clearly, something is missing. There is a famous Zen koan that addresses a key aspect of this discussion. Holding up a bamboo stick, Master Shou Shan (926-993) asked the gathering of monks, 'If you call this a stick you attach yourself to words. If you say that it is other than a stick, then you deny the fact. Tell me quick, what do you call this?'[14] And what do **you** call it?

WHICH IS ALIVE?

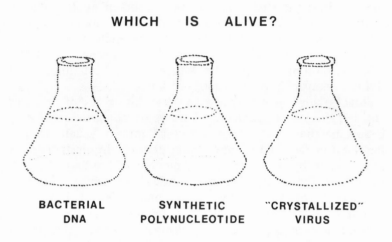

| BACTERIAL DNA | SYNTHETIC POLYNUCLEOTIDE | "CRYSTALLIZED" VIRUS |

We can not properly consider a virus separated from its milieu as alive, nor can we describe the set of genes of any chromosome as that creature. *All organisms are processes, and our separated, idle virus is no more than a snapshot, a particular momentary molecular and symbolic pattern.* Viruses are the ultimate obligate parasites, totally dependent on the metabolic organelles and operations of their cellular hosts. A virus is not a biological organism until it (the genetic program) usurps the host system while simultaneously being incorporated into it. In short, a virus lives only when it becomes a cell.

Thus, we have an outstanding example of the basic Heraclitean principle of flux. The artificially isolated and static nucleic acid genome is only an organization of matter-mind. When included in the appropriate system of free and organelle-bound biochemicals and functioning through its actions of cooperative pattern recognition, the same chain of nucleic acid—more precisely, its specific interactive activity—is awareness-mind; it is biology. However, it is the system, not the viral nor, for that matter, the host chromosome that is alive.

> A hundred dead leaves
> scurry along quiet streets—
> icy Eastern winds.

There is an exact electronic parallel in computer systems. The unauthorized insertion of a replicating and communicable program through telephone linkage could be a benign nuisance like one of the many rhinoviruses of the common cold or an act of sabotage as deadly as the rabies virus. To no surprise, computer enthusiasts call such programs *viruses*.[23,24] In both the biological and computer systems, a virus is a program of events that is encoded and requires translation, replication, release, and transmission by the host. If the computer virus is programmed appropriately, it can even mutate with succeeding generations. Lastly, both host computer and biological systems may have virus detection and defensive networks. The computer, indeed, may be an evolving new life form, according to Geoff Simons is his provocative book, *Are Computers Alive?*[25]

One of the most influential books in modern science was Erwin Schrödinger's *What is Life?*[26] Schrödinger was a physicist, the developer of wave mechanics. Published in 1944 just at the time Oswald Avery and his associates determined that DNA, not protein, was a genetic substance, the book inspired physicists to find a niche in biology and biologists to seek fresh insights in physics and physical chemistry. While Schrödinger foretold an aperiodic crystal whose atomic groups comprise a genetic code, he defined life in terms of thermodynamics as the fight against the disorder and static equilibrium of maximal entropy: 'What an organism feeds upon is negative entropy.' (Positive entropy is recognized as a young child's room five days after the parent arranged it neatly!) Schrödinger also observed that 'the unfolding of events in the life cycle of an organism exhibits an admirable regularity and orderliness, unrivalled by anything we meet with in inanimate matter.'

I regret that this view was a case of grass seeming greener on the other side of the fence. Physics, after all, with its mathematical equations and precise instruments, was once called an exact science in contrast to biology, whose investigators must suffer highly variable experimental data when testing living organisms. What impressed Schrödinger was the efficiency of an organism in translating and utilizing the information in such a small amount of material to develop, grow, and reproduce in a most complex manner.

James Lovelock had to go to Schrödinger's thermodynamic definition of life in developing his *Gaia* concept of a living planet. However, the definition had to be modified because by then certain chemical reactions described by B.P. Belousov and A.M. Zhabotinsky yielded beautiful spiral and concentric self-evolving dissipative structures.[27,28] These well-ordered patterns furthermore renewed themselves continuously. Chemistry here, therefore, closely mimics biology. Recognizing that a key difference between this local reversal or deceleration of entropy and actual living systems is the hierarchial series of boundaries, the edge of the atmosphere being one, Lovelock crafted a working definition of life. He regarded life as a self-organizing system characterized by an actively sustained low entropy within boundaries, when viewed from the outside.[11]

No one had to tell Lovelock that this definition is lifeless! Saint Augustine stated that he knew what time was until he had to explain it. Likewise, we all recognize what is overtly alive, but no suitable exception-free scientific definition has been found.

For instance, the ability to reproduce is a classic attribute of life, but obviously any man who has undergone a vasectomy is still alive, as are worker bees, which are also sterile. Nevertheless, in these cases, our logical assignment of life to the individual is in relation to the species collective or to the society, not directly to the individual. Even a crystal can grow and reproduce, if a fragment is transferred to another supersaturated solution.

Other signs of life are movement, irritability, and adaptatation, all in reference to an organism's surroundings. Again, chemistry and physics provide examples: the movement of iron filings across a surface toward a magnet; the prolonged luminescent response of phosphors to electrons and photons; and, as denoted by their name, the adaptation and structural 'memory' of plastics.

Simons, taking together the modern criteria of structure, energy- and information-processing, and reproduction, and then adopting the example of the virus, could make a case for living advanced computers. We could venture further into abstraction by treating ideas as objects, discovering that they also have the ability to replicate, move, grow, adapt, and die.

Lovelock in half-seriousness wrote that 'the answer to the question *What is life?* was deemed so important to our survival that it was classified *top secret* and kept locked up as an instinct in the automatic levels of the mind.'[11] I add as corollary that consciousness-mind deludes us as to the limits of what is alive by erecting obscuring walls of concepts.

The ancient Chinese did not develop physicochemical understandings, although from their cyclic cosmology and study of Tao they knew entropy as a principle, rather than as a heat-related mathematical relationship. Their expressions for the concepts of life, alive, or living reflect common experience and are broad in scope. One two-character phrase consists of the ideogram that means destiny and fortune coupled with a character that variously indicates being born or coming into existence; breeding, bearing, creating, producing, or causing; and—wisely—unfamiliar, strange, or unknown. A second synonymous phrase includes this last character and another that refers to survival, enduring, and existence. As in the thermodynamic definition of life, the Chinese perspective appreciates processes of development and dynamic homeostasis. It also allows certain phenomena that Western thought would not accept as life.

Incidentally, the Jewish toast, *l'khi'm,* meaning *to life,* is interesting in its use of the plural, which dramatizes the multifaceted attributes of social interactions. The singular, *khi,* emphasizes existence.

Mystics and mystical philosophers, of course, have a different point of view than most people[29] They sense that

Bibel '92

LIFE

everything is alive; they actually perceive Lovelock's hierarchies of Gaia and extend them to the cosmos. Mountains, for instance, arise, breathe (oscillate), grow, evolve, and decay in a dynamic life cycle of geologic time well beyond our normal ken. Mountains are ordered patterns, although coarsely defined. Whatever their shape, we differentiate mountains as a topographical class and identify individual ones upon finer analysis. As in higher biological organisms, where lost or dead cells are replenished, mountains may replace their mass lost by water-, wind- and heat-induced erosion through volcanic activity and plate tectonics. For instance, Chomoloungma (Mount Everest) is slowly growing higher as the Indian subcontintent continues to plow into central Asia. Eventually, entropy will prevail, and mountains will crumble into a plain. Indeed, the entire Earth may become more-or-less homogeneously flat from liquefaction, its initial condition, when it is gobbled up by the sun in supernova stage.

Thus, a mystic first may experience a mountain as any ordinary person: alien and apart. Then with study and meditation the mountain is regarded in undifferentiated unity with oneself and everything else, as observing a polar bear on the snow in a blizzard. After further practice a significant change in perspective occurs. Imagine two mirrors facing each other between which there exists absolutely nothing, not even a shadow. The student sees the mountain, the mountain sees the student. The mystic comes to appreciate the once hard and fearful mountain, projecting much like a friendly bear in repose, as distinct in form but inseparable in process/mind/life. Still, there is one more step. As one ancient Master put it, 'When I began to study Zen, mountains were mountains; when I thought I understood Zen, mountains were not mountains; but when I came to full knowledge of Zen, mountains were again mountains.'[30]

The frigid night gone,
trees and boulders stretch
creaking.

This perception of awareness-mind interpenetrates the matter-mind of earth, sky, and water through mind. Consciousness-mind may then erect philosophical structures on this foundation. Wassily Kandinsky, the pioneer of abstract art, declared, 'Even dead matter is living spirit.'[31] However, with boundary dissolution and the encompassing insight of wholeness—in Sanskrit, *tat tvam asi* (That art thou)—life and death dissolves, become at most arbitrary points in a continuing cyclic process, as the arising and subsiding of oceanic waves. Sen T'sen noted, 'When the Ten Thousand things are viewed in their oneness, we return to the Origin and remain where we have always been.' The Christian mystic Meister Eckhart pointed out that 'The knower and the known are one...God and I, we are one in knowledge.' Aldous Huxley rephrased this as 'I live, yet not I; for it is the Logos who lives me.'[29] Lastly, the Vimalakirti Nirdesa Sutra declares, 'All living beings are subject to neither death nor birth.'[32]

Our attempts to pin down life for dissection are futile. Life is as much an abstraction as the atom. We may not know the ultimate reality behind phenomena, but applying the qualifier *as if,* to these actions, occurrences, and events, we can probe the cosmic order and behaviors to attain increasingly improved approximations while furthering the evolution of our creativity.

Some philosophical and sociological critics believe that we are no closer to understanding reality than the ancient Greek or Indian civilizations and that we only change concepts.[33,34] If scientists through the ages had accepted this pessimism, there would have been no point in the adventure, and science would not have gone beyond modifying primitive technology and studying the macro phenomena of our limited senses. However, both critic and advocate would agree that the virus deserves honor as the pivot by which science was forced to shift its world view on life.

Because of its simplicity, should we also regard viruses as the first life forms? Viruses may have been necessary to evolution as a form of genetic communication, and may have been in existence shortly after the advent of complete quasi independent living organisms. They were not and could not

have been the first biological organisms. Lovelock's requirement for retentive boundaries is largely the reason.

Whatever and wherever the origin, we need to know how
DNA/RNA and the first microbe came into existence. The
classic experiment was by Stanley L. Miller and Harold C.
Urey of the University of Chicago, who agreed with pioneer
British geneticist J.B.S. Haldane that primitive Earth had a
reducing atmosphere free of toxic oxygen.[15] Beginning in
1952, they introduced various mixtures of gases into a
circuital apparatus consisting of a reaction flask, where the
gas was subjected to electric sparks, representing lightning; a
condenser to liquify newly formed products; a boiling flask
to gasify them for further treatment; and sampling ports. They
first chose an atmosphere of hydrogen, methane, ammonia,
and water vapor, which yielded aldehydes, carboxylic acids,
and amino acids. Later they substituted carbon monoxide,
carbon dioxide, and nitrogen for methane and ammonia.
Today we exclude methane from the primary atmosphere, its
appearance said to be a result of microbial life. After the
apparatus was run continuously for at least a week, they
detected hydrogen cyanide, various aldehydes, six of the
twenty typical amino acids found in proteins today, lactic and
acetic acids, urea, and other organic molecules.

The crystals of each kind of artificially synthesized amino
acid were of two varieties, mirror images, which would shift
polarized light to the right (the D configuration for dextro-
or to the left (the L form for levo-). This presented an
evolutional problem. Pasteur, again, was the trailblazer.
Although we laud Pasteur as the father of microbiology and
developer of the rabies vaccine, he began his career as a
chemist specializing in crystals of organic chemicals.[35] While
certain solutions of naturally obtained materials were
known to rotate polarized light, including tartaric acid, his
liquid preparation of synthesized paratartaric acid did not.
Curious about the failure, he crystallized the molecule, and
beheld both clockwise and counterclockwise shaped crystals,
the two crystal forms rotating light in opposite directions.
After carefully and patiently separating the two configurations one crystal at a time, Pasteur discovered why the solution

did not rotate light. The two crystal forms were produced in equal amounts. The absence of rotation was a net effect.

Working with a variety of similar opposite light-rotating configurations, or racemers, Pasteur later discovered that microorganisms would selectively metabolize only one of the forms. With few exceptions, life forms themselves contain only D sugars and L amino acids.[36] This molecular dissymmetry was an unsatiated source of intellectual irritation for Pasteur. He postulated that its origin lies with the asymmetric forces of electricity, magnetism, the rotation of Earth, sunlight, or other cosmic influence. He tried in vain to alter metabolic discrimination in growing plants using powerful magnets or a rotating heliostat with mirrors. Even with the glories of his anthrax and rabies vaccines and other medical triumphs, the old chemist longed for his crystals and a solution to this far-reaching problem.[37]

We still do not know why life forms have a particular handedness, although the mere selection of such a configuration certainly increased simplicity and efficiency. It may be a matter of chance or of an extension of a yet undiscovered (or developed) universal law.[38] Or it may relate to or through the nuclear spin vector, which also has a handedness in direction of its decay emissions.[39] Antimatter is not only opposite in charge, but spin and decay emissions are reversed. While cosmologists wonder about an unapproachable universe of antimatter, evolutionists contemplate the existence of life forms in this or other galaxies composed of L sugars and D amino acids. The two realms may be one in the same. Whatever the reason, some process of selection and incorporation took place in the first generation of self-reproducing biological forms. This event need have occurred only once. Once the die was cast, regeneration was itself selective.

There is a related phenomenon that suggests that this dissymmetry exerts a local pressure against the progress of universal entropy (or Universal entropy, if there are any quantum-connected antimatter systems.) Indeed, biological organisms continue to evolve to increasingly complicated forms while the universe tends to simplification and a return to chaos. It so happens that over long periods of time the biochemically opposite racemer of amino acids, the D configuration, appears in increasing proportions in nonrenewing and dead tissues. Attempts have been made to use the proportion of atypical racemers to date the formation of organic matter and help explain age-related dysfunction and atrophy.[40,,41]

I will refrain from describing and boring the reader with the possible chemical reactions that led to nucleic acids and other pertinent biochemicals from the apparent planetary precursors. This speculative information may be easily found elsewhere.[15,42] Andreas I. Oparin in Moscow emphasized that it was DNA, not the metabolic supporting biochemicals that was paramount in allowing life, because DNA encodes the structural and enzymatic proteins and only DNA reproduces itself. This last point is no longer true. The ability is not restricted to nucleic acids.[43] Furthermore, the matter is a chicken-or-egg problem, since the replication of DNA requires the enzyme action of polymerases to join the nucleic acids.

There are two ways out of the no-win quandary. The first, which will be described more fully in the next chapter, is that flexible RNA could itself act as an enzyme. The second is that, as any organism, there are no independent parts and that in the very beginning the reproductive and metabolic biochemicals and their corresponding DNA or RNA developed together and incorporated together. Therefore, accepting that a prebiological chemical soup had formed, we next should consider how the stuff might have avoided the curse of perpetual ineffectual diffusion and, instead, was brought into a critical mass, into a compartment suitable for rapid interactions, development, and evolution.

One tactic of boxers is to corner the opponent against the ropes to limit movement and escape. Similarly, molecules can be held and concentrated in the cavities of highly porous materials. Micas and clays, which consist of alternating layers of silicate sheets and water molecules held together by ionic bonds, adsorb molecules readily. The key is a large surface area. A one-centimeter cube of kaolinite, an aluminum clay, for instance, contains 2,800 square meters of surface area. Another aluminum clay, montmorillonite, has been shown to support the linking of adenylated amino acids into chains of greater than 50 units, which could have been an early step in the evolution of proteins. There is also a hypothesis that involves ionic bonding. Iron pyrite through its weakly positive charge could have retained and concentrated newly evolved molecules with negatively charged phosphate groups, permitting biochemical reactions.[44]

A second means of localizing organic molecules, the one which in principle succeeded, was the formation of bags. Because of efficient relationships of volume pressure and surface tension, the bag was doubtlessly spherical. *This separation of biological molecules into discrete internal and external physical environments was the first step toward the illusion of independence and utter individuality.* All present day cells, be they plant, animal, or bacterium, have a skin of lipoprotein. The cell membrane consists of two layers with the hydrophobic lipid portions facing each other and the hydrophilic proteinaceous groups facing outward to the external and internal environments. However, lipoproteins are complexes that are too advanced to have been developed at the dawn of life. As skin is an organ, the cellular membrane is an organelle.

Sidney W. Fox at the University of Miami studied the spontaneous formation of microspheroids from dissolved proteins when the solution was heated at 130° to 180° C.[41] Interestingly, their size was like that of bacteria, 1 to 2 micrometers in diameter, and they could bud and divide like yeast, drawing in more protein to form the extending wall. Furthermore, these mimes had enzymic activity, splitting esters, glucose, and peroxides.

Many biological traits, as such phenomena demonstrate, are actually physical chemistry. When I was a graduate student studying streptococcal L-form growth in human blood culture, I was mesmerized for days, observing in wonder the fairly rapid quivering, budding, and fission of red blood cells into streptococcal-like chains, an unheard of and bizarre occurrence. Red blood cells, lacking a nucleus and chromosomes, normally do not divide. I later discovered that the effect was due to lactic acid, and had been observed 40 years previously (and forgotten) with hyperbarometric pressure and other physicochemical influences. Thus, some prototype and interim limiting membrane could have arisen to permit the

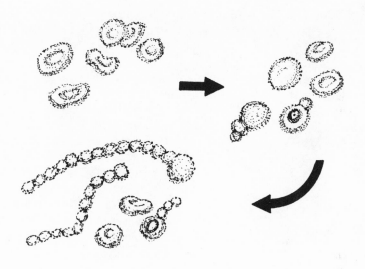

LIFE WITHOUT CHROMOSOMES.
Budding of red blood cells triggered by certain physical or chemical agents.

evolution of a biological organism and replaced in subsequent generations by DNA-directed lipoprotein

Let us accept arbitrarily the new view that over three billion years ago life evolved around thermal vents in the depths of the oceans.[44] There is a huge gap in knowledge between the formation of simple biochemicals and the first biological organism. One could make a case that the thrust of biochemistry and biophysics today is to fill that chasm. The research in protein folding and other self-organizing patterns is an example of this scientific frontier. In the next chapter, we will examine the fundamental anatomy and activity of the most primitive microorganisms surviving today and the reasons that those information storage units, DNA and RNA, are the foundation stones of biology and individuality.

Chapter 6

TRACKS IN THE OCEAN FOAM

Molecular genetics

Darest thou now O soul,
Walk out with me toward the unknown region
Where neither ground is for the feet
nor any path to follow?

Walt Whitman

And life flows on within you and
without you.

George Harrison

A code, we are told, is a system of patterns that represents or abbreviates. In the codes of many old spy novels, the letters of the alphabet are switched and the message is sent in sets of five letters. The alphabet may be more symbolically encoded as positions of objects—the semaphore system of flags or the bumps of Braille, for instance—or as a binary system of light flashes, sounds, or impulses (the Morse code). Acronyms are another form of coded information. Therefore, the sequence dash dot dot/dash dot/dot dash is decoded first as DNA and then as deoxyribonucleic acid.

DNA, as encountered in viruses and cells, is nature's own code. How scientists cracked this astonishing code is one of the greatest achievements of civilization; the intellectual adventure leading up to and continuing from James Watson and Francis Crick's puzzle-solving model in 1953 is documented thoroughly, and the reader may refer to these excellent histories.[1,2]

Regard ye well DNA, the genetic code, and its translation. For a biologist, to deeply contemplate this stuff, this elixir of life, is to become first speechless, thoughtless in awe, and then to border on laughter, grinning with a glint in the eye. I have seen staid physicists act the same way when pressed in discussions of the atom. Certain individuals, those whose left, linearly logical hemisphere of the brain is oppressively dominant, will shrug and proclaim in perfect positivistic hindsight that the code was simply an inevitable outcome of physical chemistry, confidently explaining a mystery with a mystery.

Nevertheless, this myopic view offers or at least permits the idea of self-evolution, which may be a cosmic fundamental. The scholarly Chinese scribes certainly thought so. They have several phrases for nature, as there are various meanings in English. One Chinese expression refers to phenomena: the attributes, quality, or temperament of the seasons, climate, sky, and heaven. Another focuses on activity, combining the character for *use, purpose,* and *effect* with the ideogram for *action* and *work.* The major phrase that interests us, commonly used also as a prefix, consists of two characters. The first indicates self or person; commencing at or from; and spontaneously. The second character is variously translated as *thus* or *so; certainly; permission;* or *yes.* Maintaining the tenor, we can merge these assorted contextual translations to mean *from itself, thus.* What a philosophically pregnant phrase! Everything, every action in the entire universe is of no elaborate scheme; it arises from itself for itself.

This principle, nature as self-deriving processes, hence must extend into consciousness-mind. Your very reading of this book is not only natural because it is your inclination to do so, it is Natural! You can not separate yourself from Nature, although many people try. Warfare may not be a necessary (characteristic) human trait, being unknown to some tribes or reduced in other groups to a relatively benign rite, but the existence and variety of complementary militaristic and pacifistic societies is Natural.

From the modern Western perspective (Chile, to be exact) Humberto Maturana, Francisco Varela, and Ricardo Uribe have developed a more restrictive cognitive philosophy under the banner of *autopoiesis,* a term which they derived from the Greek for self-production.[3] They regard natural systems as self-referential and primarily directed toward self-renewal. Consciousness, they believe, arises at every tier of order from

NATURE

feedback loops of an autopoietic system and its environment, i.e., activities influence experience, which in turn affect activities. (Personally, I would use the general term *mind* instead, in order not to restrict the metaphysics to consciousness-mind.) East or West, Nature evolves for itself, and DNA is its biological instrument. In the strict sense, the DNA code corresponds to a set of amino acids. However, in operation, it is more like the information complex embedded in poetry, especially haiku. Examples of this extraordinary art are presented throughout this book as instructional aids. Zen haiku requires that the impression of an incident, mood, or essence be an actual observation and, because it is more than a verbal snapshot, convey the moment-to-moment mind of the observer. Details are filled in by the imagination and experience of the reader. The poem arises simply by being alert and, like a young child, finding wonder in everything. Scientists also have this consciousness-mind, but their experience is fleeting, existing only for that moment before the first thought cascade. It is not a matter of curiosity; it is sheer interest. For instance, consider this deceptively simple scene:

A bird stands sentry
until the last beam is lost
behind Western clouds.

Encoded is that time of day—sunset—when sound is dampened and the dimming sky glows with color. We and the bird are one in motionlessly savoring the close of day, and together we move on when the glorious event is complete. Those are the dry analytical facts, *dead words,* yet the reader feels something else, something much fuller, something that can not be expressed beyond a sigh. Zen demands such *live words* and correct actions. In another example, we discover that certain sounds are silent to our ears, but not so to our heart:

Decaying deer corpse,
fracturing eroded rocks:
two songs of winter.

For us to grasp the genetic essence, the poetry encoded in DNA, we must dare to plunge into the complexity of phenomena. Too often we encounter only crude generalities of scientific knowledge that offer little insight into the awesomeness of nature. Genetics is a symphony, not a nursery rhyme. We must remember, however, that all the variety of stuctures involved in these processes are empty and ghostlike, for they exist only as activites, not as objects. New orders of phenomena arise here by complementary interactions based on shape, size, and electrical charge. Each new discrete pattern is tagged with a name. How important is nomenclature? Teiji, a seventeenth-century poet, knew:

A flowering weed:
Hearing its name
I looked again.

Molecular genetics, it may well be argued, is the most important science of this century and certainly of the first part of the next. The old description of this period as 'The Atomic Age' pales in comparison, for the might of the atom is based on the absence and fear of its application in geopolitics; furthermore, in medicine and in energy generation it remains a controlled but untamed beast, full of grave hazards. In comparison, the applications of genetic engineering in health, agriculture, and industry are of profound economic value and ethical importance. It is altering how we live and how well we live. Philosophically, the power of the gene and the processes necessary for its expression strongly influences our world view, specifically our concepts of life, death, and self. Therefore, we should have some knowledge of the fundamentals of molecular genetics to be able to make proper, informed decisions as citizens, consumers, and patients.

What follows will not be easy to follow because of its large cast of characters and subplots, but it is this complex of relationships and activities that I wish to convey. Your efforts, I trust, will be rewarded with a new perspective of nature, a new respect for yourself.

When we use the well characterized single chromosome of bacteria as a model, these are the simplified structural basics

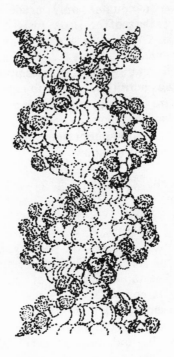

DNA: It encodes only proteins.

of DNA:[4] It is arranged as a double helix, which may be likened to parallel lines running clockwise down a barber pole, rather than to the opposite intertwining spirals of the caduseus. Both chains are composed of four sorts of nucleic acids—two purines (thymine and cytosine) and two pyrimidines (adenine and guanine)—each coupled to a sugar (deoxyribose), to which an attached phosphate group extends outward. Taken together, these three molecular components describe a nucleotide. Alternating sugar and phosphate linkages are the backbone of each chain; the nucleic acids are located inward, directly facing their opposite. The sequential arrangement of nucleotides along each chain, at first glance, seems random. However, the arrangement between the two strands are almost unerringly specific. Held together by hydrogen bonds, thymine on one chain couples only with adenine on the other chain, and cytosine joins only guanine. These complementary purine-pyrimidine pairs form overlapping plates perpendicular to the backbone. The chains of the helix run in opposite directions. Furthermore, the chromosomes of viruses and bacteria are circular, and may be supercoiled in several arrangements, depending on the extent of winding.[5] You can duplicate their appearance by twisting a long rubber band.

I said simplified, not simple! Because of the consistency and specificity in base pairing, *DNA replication is by autotemplate.* As the helix is unzipped by a protein slide, exposing the nucleic acids, newly synthesized individual nucleotide units find their partner on either chain with the guidance of a molecule of another type of enzyme that also links the sugar-phosphate groups. Thus, each cytosine is matched by a guanine, each adenine by a thymine. Because sequences of nucleotides are generally conserved, twin double-helices result. In the instance of single-strand DNA of certain viruses, a temporary double helix is formed, which serves as a template for the required single chain. The unwanted chain is later disassembled by a virus-induced enzyme.

What is truly exquisite about this already extraordinary molecule is the ternary code, which, like the I Ching, has 64 possible combinations, called *codons. The code is read as a nonoverlapping series of three nucleic acids on a chain.* Since there are 20 typical amino acids that are linked into proteins, some degeneracy or redundancy exists. For instance, both guanine-cytosine-adenine and guanine-cytosine-guanine yield the amino acid, alanine, but guanine-adenine-guanine is one of the codes for the amino acid glutamine. A series of codons that leads to a given polypeptide chain composes a gene; a protein consists of one or more polypeptide chains. The average gene contains over 1,000 nucleotide pairs, or about 350 codons. Some codons are not associated with any

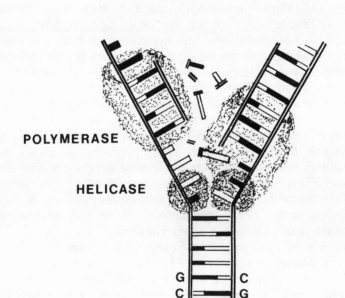

POLYMERASE

HELICASE

G | C
C | G
A | T
T | A

REPLICATION OF DNA THROUGH THE AGENCY OF PROTEINS.

particular amino acid; instead, they serve as punctuation, initiating and terminating a gene message.

What delivers the message? Messenger RNA (mRNA), of course. RNA is similar to DNA, differing in its sugar, ribose, and the substitution of the nucleic acid uracil for thymine. In addition, mRNA is single stranded. However, when RNA, single or double stranded, is the viral chromosome, *the messenger is the message*. (Does that sound familiar? Historian and mass-communications philosopher Marshall McLuhan is remembered for his phrase *global village* and his slogan, 'The medium is the message,' referring to the psychological differences of cold newspapers and hot television.) As, in the usual case, complementary DNA chains form on both unwound DNA strands for replication, individual RNA nucleotides find their corresponding exposed chromosomal nucleic acid but only on one of the chains. This selection depends on the gene, and is determined by the presence of an attached promoting protein. If messengers were instead layered upon opposite regions of both DNA chains, two types of proteins would result, the codons being different. An enzyme recognizes the marker protein and helps guide and link the RNA nucleotides into the gene messenger. This process of message copying is termed *transcription*. The above described amino acid equivalents are based on the translation of the codons of messenger RNA. *In other words, chromosomal DNA has an agent to represent it in fulfilling contractual obligations.*

Manfred Eigen and his colleagues have made a strong case for single-stranded RNA, not the double helix of DNA, as the first evolved carrier of genetic information.[6] They based their very reasonable belief on the structural flexibility and functional versatility of RNA along with its comparative advantages in synthesis. Additional studies provided another point in favor of RNA: RNA can be catalytic and, remarkably, autocatalytic, as a snake twisting around to remove a chunk of itself.[7-9] As fantastic as lifting yourself by your own bootstraps, RNA, to an extremely limited degree, can also act as an enzyme to replicate itself. In the case of the viral RNA chromosome, a viral enzyme, reverse transcriptase, induces the formation of a complementary DNA chain onto the RNA. Later this viral hybrid unwinds, and the single DNA chain becomes a template for its DNA complement. *Thus, we have DNA leading to DNA; DNA leading to RNA; RNA leading to DNA; and RNA leading to RNA.* 'Curiouser and curiouser!' cried Alice.

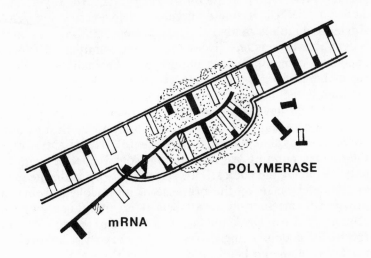

TRANSCRIPTION OF THE GENE CODE INTO mRNA. (Adenine is matched by thymine in DNA, uracil in RNA.)

RNA, which we have seen can serve as both chromosome message center and transcribed messenger, is also involved in the translation of the code in two interactive but structurally different forms—transfer RNA (tRNA) and ribosomal RNA (rRNA). The function of tRNA is to bring amino acids to the polypeptide assembly organelle, the ribosome, and properly situate them for coupling. *t* can also stand for teamster. A given amino acid will bind specifically to a corresponding transfer RNA.

Messenger RNA is a linear molecule, but tRNA is globular.[10] How does this happen? A globular protein, in comparison, is usually so because the chain folds upon itself, allowing the now spatially adjacent sulfur atoms of certain amino acids to form strong crosslinking covalent bonds. Similarly, tRNA folds its chain in such a way that eight sequentially separate areas will form weak hydrogen bonds with their complementary sequence. The shape is a twisted and bent cloverleaf. At the end of the farthest loop is an anticodon that is complementary to the codon of the messager. Such loops, which resemble the Greek letter omega, are also found on the surface of proteins and likewise serve as recognition sites.[11]

A given amino acid is joined to the stem of its respective tRNA through the catalytic activity of a corresponding enzyme. Since proteins may contain up to 20 different amino acids, there are 20 different enzymes. These combined units of amino acids and their carriers are on-call for any messenger. The messenger RNA situates itself within the ribosome, which has two adjacent regions for processing, and a unit of tRNA-amino acid then couples to the appropriate codon. When the ribosome moves tothe next codon, a new transfer RNA arrives. The amino acid of the first tRNA is enzymically removed and linked to the free end of the amino acid of the second tRNA. The first tRNA, empty of its burden, is freed. Again the ribosome moves to the next codon, and the cycle repeats until the message is completed and all the links of the polypeptide chain are connected, which may take seconds in bacteria or up to several minutes in mammals.

The genetic process as discussed so far is a series of *complementary transfers of information,* and it is difficult to know which pattern is the original. Remembering that both strands of DNA are involved in transcription, depending on the gene, let us consider the gene sequence on one strand of DNA (call it B) that is transcribed by mRNA into its complementary sequence (A"). The uninvolved chain (A), represented by mRNA (A"), would be protected from any injury due to faulty transcription and would thereby be more apt to replicate true. The anticodon of tRNA (B") is equivalent to the transcribed DNA codon (B). Thus, the conserved sequence (A) would be the master code. On the other hand, a faulty transcription leading to a mutant protein may be instrumental in evolution. If the active is deemed more important, then the transcribed sequence (B) would be the master. Taoists, who emphasize the metaphysic of complementarity, prefer the female or conservative principle, which implies the receptive, the passive, the unobtrusive: 'He who is conscious of the light, but keeps to the dark, becomes the model for the world.'[12]

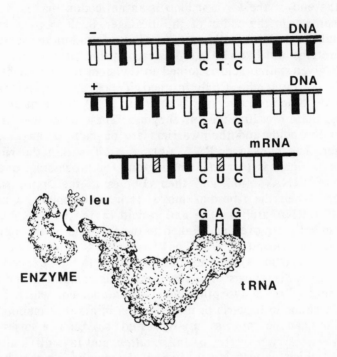

THE MIND OF tRNA:
Translating the code to amino acids, e.g., leucine.
(Which DNA chain is the master, which is the agent?)

We now come to the factory, the organelle called a ribosome. As an *organ* is composed of various tissues and is chiefly dedicated to a primary bodily function, such as digestion or respiration, an *organelle* consists of various molecular structures organized to provide a specialized cellular function. The ribosome consists of RNA and numerous smaller proteins. Bacteria and related primitive organisms have few types of organelles compared to molds and protozoa, but they are nevertheless crammed with some 10,000 ribosomes. Each ribosome is a composite of two asymmetric subunits.[13] When aggregated, the clefts, platforms, and protuberances of the ribosome subunits provide restrictive and protected channels for messenger and transfer RNAs and proteins.

The larger subunit includes two RNA chains. They are associated with 34 different proteins. The smaller subunit, which is mainly involved in the codon—anticodon interaction, has at its core a long, multifolded chain of RNA. In addition, 21 different ribosomal proteins are located around the RNA, held together by hydrogen and ionic bonds. What is marvelous about these assorted structural molecules is that *they are assembled in a particular sequence that is dependent on mutual cooperation.*[14] Some proteins directly bind to the RNA; others follow as a cascade. While assembly takes place, the components, especially RNA, progressively fold into a compact structure, a process that exposes new protein-binding sites on already attached proteins or on RNA. Folding stabilizes the structures and protects certain nucleotide regions, constraining the path of the RNA chain.

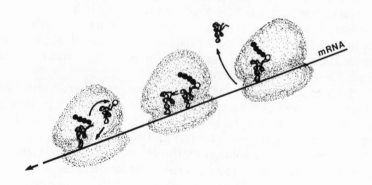

THE RIBOSOME:
A protein-forming organelle composed, in part, of protein.

Thus, the ribosome is not a jigsaw puzzle of rigid pieces. *The organelle is itself an organism.* As the attachment of each protein in turn alters the conformation of the unit, the fluid pattern increasingly becomes limited in freedom of movement. However, some flexibility remains to permit enzymic activity in translation of the genetic code. *The self-development of the ribosome, in short, is a process of awareness-mind involving pattern recognition and feedback control of movement and chemical bonding.* Barring the rare mutation, the 10,000 bacterial ribosomes are all identical.

This arduous presentation, which resembles the pages of a college textbook, only hints of the amazing number and variety of molecules and interactions that occur in the transfer and translation of information and its transformation into activity. Nuclear physics is complicated by the mathematics and the engineering of instruments necessary for its research, but the subject under study is limited and can be isolated without apparent loss of comprehension. In cellular biology, the level of mathematics and the sophistication of apparatus is more elementary; however, molecular biology (in its proper sense) is extraordinarily complicated by the 100,000 actors and simultaneously spoken lines in the drama of life, every one essential to the plot. Through reductive science, we attain a fair appreciation of how each unit routinely behaves, usually in isolation, but we often fail to recognize its properties and activities that relate to coordination and cooperation. Holistic, organismic science is primary despite the indifference rampant in research today.

I have described some intricate molecular structures and operations, and it seems appropriate to pause here to reflect on the underlying principles discussed earlier. We find that the genetic code depends on recognition of structural patterns on one molecule by another molecule having a complementary pattern. Furthermore, the pattern is unusual because it is composed of three joined units, which may be the same or different. The process of recognition requires weak hydrogen bonding and moderate structural flexibility. Like any code, the message must be transcribed and translated; no unit of the system is expendable and each requires the other for maintaining itself. In the living organism, no biological molecule, no organelle is an island entire of itself!

Richard Dawkins, a behavioral biologist, caused a stir with his book, *The Selfish Gene,* which could be epitomized as a variation of the chicken-and-egg argument: an organism is a gene's way of reproducing itself.[15] His study, an alterative to socially determined behaviorism, concerned the genetic and sexual basis of selfishness and altruism, especially towards relatives with whom we share 100%, 50%, 25%, and fewer genes. It is an interesting thesis, which unfortunately is flawed, as I see it, by its rigid reductionistic and materialistic tenents. He regarded organisms as 'survival machines', the body as a colony of genes, and the true objective of DNA as mere survival. 'Vanity of vanities, saith the Preacher, vanity of vanities; all is vanity,' saith the Bible. A classical teleologist might say that the purpose is not to maintain but to evolve. Concepts of any such goals are cast off by Buddhists, as indicated in Buson's haiku:[16]

Fallen leaves—
When the wind blows from the west
they gather in the east.

Dawkin's preeminence of genes ignores the simple fact that the genetic material did not evolve into a biological form alone. Although primordial RNA could have acted as enzymes to replicate itself or as crude tRNA to bind environmental peptides, these separate and uncoordinated effects were closer to physical chemistry and crystal formation than biology. It would be as reasonable and as wrong to say that in a biological organism a gene is a protein's way of reproducing itself. After all, enzymes and other proteins that serve a given function evolve, differing in composition among species; in addition, enzymes are essential to code replication, transcription, and translation. Or, in striving toward a cellular perspective, we can give dominance in purpose to the organism-as-structure. However, none of these isolated objects can dictate organismal behavior as consciousness-mind or even as awareness-mind. Co-evolution had to take place.

The rainbow is a classic example of holism. It is not an object but, rather, a ghostlike entity. It does not occupy space, nor is it an abstraction. The phenomenon requires diffractive beads of rain, the proper geometry of sun and observer (or the observer's intermediate proxy, such as a camera), and the interpretative sensory system of the observer. The elimination of any component will prohibit the manifestation. So, too, there is no genetic code without the existence and activity of transfer RNA and the enzyme that links it with its corresponding amino acid. Unfortunately, they are too often regarded as mere accessories to DNA.

So conditioned are we to reductive scientific thinking that I continually need to emphasize this principle of dynamic and developmental holism. It is easy to fall back to our old and comfortable perspectives. Many critics have unjustly placed the onus of reductionism solely upon Western civilization; mutual arising, interdependency, and organismic processes are not readily perceived by any people. They are interpretative consequences of the religious experience and of philosophical insights.[12]

The student of knowledge aims at acquiring day by day; the student of Tao aims at disburdening day by day.

Although cultures of Southeast Asia and the Far East developed in part around this philosophy, individuals still required extensive training to personally validate it.

As the temple bell was struck, the Buddha asked Ananda (the everyman of Buddhism), 'What produces the sound of the bell?'

'The bell,' answered the student.

'How could there be sound without the striker?'

'Of course, the striker causes the bell to resonate.'

'What about air?' reminded Buddha. 'There is no sound in a vacuum.'

Ananda stroked his forehead and replied, 'Yes, the sound is the motion of molecules transmitted in the air.'

'Then,' smiled Buddha, 'how is it that an ear is necesssary to hear the sound?'

'Yes, the sound of the bell comes from the sense of hearing.'

'Ananda, how can you say that the sound is of the bell without having consciousness-mind?'

'I see now.' Ananda responded, 'The bell sound arises in consciousness.'

Taking his student to the limit of the causality series, the Buddha in great compassion said, 'Ananda, consciousness-mind is but a name. It has no form or location. It is of no substance. Nonetheless, long after the bell has sounded you are able to recall its qualities. Tell me, Ananda, if you have no consciousness-mind, how does the sound of the bell arise?'

Bong!

Returning to genetic operations, we encounter a form of intelligence in biochemical communications and cybernetics. Again, the technical information, with descriptions of diverse agents and functions, may be formidable for some readers. This chapter is the most difficult, and the details need not be assimilated. What is important are the principles that these examples illustrate. Nevertheless, a list of key concepts without the evidence necessitates faith, which is contrary to both science and Buddhism. Like Ananda, readers must explore and discover for themselves.

Transcription is governed by a wide variety of regulators and processes. The earliest, the concept of the operator and repressor, was developed in the late 1950s by three researchers at the Pasteur Institute—Arthur Pardee, François Jacob, and Jacque Monod—and over the ensuing years evidence has repeatedly substantiated it.[2,4] Many genes that provide non-constitutive proteins (the products, typically enzymes, that need to be induced) are associated with an adjacent region of DNA called the *operator*. Another portion of the chromosome leads to the synthesis of a protein, called the *repressor*, that specifically couples with the nucleotides of the operator through hydrogen bonding. Because the repressor physically blocks an enzyme from acting on the gene promotor portion, no mRNA is initiated; the gene is inactive. An *inducer*, which is often the target or end product of the enzyme coded by the gene, can neutralize the repressor, preventing its attachment to the operator, and hence permit the transcription of the

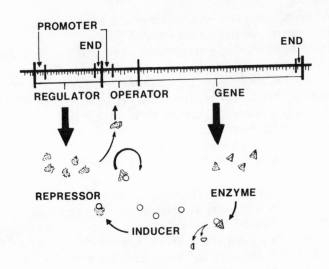

PROMOTER

END   END

REGULATOR OPERATOR   GENE

REPRESSOR   ENZYME

INDUCER

REGULATION OF TRANSCRIPTION BY
INTRACELLULAR ECONOMICS :
Supply-demand feedback loops.

gene.The inducer forms hydrogen and ionic bonds with complementary areas of the repressor. The hazard of metabolic
suffocation through an infinite series of regulatory loops is
avoided by the absence of operators that are repressor genes.

We have been dealing with genetic systems in bacteria. Life
made several quantum-like leaps in its evolution: the rise of
eukaryotic organisms from bacteria or other prokaryotes, the
evolution of vertebrates from the invertebrates, and the
emergence of consciousness-mind. Eukaryotic cells have
additional gene regulators, including another RNA-protein
organelle, the *spliceosome*.[17] This comical word, a Dutch-
Greek hybrid, is reminiscent of the old notorious advertise-
ments on television for the Vege-Matic[tm] kitchen appliance;
the spliceosome both slices and splices messenger RNA. The

reason for its existence is strange indeed. *Most of the coded gene sequences of nucleotides in eukaryotic cells are not continuous;* they are split along the strands into numerous well-separated fragments, the record thus far being 52! The nucleotides between fragments are nonsense or punctuation codons. A small number of split genes may also exist in the DNA of cyanobacteria, archebacteria, viruses, and mitochondria and chloroplasts of eukaryotic cells. [18-20]

Split or mosaic genes are a recent discovery of genetic engineering, and their unexpected complexity have been a significant factor in holding back therapeutic applications in humans and animals. Messenger RNA is formed along the chromosome, beginning at the promoter region; it is then capped with a small phosphated chemical to aid in ribosome attachment and enzymatically stuck with a kite tail of some 200 adenine nucelotides! The spliceosome is the editor that cuts away the stretches of connecting sequences, called *introns,* while sealing the ends of the fragments to form a united gene. (Prokaryotic introns are self-splicing.) The revised messenger must now overcome a physical barrier. Chromosomes of eukaryotic cells are located within a large organelle called the nucleus, which is bound by a porous membrane.

The spliceosome is a true holistic organelle. Damage to even one of its proteins will prohibit splicing, and none can act alone. Each has its special function. The coordinated activity of these proteins ultimately leads to their own replication.

Despite their nonsense, the intervening sequences between the gene fragments, the introns, are important to the eukaryotic transcription system. The experimental deletion of all the introns will prevent transcription! Keeping all but one intron will still prevent mRNA from exiting the nucleus. The spliceosome remaining on the messenger is too large to cross the membrane.

Why would such an elaborate and seemingly wasteful system develop? The short answer is to hasten evolution.[18,21] Dispersed fragments, like a deck of cards, can be more easily and safely shuffled, and the more distant fragments, or cards, are more apt to be mixed than those close together. Eukaryotic introns are 65 to 100,000 nucleotides long, ample for promoting nature's experiment, the mutation. The patches of non-sense codes are useful because recombinations taking place at such areas do not throw the triplet code out of phase. Walter Gilbert at Harvard University was first to suggest that each gene fragment, rather than being random, was responsible for active recognition regions of proteins. The recombination or random mixture of such fragments could provide new functional genes or novel proteins. The diversification of antibodies do fulfill this scheme, although the concept may not be universal.[22]

I should also note that chromosomes of viruses that enter the nucleus, in contrast to those that replicate exclusively in the cytoplasm, have split genes also. This is a clue of evolutional importance both to the rise of viruses and to the advancement of biological life.

Finally, methylation of the nucleic acid cytosine has sparked much interest as a gene regulator.[23,24] The cells of mammals have two nonidentical sets of chromosomes, one set from each parent. Are the genes on both sets of chromosomes expressed? Is there genetic competition? Generally, maternal genes are more methylated, and since methylation inactivates genes, the paternal chromosomes dominate. This may seem a plot of disinformation from male chauvinistic scientists. However, the static condition is not representational of life, which is a process. Demethylation and methylation of the gene may be an on/off switch, activating the appropriate gene at the appropriate time.

Although more paternal genes are active at any given moment, both parental sets are required, a conclusion of the experiment in which fertilized eggs of mice were manipulated to contain either two female or two male nuclei.[23] None of the embryos fully developed. Furthermore, the male chromosomes are associated with the formation of the placenta and amniotic membranes around the embryo; the skeleton, and skeletal muscle; however, the embryo itself, especially the brain, is directed by the female set of genes. Incidentally, only one of the two X chromosomes of females is active, but it may be of either paternal or maternal origin.

Genetic engineering also provided evidence for this regulator. When a methylated or nonmethylated foreign gene was introduced into a cell, only the nonmethylated form was expressed. If, for example, a gene for muscle protein was inserted into a muscle cell, the methylated form was de-methylated. The same gene within a liver cell would not be activated.

Methylation may also have a role in aging and death. The number of generations of cellular divisions is limited for normal tissue (cancer cells are immortal). Leonard Hayflick, while at the Wistar Institute in Philadelphia, established in cell culture that 40 to 60 generations describe the life span of human cells.[25] A fertilized egg, splitting into two at each generation, will, after 50 cycles, yield a total of some 10^{15} cells. Since a human on average consists of a like number of cells, there is little room for efficient tissue repair, as known to any adult who remembers how cleanly wounds healed as a child. To explain the Hayflick phenomenon, various mechanisms have been proposed.[24,26,27] Demethylation of genes may be listed among the genetic causes. Some researchers have observed a corresponding decline in methylated cytosine in DNA with the number of cell divisions. The loss of regulation and cellular coordination may lead to harmful mutations or autotoxicity.

Having sketched the main material components of inheritance and the normal operations of the genetic system, we need to probe them with the needle of individuality, which, you may recall, refers to uniqueness, completeness, and independence as well as to nonreducibility. Among a large population of apparently similar organisms, where is the key (which we now know to be an activity rather than a structure) that opens the door to individuality? It will be precise but irrelevant if we differentiate like cells according to their age, the number of molecules or atoms, or their quantum levels of energy. *As we proceed higher in orders of organization, the influence of variation in lower tiers is diluted, although it can never be totally excluded. Functional individuality, therefore, should be regarded only within a given hierarchy.* At the cellular level, the distinctive element among organisms is the sequence of nucleic acids in DNA.

So long as we qualify them as only a contributor to individuality, the encoded chromosomes make us unique. To put this concept to a most stringent test, let us inspect a broth culture containing a billion bacteria of the species *Escherichia coli*, which normally resides in our intestines. More is known about this simple microorganism than any other life form, including ourselves. Assuming that the source of the inoculum is a colony grown on nutrient agar in a Petri dish, are all the bacterial cells in the test tube exactly the same? That is to say, are these individual cells one individual? If this were so, we would have a paradox. We have a paradox. Should we remove 100,000 cells and kill them, we would not be killing them! They, rather, it would still survive in the broth. Although each cell is a separate organism, it is not unique. Providing homogeneous environmental conditions (achieved by constant mixing), there can be no intercellular actions or higher social order, only cumulative activities. There is a saying that a cat has nine lives, all in series; within the glass vessel, this clone has one billion lives, all parallel. Within the human and animal reservoir, its serial life may have existed for eons and may continue for eons more.

Now the caveat. If such a circumstance persists, how can evolution occur? Actually, not all of these billion bacteria are identical. Most are, without a doubt; but the odds of finding a mutant for a plausible characteristic, such as failure to synthesize a certain structural protein or an enzyme, are about one in 10^7 to 10^{11}. (In humans, the average odds are one in 10 billion.) Therefore, chances are excellent that the culture contains a fair number of unique cells, perhaps some thousands. Most of these can not reproduce. Another proportion can not compete with the surrounding horde. In practice, it is difficult to isolate the rare cell even by utilizing selective culture media and altering environmental conditions. Nature is patient, however, and eventually as conditions change, new varieties will endure and thrive, while older forms decline and disappear.

The reader can readily point to areas in which mutations or genetic modifications arise. Errors in translation can occur; indeed, they are built into the system as wobbles in the coupling of tRNA anticodons with mRNA.[10] Improper reading of the codon while forming mRNA is also likely. In both situations, the attributes of the individual may change, perhaps with repercussions in higher social systems that could influence the behavior of future generations of individuals, but they are not directly inheritable at the level of unicellular organisms. Efficiency in evolution requires change in the genome. The means by which DNA is altered prior to and during replication are numerous, and if it were not for repair systems, we humans, if evolved at all, would probably not be as we are today.[28]

Mutagenic agents are everywhere: cosmic rays, ultra violet light, chromium and nickel, asbestos, fried meat, the natural radioactivity of bricks, cosmetics, pesticides, industrial chemicals, tobacco smoke, and even by-products of intestinal metabolism.[29,30] As you may already have inferred from this excerpted list, most mutagens are also apt to be carcinogens. Sometimes mutations occur spontaneously in 'hot' spots of the DNA chain, a result perhaps of certain sequential or chemically unstable structural patterns. Alterations also may happen at the time enzymes are in their chemically active transitional configuration. Mutations are usually a failure to achieve complementarity in forming new strands of DNA. Bases are substituted, added, or deleted. (Sickle cell anemia, for instance, is a mutation of the hemoglobin gene, the substitution of one nucleotide, that leads to a different amino acid in the red blood cell protein.) As an indirect agency, repair enzymes and systems, the proofreaders of the cell, may themselves be rendered ineffective, allowing any mutations in DNA to have the opportunity of being transcribed and translated.

Other genetic changes may take place by shuffling genes. In eukaryotic cells parallel sections of chromosomes can switch places by breaking and recombining. In meiosis, which is the process by which the double sets of chromosomes are reduced to single sets in egg or sperm, sections of whole chromosomes can also crossover. As any military commander, any electronic engineer, or any other systems analyst is well familiar, increases in system complexity are accompanied by additional sites at which the organization may be compromised. And according to Murphy, it does happen.

Sexual intercourse is the most common means for transferring the genes of one individual to another. In humans and most eukaryotic organisms, two individuals are donors but there is no recipient. That third individual arises from a fusion of the donors' cells and gene pool. Sex or, more properly, conjugation in bacteria, however, is a simple transfer of duplicated genes.

Its characteristics were first disclosed in 1946 by Joshua Lederberg and Edward Tatum and later by William Hayes in the early 1950s.[31,32] The donor cell contains a small loop of nonchromosomal DNA, called a *plasmid*, that codes for fertility factors. One result is a special organelle, the bacterial equivalent of a penis, called the F pilus. Conjugation often results in the transfer of only this plasmid, which renders the recipient a potential donor. At times the plasmid becomes incorported into the chromosome and is duplicated with it. Upon conjugation, the fused DNA loop is broken and the leading edge, a portion of the F plasmid, slowly enters the

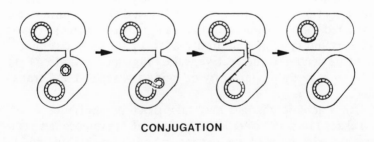

CONJUGATION

GENETIC RECOMBINATION BETWEEN BACTERIA: Bacterial sex.

receiving bacterium. *Coitus interruptus* may easily happen over the 100-minute period, but occasionally most of the set of donor genes is transferred. Related genes may be exchanged or simply added to the recipient chromosome by breakage and recombination before the visiting DNA is degraded. Since the F factor is not completely transferred, the recipient cell remains infertile.

A similar process, *transduction*, has been established in viral infections of bacteria. In 1949 Lederberg and Norton Zinder stumbled upon the phenomenon.[32,33] The viral loop of DNA typically remains independent while reproducing itself and the viral proteins that encase it. These viruses are *bacteriophages*, meaning bacteria eaters—the parasitic way, from the inside, rather than the predatory way, from the outside. The mass of reproduced bacteriophages literally bust out, dissolving the cell wall and killing its host. However, viral infection does not alway lead to bacterial death, at least not immediately. The viral DNA, like the plasmid, insidiously infuses itself into the bacterial chromosome. Generation after generation of bacteria will harbor the occluded viral genes.

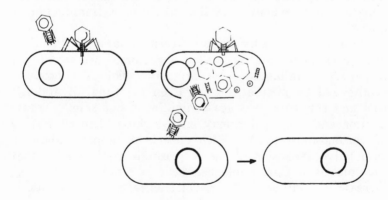

TRANSDUCTION

GENETIC RECOMBINATION BETWEEN BACTERIA:
Virus as gene vector (not to scale).

Do not regard the genes as simply passive passengers. The genes are active and it is they which are responsible, for instance, for the toxins of diphtheria, botulism, and scarlet fever. Occasionally, but especially after exposure to ultra violet light, the viral component of the chromosome—the *provirus*—loops off, and viral genes are activated to induce formation of structural products as well as copies of themselves. The loop infrequently may contain adjacent bacterial genes, and thus upon release of the viruses and subsequent infection of a new host, the bacterial genes are introduced into the host genome. In this way, bacteriophages are vectors. However, there is limited room for DNA within the protein shell of the virus, and the hybrid DNA does not include a complete set of viral genes. No new virus particles can be produced in the new host.

Can bacterial transduction serve as a model for human genetic recombination or disorders? Retroviruses, the RNA tumor viruses of animals that include the virus of AIDS, also incorporate themselves as proviruses into the host chromosome through a DNA intermediate.[34] They may infect germ cells as well as body cells, and are subject to the various means of mutation and regulation. A limited form of transduction is possible.

Because they render bacteria resistant to specific antibiotics, certain plasmids are called R factors.[35] We should not forget that antibiotics were originally biological products synthesized by microorganisms. Even the fungi of athlete's foot and ringworm produce penicillin on our skin.[36] Transduction and conjugation may involve these plasmids instead of chromosomal DNA. Each episode of transfer allows a cumulative expansion of the R plasmids as they join other such plasmids. Epidemiologists have observed an alarming increase in multiple drug resistance as each new antibiotic is introduced into the clinic. R factors now commonly destroy or interfere with five to as many as 10 unrelated antibiotics..

Other plasmids produce specific nonantibiotic agents, *bacteriocins*, that attack other bacteria; enzymes that ferment milk; and substances that degrade industrial hydrocarbons. Many bacteria carry several plasmids. *Staphylococcus aureus*, the bacterium of pimples and boils, harbors, on average, five plasmids that provide toxins, antibiotic resistance, and bacteriocins. This hardy microorganism is reknown for being the leading opportunistic pathogen, and its ecological survival kit of plasmids enhances its ability to overwhelm competition.

The third means of transferring genes is the most direct. It was discovered in studies of *Streptococcus pneumonia*, whose capsular outer covering, when present, protects it against host defenses in the lung. Called *transformation*, it explained why, in 1928, Fred Griffith found live, virulent, encapsulated pneumococci in mice, after injecting the animals with dead, virulent, encapsulated bacteria mixed with live, avirulent, nonencapsulated pneumococci.[37] In 1944, Oswald Avery, Colin MacLeod, and Maclyn McCarty discovered that free DNA from the dead strain was taken up by the living bacteria, where the gene for the capsule was incorporated into the host.

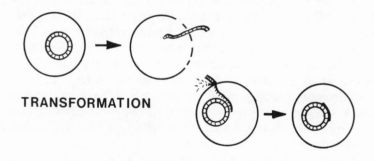

TRANSFORMATION

GENETIC RECOMBINATION BETWEEN BACTERIA:
Bacterial DNA mimics an infectious virus.

These jumping genes give us several conceptual problems. Richard Novick has argued that plasmids are *endosymbionts, internal ecological beings, protoviruses* if you will.[35] Like Dawkins, he defines a living organism as a nucleic acid system that controls its own replication. Setting aside this limited conventional perspective, there is yet merit to the notion of plasmid as organism. Like a virus, they exist only by integrating with host transcription and translation cognitive systems, as business executives sharing a secretary pool. *Plasmids are thus quasi independent, nonessential, self-directed, replicative forms that at times provide benefit to their host.* Furthermore, they may harmlessly 'infect' other bacteria. We will encounter similar endosymbionts when we discuss the eukaryotic cell in detail.

This is a good place to improve the description of viroids and how they fit into the spectrum of genetic life. These infectious agents are very odd.[38] The circular RNA chromosome is composed of fewer than 400 nucleotides, which are almost completely self-complementary. Moreover, since the sequences have no promoter codes and are rampant with nonsense codons, *viroids do not code for any proteins,* and seem to depend entirely on host-directed metabolism for a peculiar form of template replication. (A controversial form of infectious proteinaceous agent that lacks any nucleic acids, called a *prion,* may also be replicated from innate host materials.[39]) Now, it so happens mRNA, chloroplast tRNA, and other nonchromosomal structures, some of which have autosplitting properties, consist of sequences found in viroids. Some researchers have speculated on whether viroids are escaped introns or perhaps close relatives.

Another difficulty is the idea of species. For example, a certain family of gut bacteria is frequently reclassified. Clinical microbiologists find that while their diagnostic tests can identify most isolates, a fair number give ambivalent results. These bacteria transfer genes to each other, even across genera, by conjugation and transduction. Taxonomy in general is often a controversial and arbitrary matter overseen by international commissions, and bacterial taxonomy is especially soft-edged. All bacteria today have a common genetic endowment of billions of years of evolution and gene swapping. In a contiguous mountain range complicated by spurs, saddles, aretes, and plateaus, where exactly does one mountain become another? Only the summits are certain.

When considering bacteria, those ubiquitous primitive unicellular organisms, do we see a singular object, or do we perceive a society of genes with their support network? We have been trained to see a static unit; a change in perspective is in order. *The organisms of each hierarchy are collectives of lower order organisms whose relationships provide new patterns of structure, recognition, and behavior—patterns of mind—that in turn influence the behavior of the agents of the lower hierarchy.* These hierarchies, hence, are not independent or isolated. Moreover, we have no sword to cut the strange interpenetrative loops that mesh them, except for the blade of delusion.

In conclusion, can we rest on the sequential pattern of DNA as defining our individuality? Legally, yes. *DNA fingerprints* have achieved legal standing in some 100 forensic cases as of June 1989.[40,41] Developed by Alec Jeffreys at Leicester University, the technique compares the hyper-variable patterns in size and sequence of certain introns [!] in cell samples from the suspect and in the crime or contested material, which may be bloodstains and sperm nuclei. Using two intron probes, the odds of a match between unrelated persons within ethnic or national groups were estimated as one in 10^4 to 10^7.

This approach is most interesting in that it does not consider the genes, but rather the stuff between them. It is as if looking at a bird in flight, the observer confers individuality to the animal by describing the sky around it!

Hui-Neng (638-713), the future sixth Chinese patriarch of Zen, overheard two monks arguing about a nearby banner. 'The banner is moving,' said one. 'No, it is the wind that is moving,' replied the other. Hui-Neng came up to them and declared, 'You are both wrong. It is your mind that moves.'[42]

Yun Nan T'ien (1633-1690) commented, 'Modern painters apply their mind only to brush and ink, whereas the ancients paid attention to the absence of brush and ink.'[43] When asked what is the most difficult aspect of painting, Ike-no Taiga

(1723-1776) replied, 'Drawing a white space where absolutely nothing is drawn.'[43]

There is also the matter of twins, who like *E. coli* in our broth culture, have essentially the same chromosomal patterns. However, DNA fingerprints are not fingerprints; genotypes are not phenotypes. Much can happen after mRNA transcribes the codon. Distinctions arise in developmental mutations, in selection and recombination of gene sets, and in expression of genes. 'Identical' twins on closer inspection differ physically, including fingerprints, and, of course, they have unique consciousness-minds, although some have a sense of overlapping selves. Gene sequences, besides being material codes for proteins, are, for us, representations of biological organisms. Knowing not to equate the map with the territory, we must proceed to a higher level of organization to further refine our definition and comprehension of individuality and self.

Chapter 7

ACROSS THE GREAT DIVIDE

The biological organism

What a chimera then is man! What a novelty!
What a monster, what a chaos, what a contradiction,
what a prodigy! Judge of all things, feeble earthworm,
depository of truth, a sink of uncertainty and error,
the glory and the shame of the universe.

Blaise Pascal

Homeowners, real estate agents, and exterminators may make war upon them; sharp-clawed and stilleto-tongued aardvarks and anteaters as well as stick-wielding chimpanzees may find them to be tasty treats; however, with scientists and naturalists, both experimentalists and *in situ* observers, termites are spared as fascinating subjects of investigation. For some biologists, these ubiquitous but concealed insects, so exceedingly ancient like their close relative, the hardy—and pesty—cockroach, are the epitome of evolution. This may strike the reader as odd, since humankind might seem a better choice, we being the most advanced species. One may also protest that the termite appears unremarkable, forgetting or ignoring the obvious fact that we ourselves are the brilliant, hairless variation on a primate theme. However, evolution concerns more than shape and organization; it includes organismal behavior and, especially, functional interrelationships. The lowly termite is a prime example of symbiosis, life in mutual association with life, while twentieth-century humans absurdly tend to separate themselves from other life forms, except for their pets.

The architecture of termite colonial abodes towering up to 20 feet over the savannahs of Africa and Australia, a wonder of form and engineering, is a befitting enterprise of cooperative behavior, because termites, like ants and bees, are social insects. Termites vary in form and behavior around the planet, comprising over 2,000 species, 40 of which are in North America. Some produce flamboyant ventilation shafts; others merely divide their living space into small apartments with walls constructed from their own excrement. A large nest may be inhabited by some 4,000,000 termites, which, like other social insects, are differentiated by form and function. Most are infertile workers. They build and clean the nest, tend the eggs, collect and process food, and through regurgitation, feed the guardian soldiers at the entrances. In some species, soldiers may have mandibles shaped like large pinchers; in others the jaw forms a nozzle for squirting a sticky gum. Within the catacombs, the huge immobile queen and her smaller consort king have the duty of reproduction, and in one species the queen lays an egg every ten seconds for nearly 10 years. The workers need also to feed and to clean their royalty. Finally, there is one type, fertile winged reproductives, which develop only under particular circumstances. Their task, like dandelion seeds in the wind, is to leave the nest and establish new colonies. These pilgrim adventurers are the termite elite, able to reproduce and to feed themselves as well as to fly, but they are the most vulnerable to the onslaughts of the environment outside their nest. Hence, even with this exception, a single isolated termite, besides being unemployed, may be doomed to starvation or, alternatively, may be the end of its genetic line. Furthermore, a single termite can not initiate nest building; this collective- dependent activity requires both a minimal number of workers and the overcoming of a behavioral threshold.

Such interdependent relationships play havoc with ordinary definitions of life. Those colonial termites that can feed themselves can not reproduce; those that can reproduce can not feed themselves. Where is individuality? The colony acts as a unit, and it, not the single termite, is the stable organism. However, a given colony is not unique; other colonies of the same species behave in the same way, producing like nests and like inhabitants. Variation in the number of workers in a colony is as useless a criterion of self as the number of hydrogen atoms in a star; the presence of a genetically altered soldier has as little bearing on termite singularity as a different energy state of a stellar electron has on a star. Furthermore, slight differences in nest shape reflect environmental influences. Such absolute distinctions are functionally insignificant. We seek meaningful uniqueness.

The termite is an isolationist, and its nest—its fortress— affords protection and seclusion from the hazards of weather and predator, although the cloister can shelter other life forms, some of which compensate their host with nutritive secretions. According to Gaian principles, termites have the entropic function of recycling wood matter into soil. Fallen timber in rain forests do not remain long on the ground where termites abound.

We know the termite as a wood-eating insect, but is it a wood-digesting insect? One must take care here in answering such a seemingly self-evident question. It depends on how you define or delimit the insect, because, in fact, the wood is broken down into nutrient carbohydrates not by the digestive enzymes of termite tissue, but by particular protozoans living in its digestive tract. To make matters even more complicated, these protozoans live only in termites and are themselves dependent for motility on an astonishing coordinated undulating organization of surface-attached spirochetes (a kind of bacteria) and for assistance in digestion on a variety of other intestinal bacteria. Furthermore, if that buck-passing is not sufficiently perplexing, then we must also contend with the evidence that this peculiar protozoan, like all eukaryotic cells (including termite tissue), is a composite of vestigial bacteria.

Having lost the individual insect outwardly within the necessary higher order of colony, we now find the single termite inwardly dissolving into a series of enveloping boxes. Here we have the biological equivalent of the atomic ghost and its indistinct edges. In most ecological textbooks, organisms in symbiosis functionally interpenetrate each other horizontally within each hierarchy; the contiguous association of alga and fungus in lichens and of plant and bacteria in root nodules of legumes are the classic examples. However, such relationships must also be considered vertically through tiers of order. In this holistic fashion, *all life activity is fundamentally symbiotic.* You, I, and the termite have much in common. To examine this principle, let us plunge into the termite to look closer at the protozoan eukaryotic cell.

A eukaryotic cell, as the term indicates, has a nucleus. Within the cytoplasm are numerous *mitochondria* (Greek for granular threads), which mint the energy currency of the cell, adenosine triphosphate. During cell division, the nuclear membrane breaks down, and the chromosomes are sorted out by the mitotic spindle, filamentous attachments to wheel—like structures called *centrioles.* (In bacteria, a membranous whirl, the mesosome, does similar duty.) The cell may contain any of a variety of membrane—enclosed vacuoles containing food stuffs, enzymes, and other products. If the cell is a plant, it will include *chloroplasts,* organelles responsible for photosynthesis. Depending on cell type, the exterior surface may be characterized by appendages, such as a flagellum whip or a galley pattern of cilia oars, which provide locomotion for the cell or its surroundings. The corresponding examples in humans are sperm and the ciliated cells lining the respiratory system that push mucus and debris up into the throat for swallowing or forceful expulsion by coughing. Animal cells have no cell wall.

Besides having greater size and more genes than bacteria, eukaryotic cells are noteworthy for their organized chromosomes and hefty ribosomes. DNA in the nucleus is at intervals wrapped around globular proteins as beads on a string; together they are enfolded into chromatin strands, and during cell division they are further condensed into large well-defined chromosomes. Although ribosomes in prokaryotic and eukaryotic cells are of similar appearance, the eukaryotic ribosomes in the cytoplasm are larger and consist of different proteins. Differences in the regulation of gene expression were previously described.

Clearly, there is a huge chasm between the cells of bacteria and the cells of their predators, the protozoa. Biologists have long sought to bridge the gap with hypothetical evolutionary intermediates, but all attempts of applying simple Darwinian variation and natural selection have failed. The differences are too extensive. An ecological approach, championed by Lynn Margulis among others, has yielded plausible evidence of at least the early part of the process.[1-3]

About 2 billion years ago nature did something extraordinary, something that opened the floodgates of biology: symbiotic synergistic fusion.[4] It was not the fusion of egg and sperm, since sex did not yet exist. It was not the fusion of an invading viral genome into a bacterial chromosome, since dependence was not mutual. It was the fusion—probably a short series of fusions—and then degeneration of different bacteria into an entirely new biological form.

There exists a group of bacteria, the mycoplasmas, which, lacking a cell wall, are plastic in shape and irregular in reproduction, dividing by fission or by the formation of internal elementary bodies. Through the use of penicillin and other antibiotics that interfere with wall formation and of solutions to balance internal osmotic pressure to prevent membrane rupture, researchers have easily produced analogous wall-deficient bacteria, the L-forms, from otherwise normal bacteria.[5] Some of the interesting features of these atypical bacteria are the formation of membrane-lined vacuoles (an apparent result of invagination) and the significant enlargement of the cell.[6] According to one scenario, an ancestor of such a flexible wall-deficient organism could have been the foundation of the eukaryotic cell.

This organism might have engulfed a regular bacterium that at first had an indifferent commensual relationship with its host, neither party gaining any particular benefit and certainly neither suffering any harm. Nevertheless, the internalized microorganism replicated in tandem with the wallless large body. After generations, otherwise lethal mutations in the small bacterium allowed the organism to survive without a cell wall and certain enzymes; it became dependent on the host in benign parasitism. The host cell, however, received benefit through the guest's more efficient oxidative metabolism, and in due course it, too, lost the genes for now unnecessary enzymes. Mutualism now characterized the endosymbiotic relationship. The internalized bacterium became the mitochondrion. Similarly, an engulfed photosynthethic cyanobacterium (a blue-green alga) was the source of the chloroplast.

The concept of endosymbiosis was adopted in the late 1960s as the origin of the eukaryotic cells, although there was little laboratory evidence to support it. The notion was attacked mainly from biochemical perspectives.[7,8] Molecular genetics, then in its infancy, could not confidently offer support either way. Today most scientists accept the principle and only argue about the steps. The circumstantial data are overwhelming. Mitochondria are bounded by two membranes, as would occur if a microorganism was engulfed by another. Like bacteria, mitochondria and chloroplasts possess their own circular DNA and divide independently of the cell, although the replicative enzymes may come from the nucleus. The mitochondria, which grow in size and internal complexity, can number up to thousands in the more active cells of vertebrates.

As one would expect in symbiotic evolution, the extent of genetic degeneration advances with the emergence of higher phyla, such that yeast mitochondria DNA is five-fold the length of its human counterpart. Some of the genes are eliminated, being no longer necessary, but others are transferred to nuclear DNA.[3] For instance, mRNA for most of the special enzymes that are involved in respiration, and which are bound to the pleats of the mitochondrial membrane, are produced in the nucleus. Chloroplast DNA is also translocated to the nucleus as well as to the mitochondria.[9] Mitochondrial DNA codes for two ribosomal RNA chains and tRNA of unique structure. The organelle contains not the large ribosomes of the endoplasmic reticulum, but rather the smaller prokaryotic forms. The sequences of animal mitochondria rRNA do not readily compare to contemporary bacteria, but the chloroplast rRNA do resemble that of purple bacteria, rhizobacteria, and the obligate parasitic prokaryotes, the rickettsiae. The conservation of genes suggest that chloroplasts and higher plants are comparatively more recent biological forms.

Most remarkable is the finding that the genetic code differs slightly in mitochondria. In mammals, the codon uracil-guanine-adenine in the nucleus is a messenger-terminating sequence, but in the organelle it yields tryptophan; instead of coding arginine, adenine-guanine-guanine is a terminating codon. In yeast, the mitochondrial code differs from both eubacterial and eukaryotic chromosomal systems and also animal mitochondrial genetic systems. *The genetic code, therefore, is not quite universal; there are dialects.* Differences in the archaebacterial code are yet to be determined. When that great day comes when we encounter extraterrestial microbial life, its genetic code will probably vary further, existing as a different but related language. *Mitochondria and chloroplasts, hence, apparently have evolved independently,* the evolution of mitochondria in animals being longer and more extensive.

Finally, in those organisms that reproduce sexually, mitochondria are inherited maternally.[3,10] Although a few mitochondria power sperm of some species, they do not enter and replicate in the zygote. Thus, while methylation represses the transcription of most maternal chromosomal genes, we safely breath oxygen thanks to our mother's endosymbionts.

The next probable biological fusion was the incorporation of spirochetes, whose shape resemble long slender corkscrews. Although their notorious representive is the agent of syphilis, spirochetes are generally not associated with disease. Spirochetes, which move by rotation and bending, may have adhered to the surface of the eukaryotic prototype in the same manner they cling to the termite protozoan today, giving it the appearance of a minute hairy eggplant.[11]

Flagella in prokaryotes, if present, are single protein fibers that may be situated at one or both poles or entirely around the microorganism. Whether long flagella or short cilia, the eukaryotic appendages are, instead, a complex of tubules. Two central microtubules are surrounded by nine other pairs. This pattern is nearly duplicated by the centriole, the organelle of chromosomal division, which consists of only the circular array of paired microtubules. No one has adequately explained how a symbiotic spirochete could transform to a eukaryotic flagellum and then to centrioles, nor is there scientific evidence of correspondence between these prokaryotic cells and the organelles, although eukaryotic flagella, cilia, and centrioles are structurally and biochemically related. The distribution pattern of spirochetes on the termite protozoan and their entrained undulations that yield motility may only

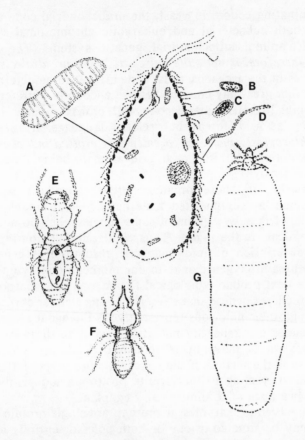

FIND THE INDEPENDENT TERMITE.

WOOD—DIGESTING INTESTINAL PROTOZOAN:
(A) Respiratory mitochondrion, a vestigial bacterium.
(B) Bacterial cobblestone.
(C) Digestive bacterium.
(D) Spirochetal oar.

SOCIALLY DIFFERENTIATED CASTE:
(E) *x10* Worker.
(F) *x15* Soldier.
(G) *x 4* Queen.

be a coincidental analogue, but the possibility of a spirochetal origin of flagella and cilia remains tantalizing. *While we do not live in the past, the past literally lives in us.*

Our example termite protozoan, appropriately named *Myxotrichia paradoxa,* is therefore a very strange creature worthy of inclusion in one of the fanciful medieval bestiaries. We find it covered with a mat of small and occasional large spirochetes that are evenly interspersed, as a checkerboard, with adherent bacilli. We know that it consists in part of vestigial bacteria, the mitochondria, and that it is endowed with countless generations, a continuum, of genetic improvisation. We recognize the entire group pattern and give it a name, but where exactly is the organism? Where is the individual? The protozoan chromosome and cytoplasm divide independently of internal and external symbionts, but these associates then replicate to keep pace with protozoan growth. Furthermore, the process is a feedback cycle, since their related activity allows cell division. This protozoan, thus, is a composite, a committee, a society of awareness-mind rooted in matter-mind. *This protozoan is an organism of organisms.*

A jump to the higher tier of termite gives us further pause. A germ-free termite worker (without any artifical feeding) is a dead termite. It will chomp on wood to no avail until dead of malnutrition. Thus, the protozoan is a mutually evolved endosymbiont of the termite worker. Except for human intervention, the two are inseparable, ecologically defining each other. The singular termite itself is largely dependent on its society. And the termite colony is an important node of the Gaian network. So what is a termite? Despite our cultural conditioning, it is not a form nor a complex of forms; it is a *pattern of multitiered relationships and activities that is symbolized by forms.*

As the reader can readily apprehend, I am reluctant to isolate any pattern in time-space. We separate structures and functions because it is useful in describing the contributors and influences of phenomena. We do so for advancing technology and medicine. We do so for the pleasure of discovery and the social power and prestige of expert specialization. Paradoxically, we reduce and isolate to fully savor and comprehend the whole. Prajña transcendental wisdom *through* knowledge, an approach of jñana yoga and Tibetan Buddhism, is the mystic path typically favored by scholars and scientists, if so inclined. Whitman understood this when he wrote,[12]

> Hurrah for positive science! Long live exact
>   demonstration!..
> This is the geologist, and this works with the scalpel, and
>   this is a mathematician.
> Gentlemen I receive you, and attach and clasp hands
>   with you,
> The facts are useful and real....they are not my dwelling....I
>   enter by them to an area of the dwelling.

Most knowledge is derived from taking things apart, naming and describing and, to a small extent, creating components. However, the activity and form we call *termite,* no matter how well defined, is ultimately arbitrary, a convention. The Tao Te Ching puts it this way:

> The nameless is the origin of heaven and earth; the named is the mother of all things. When we cast off intentions, we behold the mystery of existence; when we surrender to desire, we behold manifestations. Fundamentally the same, the two are differentiated by naming.

All of life is like the termite. We, too, are endosymbionts and exosymbionts. We are mitochondria of human cells. We are the microorganisms that live and interact in skin, nose, mouth, intestine and genital-urinary openings. We are family. We are the commerce, communication, and cultural activities of peoples and nations. We are the beleaguerers of Earth, and we are the beleaguered planet. We are cosmos. We are mind.

> Constant companion
> however alone my path:
> footsteps.

The termite society must be construed as an organism. Within Gaia, termites are collectively a behavioral unit interacting with other organized processes. Indeed, all hierarchies are evolutionary substrates. Stephen Jay Gould, seeking to construct a more powerful and versatile edifice on the reductionistic Darwinian foundation of variation and natural selection among individuals, proposed the concepts of dynamic 'punctuated equilibrium' and hierarchial influence as an approach to the significant jumps and bifurcations in the biological record. The nature of the creative force providing optimal amount and scope of genetic variation is the crux.

Traditional Darwinian processes of step-by-step modifications through mutation and recombination, *gradualism,* is unquestioned when restricted to microevolution. Evolutionary direction here is determined and channeled by inherited forms and developmental operations. A species may survive new stressful environmental conditions through the selection and proliferation of resistant mutants. Gould associated macroevolution, the differential spread of a combination of various features, with geological events, and further recognized that *evolution could act on species as a unit as well as on single animals and plants.* 'Our language and culture include a prejudice for applying he concept of individual only to bodies, but any coherent entity that has a unique origin, sufficient temporal stability, and a capacity for reproduction with change can serve as an evolutionary agent,' he observed.[13]   After all, species arise, modify, and become extinct. While retaining the principle of selection as universal, he speculated that each level below as well as above traditional organisms generates variation by diverse mechanisms among its individuals.

In his scheme, hierarchies interact. Stability of individuals is maintained with higher level suppression. While species may be ecologically disadvantaged by overspecialization (prone to extinction with modest environmental flux) individuals are often favored in overly competitive or otherwise inhospitable conditions. When supportive hierarchial interactions occur, an individual trait may spread across the tier. He further accepted the notion of directed speciation. At the species level, there may exist a directional bias toward the rise of certain *phenotypes,* which are manifested individual characteristics that result from the influence of environment on genetic expression.

There appeared a possibly related report that could not only support Gould's views, but could open the door for the ghost of Jean-Baptiste Lamarck, an early nineteenth-century biologist who suggested that the physically acquired characteristics of an organism, such as calluses on camels' knees, can be inherited by the next generation. Growing *E. coli* on essential nutrient-deficient solid culture media, John Cairns, Julie Overbaugh, and Stephan Miller at Harvard University found that genetic variation is not always random, that product-induced mutations can occur.[14]

Normally, a certain number of bacteria have preexisting random mutations that can render them fit to survive otherwise lethal conditions. For instance, while the parent strain, containing terminating codons through genetic engineering, can no longer use lactose for growth, mutant daughter cells that delete the interfering nucletotide sequences may do so. If, however, the environmental conditions prevent only replication, the bacteria may undergo nonrandom, directed mutations to permit continued growth and division. The research group discovered this anomaly when agar plates containing lactose, but hardly anything else, were inoculated with the altered parent bacteria. As expected, only preexisting mutants grew. Several days later a new wave of colonies began to appear. By mutating—only in the presence of lactose—the bacteria now could consume the sugar and replicate.

Barry G. Hall at the University of Rochester has substantiated and expanded this work.[15] To avoid an organismal instruction concept, he proposed and found evidence for the induction of a hypermutable state in some cells whereby many genes mutate randomly.[16] Selection then follows. However, Hall maintains the regulatory link of environment and mutagenesis whatever the underlying mechanism.

Gould placed species and other hierarchies on an equal footing, but to concretize them, as in Arthur Koestler's scheme of holons and holarchy, is to be blind to the flowing processes, the Tao, if you will, of evolution.[17] In his desire to accommodate both holism and reductionism, Koestler chose as symbol Janus, the double-faced Roman god, whose youthful countenance looked to and controlled the beginning and whose aged half represented the end of all matters.

For Koestler, a holon is a system of relations, with each level 'interlocking' or 'entwining' the holons below and above. To those above it is a dependent part; to those below it is the autonomous whole. The input holon 'abstracts'; the output 'concretizes'. Regulatory information must pass through each adjacent level, there being no direct communication between a tier and a holon several steps lower. The exception is through attentive consciousness (a condition Koestler erroneously considered pathological as did Erich Jantsch, a systems scientist who was aghast at willful control of blood pressure, skin temperature, electrical brain waves, and other body functions once thought to be autonomous.[18] This power is an unwarranted fear. Such purposeful control can be therapeutic when facing mental and environmental stress as well as useful as a tool in neurophysiological and noetic exploration.

The image of intertwining threads or interlocking machinery to represent hierarchial relationships emphasizes the separation and independence of orders. I do not see hierarchies in this way, preferring to accentuate those aspects that unite them into a single system. I therefore edge closer to Jantsch, who described each hierarchy as being self-organizing through its own dynamics, which he equated with mind. For him, higher orders of organization both coordinate and reinforce processes at lower levels, but they do not dictate behavior. The regulatory role of lower levels on higher tiers, except for providing information, is less clear.

My perspective is particularly close to Douglas Hofstadter's, who offered the symbol of the Möbius strip to describe hierarchies.[19] Hofstadter is a mathematician, computer scientist, and, fittingly, a devotee of the delightful mathematical music of Johann Sebastian Bach. He is also haunted by self-referential systems and by Zen Buddhism, although evidently he has not undergone any formal training. While his overly intellectual analyses of Zen and its koans in his brilliant synthesis, *Gödel, Escher, Bach,* generally are wide of the mark, he may have hit squarely upon a deep metaphysic of hierarchial relationships.

He referred to *Strange Loops* and *Tangled Hierarchies.* In studying a system, such as artistically and playfully provided by M.C. Escher and Rene Magritte, one may be taken aback by discovering something that leaps out and acts on the system in which it belongs. 'The top level reaches back down toward the bottom level and influences it, while at the same time being itself determined by the bottom level.'[19] The background becomes the subject, which becomes the background; the observer observes the observer observing. Hofstadter also noted a self-reinforcing resonance between different levels, as a television camera focused on its own monitor will induce a distorted yet harmonic image. He differentiated Strange Loops, which are *transforming* and *qualitative paths,* from feedback loops, which are *quantitative regulatory circuits.* His provided examples of entanglement in molecular genetics and biochemistry were the DNA codons that lead to the synthesis of an enzyme that lead to the replication of the nucleotide codons for the same enzyme; overlapping and nesting of genes within DNA (achieved as reading frame shifts in a particular bacterial virus); and a given pivotal molecule serving unrelated functions in different physiological systems. Most of his discussion, however, centered on conceptual frameworks, cybernetics, mathematics and logic, language, and consciousness-mind. Well before Hofstadter, the creator of haiku, Matsuo Basho (1644-1694), encountered a Strange Loop:

Here in Kyo
I yet long for Kyo.
Oh, cuckoo!

If we were to adopt and expand his Möbius strip analogy, each organismal hierarchy would be connected to the ones above and below by Strange Loops. Furthermore, all hierachies would be united in a master loop, with each tier represented by a twist in the Möbius strip. No matter how many twists, or hierachies, there is but one side, one edge, one path. Thus, from an outside reference point there would be distinct tiers flowing into each other; from within the system hierarchies would be but diffused zones in a continuum. A major alteration along the path (in a hierarchy) may eventually affect other tightly curved areas (hierarchies), and the influences up or down the circuit eventually return to affect the source. Recognitive processes of behavioral patterns is the currency. The system, although closed, may enlarge and increase in complexity.

By this scheme, the behavior of atoms combining to molecules is modified by the restrictive relationships of the molecule, as people coming together into a society are governed by the rules of the society. Furthermore, atoms and human society, while categorized as extremely distant levels, are nevertheless unitary, being of the time-space evolution of this universe. In the Grand Strange Loop, the highest levels of consciousness-mind and awareness-mind can influence the lowest tiers of matter-mind, phenomena whose purview is the novel science of psychophysics and psychokinesis. [20,21] Instead of meshed gears as the analogy of hierarchial bonding, we have holistic hydraulics.

In the Taoist and Buddhist perspective, opposites interpenetrate, not interlock: the seed of yin exists in yang, as yang is intrinsicly present in yin. The same may be said for hierarchies. The welfare of the termite worker's protozoan is dependent on the health of termite society, and, of course, there would be no termite society without the protozoan. If one does not objectify, the protozoan is every much that termite colony as the colony is the protozoan.

Perhaps the most famous story of Chuang Tzu, a boggling sort of tangled hierarchy of mind, is when he dreamt that he was a fluttering butterfly happily unaware of being Chuang Chou. When he awoke, he found himself again as Chuang Chou, but was not quite certain whether he was then a man dreaming that he was a butterfly or now a butterfly dreaming that it was a man. For us who have had the experience of lucid dreaming, of being conscious of the fact of dreaming while dreaming, and, thus, being able to redirect the dream, the butterfly tale is more than a parable of transformation.[22] Even more peculiar is to have a dream in which one is dreaming and then 'awakened'. When afterwards awakening fully to consciousness-mind, the roused sleeper is completely but fortunately temporarily disoriented as to identity, place, and reality.

Remarkably, the Chinese, whose practical bureaucratic bent instituted the first civil service examination (which, besides testing the knowledge of Confucian principles, included poetry and calligraphy!), do not have a single character or short phrase signifying hierarchy. True, there are ideograms referring to rank or class, but phrases of six to eight characters are needed to instill the organizational and systematic features.

I enter as last exhibit George Herbert's teaching of cascading dependency as coupled to Shakespeare's prose at the end of either a movie or television version (it was so long ago) of *Richard III:* For want of a nail the shoe is lost; for want of a shoe the horse is lost; for want of a horse the rider is lost. Because chaos theory tells us that no long-term prediction in complex physical or biological systems is possible (even the orbits of planets are chaotic) and that there is mutual and sensitive dependency of every world event, which yet can be modeled by moderately simple mathematics, it would not be such a brazenly wild and comical exaggeration to surmise that the turbulence of a million people in Tiananmen Square in Beijing might have influenced the weather experienced several months later in Washington, D.C., both meteorologically and politically.

Up to this point the discussion has dealt with taxonomic hierarchies. Although the description of loops implies activity and change, the emphasis on relationships has probably imparted a feeling of static conditions. There is another form of hierarchy that does not concern evolutionary order, nor does it rest on any structural organization. It is a mutually dependent but ranked system of flux, the temporal order of circadian (meaning about a day) and other biological rhythms.

I Got Rhythm and *Fascinating Rhythm* were hits for the Gershwin brothers, but we do not only have rhythm, we *are* rhythm. More than the hills are alive with music; the entire universe is a symphony of vibrating and oscillating organisms often in resonance.[23] I am not being poetic. Everything pulses and cycles, from quantum waves of protons to sunspots and tides to our spinning galaxy, from the dividing cell to our breathing and skin temperature to the electrical activity of the brain and nervous system. Prophetically, the familiar philosophically powerful and ancient symbol of Taoism, which emphasizes natural cycles, is a modified sine wave.

Before I briefly review the evidence for this multitudinous sound, I will mention in passing that Buddhist religio-philosophy recognizes such silent sounds. The name of the bodhisattva of compassion—Kwan Shi Yin or Kwan Yin, for short (Chinese); Kwan Seum or Kwan Um (Korean); or Kanzeon or Kannon (Japanese)—literally means *perceive world sound*. Mainstream and romantic Buddhists may take it as the bodhisattva's harkening to the cries of suffering sentient beings, since Kwan Yin predates Buddhism as the Chinese goddess of mercy. However, Kwan Shi Yin, according to some scholars, was improperly derived from Avalokitesvara, rather than Avalokitasvara, the Indian male bodhisattva of compassion, whose name means *lord of the beholding sound*.[24] Thus, the original and more difficult intent was for us to perceive the sound of the bodhisattva, not the reverse. Zen students in either case emulate the ideal from the broad sense, learning to hear the holeless flute with their nose. Seriously.

John Cage, an admirer of Zen Buddhism, composed a four-minute and thirty-three second long piano piece (appropriately entitled *4'33"*) consisting of nothing but rests, and once performed it outdoors in New York City, accompanied by an aide to turn the pages. It was marvelous theater as he lifted the cover to expose the keyboard, positioned his hands, and then followed the score. Needless to say, only a few spectators understood, perceiving the music of themselves and the world of their urban street.

Painters also understand the depths of sound. Paul Klee's painting *Ancient Sound* is a grid of muted earth tones emerging from a dark background. Wassily Kandinsky expressed the mysticism in an essay: 'It must become possible to hear the whole world as it is without representational interpretation... The world sounds.'[25]

Physically and neurophysiologically, sound for us is far more limited. It is a vibration of air, from about 20 to 20,000 cycles per second, that stimulates the tuned hair cells of our ears, from which electrical impulses travel the neurological pathway to the cortex of the brain, where the pattern is transformed and interpreted. Dolphins, bats, and dogs can perceive pitches much higher than our hearing sense (up to 100,000 cycles per second) and although our ears can not register certain low pitches, we nevertheless feel them resonating with our body cavities. Because of memory, many experienced musicians can merely pick up a score and hear the soundless 'sound' of its notes; Mozart was able to hear a particular music before he encoded it. We should therefore not restrict the definition of sound to our very limited human auditory organ. *Sound is any vibration or oscillation whose behavioral pattern interacts with and is recognized by a receiver, which is a vibrational pattern of a greater complexity or hierarchy.*

If we know the frequency of vibration, we can state its source or its name. This could be a new parlor game for bored bioengineering students. Approximately 7.8 cycles per second are both the magnetic oscillation between the surface of the earth and the ionosphere and an alpha frequency of the human brain. A frequency of 0.00001160577 cycle per second is the rotating Earth. What is one cycle per second? Your resting arterial pulse. X-rays are around 10^{18} cycles per second. In the equal tempered scale, 261.6 cycles per second describes middle C.

Having evolved on a planet with an approximately 24-hour day and 365.25-day year, we and all other higher biological organisms function to the beat of these astronomical clocks, a concern of scientists and other visionaries who are planning our first primitive interplanetary trek. A Chinese phrase that refers to the various forms of rhythm consists of two characters: one, whose radicals or roots point to the segment of bamboo between two nodes, now means, in addition, season and term; section, paragraph, and verse; melody; constancy and integrity; and to restrict, control, or economize. The second character indicates offering of oneself to a superior for information or, especially, the playing of a musical instrument. Related is another Chinese phrase for melody whose characters are separately translated as the laws and regulations that govern orbits and revolutions, urination, and cyclic return. Astronomy, mechanics, the arts, and biology: the universe is like a Brazilian percussion band at carnival!

The pioneer of the inner realm of circadian and seasonal rhythms was Jean Jacques d'Ortous de Mairan, who in 1729 discovered that the daily opening and closing of leaves of a

Bibel '92

RHYTHM

sun-following plant (probably *Mimosa pudica*) continued to do so when he relocated the plant away from sunlight.[26] No longer deemed a passive cylic phenomenon, the botanical active and resting states were as basic to the organism as the sleep cycle of bedridden patients oblivious to time. A hundred years later it was established that the leaf movements of *Mimosa* maintained in the dark have a cycle of 22 to 23 hours, indicating that the biological clock is inherent and recalibrated when exposed to the proper environment. In 1866 William Ogle recognized that humans also have rhythms when he followed body temperature over the course of a day. The search for other biological rhythms and their oscillators did not and could not advance significantly until the physiological basis of life was sufficiently described and understood, which is to say, until some forty years ago.

Have you ever awakened just before the alarm goes off, especially if you had reminded yourself of the time prior to turning out the bedroom light? We have a biological clock, and so does the honey bee. The insect can be trained to come to a feeding table at a certain evening hour when the sun can offer no cue. This is important, since the bee normally uses the sun as a directional reference point in its circular wiggle dance that communicates to fellow workers the position of a food source. When such a trained bee was transferred to a distant time zone, it came to the similarly positioned feeding table at the prescribed time occuring in the original time zone.[26] We human jet travelers know the sensation of being out of phase to local events.

Circadian is not a hedging but an accurate description because, like the *Mimosa,* our free-running, unsynchronized biological cycle is not 24 hours; for humans it is 25 hours. However, when subjects are shielded from the electomagnetic field of the Earth, the basic biocycle may be longer and more irregular.[27] What, besides sleep and body temperature, follows a circadian rhythm? Just about everything: enzyme and hormone synthesis; antibody formation; populations of red and white blood cells; blood potassium; phagocytosis (the engulfment of particles by white cells); urine output; blood pressure and cell division.[28,29] Also, natural death and birth tend toward the early morning hours of the day. When a physiological characteristic appears to be constant, it is usually because two rhythmic systems are counterbalanced. Superimposed are seasonal rhythms, such as 'spring fever', hibernation, molting and hair growth.

Other biological rhythms include the reproductive cycles of estrous in rodents (4 to 5 day cycles) and primate menstruation (25 to 35 day cycles) and the alternating sleep cycles of rapid eye movement and non-REM episodes, which in adult humans is 90 to 100 minutes; in infants, 50 to 60 minutes; in elephants, 120 minutes; and in mice, 20 to 30 minutes. The rhythm and quality of arterial pulse figure prominently in Chinese medicine, and Indian yogis have long been familiar with cycles in respiration. For example, the underlying tissue of the right and left nostrils alternately swell and contract in cycles of 100 to 120 minutes.[30] (The stimulation of the left side with increased air flow is preferred for meditation.)

Biological rhythms are synchronized or entrained by a variety of environmental influences. Bright daylight is the most important; in fact, it has been found that intense artificial lighting can help alleviate jet lag, reset the sleep cycle, and help in depression.[31,32] Some species are affected by both daily and seasonal environmental temperature cycles. The availability of food is a well-known means to reset the clock as well as to induce Pavlovian conditioning. We experience desynchronization with willful extended fasting. Social cues, such as sounds, body language, and smells, are also influential. Pheromones are always powerful and subtle agents, as seen in the case of small groups of women in close association who find that their menstrual cycle has become mutually synchronized. As noted above, another interesting entraining factor is electromagnetic fields. Of course, drugs can alter the cycle, and caffein is notorious for resetting the clock.

I have mentioned clock in the singular, but in fact there are at least two in most species examined. This was established experimentally when the sleep/wake cycle was in its free-running 25-hour periodicity; certain other rhythms followed an independent course to the extent that after a while, they completed more circadian days. In addition, organ cultures and tissue cultures followed their own beat. Here, liver cells manifested rhythms of protein synthesis and oxygen consumption, and the contractions of intestinal sections varied over the day.[26] The period of cultured cardiac cells, which are self-entrained in their beating, varies with the number of cells.[33] While it is clear that many physiological cycles are coupled, since their pathways intersect, the question whether they are dependent on a master pacemaker remains; and if there is such a command center, what and where is it?

Curt Richter zeroed in on the major pacemaker that is synchronized to light/dark cycles.[26] He found it located in the two suprachiasmatic nuclei, which are near the brain stem in the hypothalamus adjacent to the convergence of the optic nerves. Indeed, there are nerve connections between the eyes and this region.[33] Blinded rats have dissynchronated biological rhythms. The pacemaker nuclei contain some 10,000 compacted neurons.

Other researchers observed that the fetus of animals has its oscillator entrained by its mother.[34] Using several pregnant animals, they removed either the adrenal, pituitary, or thyroid glands or the ovaries to determine the effect on the fetal biological rhythm. There was none. However, the removal of the mother's suprachiasmatic nuclei early in pregnancy eliminated her circadian rhythms, and caused the fetal pacemaker to run free.

When excised and cultured, nerve tissue containing the suprachiasmatic nuclei maintains its electrochemical beat.[35] The next step is to transplant such tissue in compatible animals with different rhythms. Martin R. Ralph and his colleagues at the University of Virginia did just that.[35] Normally, hamsters have a 24-hour cycle. Certain mutant hamsters have a circadian rhythm of 20 hours, if the altered gene is present on both chromosomes, and of 22 hours, if the mutation is found on only one chromosome. Removing the pacemaker tissue from these various animals renders them arhythmic. The research team traded suprachaismatic nuclei between the different hamsters. The circadian rhythms that were restored to these grafted animals were those of the donor, not the recipient.

Some intriguing evidence has come from the independent laboratories of Ronald Konopka at Clarkson University and

Michael Young at Rockefeller University that may provide a genetic and biochemical basis for the major pacemaker.[36] The male fruit fly *Drosophila* was the test subject.

Different mutant fruit flies were found that certainly followed the beat of different drummers. All mutations were located in the same region of the X chromosome. Normally, the male fruit fly momentarily beats its wings every 60 seconds as a mating song. One mutant had no pacemaker and did not seem to sleep. (Interestingly, a few rare humans also do not need to sleep or require only one or two hours.) Its mating serenade had no particular rhythm, a free-form song. Another mutant had wake/sleep cycles of 18 to 20 hours and 40-second mating songs; a third mutant had 28- to 30-hour days and 80-second song cycles. *The investigators discovered that the quantity of the gene product is correlated with clock speed and that the circadian oscillator is situated in the insect's head while the song clock lies in the thorax.*

The repetitive sequences of the fruit fly gene, which code for alternating amino acids, have also been found in humans, mice, and chickens. The sites of activity and the biochemical mechanism of timing remain mysterious. What is food for speculation is that the gene product is similar to molecules found on the outside of the cell and may be involved in intercellular adhesion and the development of the embryo.[37] I will have more to say about this.

The organization of the biorhythm complex commences with environmental cycles (mainly the dominant light/dark alternator of the revolving Earth) and continues to an apparently interactive hierarchy of a major and minor pacemaker, whose units communicate, and of respective subordinate oscillators, which are usually coupled.[26,33] The major pacemaker regulates REM sleep, core body temperature, plasma cortisol, and the excretion of urinary potassium; the minor pacemaker controls slow brain wave sleep, skin temperature, plasma growth hormone, and the excretion of urinary calcium. The field is ripe for breakthroughs.

When we have an assortment of oscillators, we are sure to have *resonance*.[23] Imagine a cymbal or drum coated with a thin layer of sand. Strike the instrument. What occurs is a rearrangement of the grains to nearly symmetrical areas of concentration and emptiness, nodes and troughs. This is a pattern of system resonance. It may be responsible for the arrangement of stars in arms of a spinning spiral galaxy and, with the gravitational help of herding moons, the rock and pebble rings of Saturn. Sheldrake's idea of sequence-related self-resonance in morphogenesis and perhaps in the expression of instincts has been mentioned earlier. A demonstration of entrainment toward resonance of oscillators may be achieved by placing several grandfather pendulum clocks along a wall; given sufficient time the different phased pendulums will synchronize by the vibrational field. Sympathetic strings are a characteristic of Hindustani musical instruments, such as the sitar and sarod; striking a playing string will cause the unplucked atuned sympathetic string to resonate.

In terms of our own psychology of consciousness-mind and awareness-mind, we informally speak of feeling good or bad vibrations, and most of us have experiences of being in synchrony or resonance with a comrade or the events of the environment. This not mere mentation; we actually are! People in conversation or communication, including infants and their mother and preachers and their audience, synchronize their body movements and speech patterns.[38] In Chinese, the phrase for resonance is composed of two characters meaning shared or collective weeping, which is to say, sympathy.

Resonance among subatomic particles, atoms, and crystals is not difficult to find: their very nature of form and interaction is defined as resonance. The occurrence of resonance among more complex, multicomponent systems varies from moderately infrequent to exceedingly rare. This is especially evident within and between biological organisms. Heartbeats are cyclic but not precisely periodic. Brain waves are normally irregular. Indeed, uniform rates of biological oscillations are associated with disease and even death.[39] It may be a matter of chaos.

Imagine two turbulent flows of water, forms in chaos, and consider the chance that even for a moment they will be in resonance. Is resonance in chaotic systems possible? Yes. William Ditto, Steven Rauseo, and Mark Spano of the Naval Surface Warfare Center and Louis Pecora and Thomas Carroll of the Naval Research Laboratory have experimentally

RESONANCE

controlled chaos with chaos in the bending of an iron ribbon in competing magnetic fields and in interfering circuits of fluctuating voltage.[40,41]

Resonance or synchrony of a system and subsystem may involve their *Strange Attractors,* the mysterious and untouchable hubs around which the mathematical graphic plots of dynamic relationships of components orbit to form the orderly patterns of chaos. The rarity in achieving natural resonance of complex systems indicate why laboratory demonstration of certain controversial psychological phenomena, such as precognition, clairvoyance, and remote viewing, are at times difficult for the experienced subject. The use of subsystems to synchronize and control chaos may offer a strategy to ease such practices. Chaos also explains, in part, why even standard experiments of accepted materialistic biological phenomena sometimes go awry. Each musical instrument and the orchestra as a whole must retune, return to resonance, after the performance of every work. Human awareness-mind and consciousness-mind are like that; like the musician, the greatest Zen master still needs to practice.

Whispering breeze,
yet the curtain performs
a spirited dance.

We dance to the rhythm of the environment, the rhythm of ourselves. Even in the flux of chaos there is deep order and the capacity of resonance. The tangibly solid structure of existence becomes more and more a conceptual mirage. Seeing how the hierarchies of organisms, simple matter as well as life, are an inseparable evolutionary continuum, finding that internal processes are conjoined at common sources and regulated by external agencies, can we then truly separate what is above from what is below, what is without from what is within? Let us eliminate *we,* eliminate *environment.* What remains is only the dance, *mind,* in resonance with itself, the sound of cosmos.[42]

Chapter 8

ALL FOR ONE, ONE FOR ALL

Development/Cell biology

So we grew together,
Like to a double cherry, seeming parted,
But yet an union in partition;
Two lovely berries moulded on one stem.
William Shakespeare

Whatever I do has come from doing and
only relates to what's done.
Ad Reinhardt

When, in the last century, Chinese scientists and scholars had to deal with Darwin's novel evolutional concepts of natural selection and fitness, they needed a suitable phrase. Their practical lexicographers joined the character for nature with those for cleaning and washing rice in a sieve. As with Western languages, evolution itself is not cleanly differentiated from development of the unit organism. To *evolve* is to unroll, as if the origins and variations in biology were already written implicitly on a scroll. The term *develop,* the opposite of to wrap up or surround, hence, means to disclose or uncover. The nuance is the flow and extension in time of evolution and the condition and locality of development. The Chinese use at least six synonymous phrases. The most specific—applied to scientific concepts of evolution—indicates improvement. Four start with a character whose roots refer to pulling back the string of a bow (a simile used by Kahlil Gibran in 'You are the bows from which your children as living arrows are sent forth.'[1]); the character itself denotes

DEVELOPMENT/EVOLUTION

issue and *originate,* as well as *become* and *reveal.* Some second ideograms are translated as *extend, unfold,* and *dilate; beget;* and *intelligent, successful, arrive at,* and *inform.* Thus, not only is evolution a streaming—sometimes, as we now know, with an increase in the number and complexity of formed channels, at other times with terminations and simplifications of the diverse flows—it is also a destined progression (forward movement) through self-knowledge.

This interpretation of the Chinese phrases does not mean that the rise of human beings from the spontaneous formation of the first RNA molecule was inevitable. Rather, the direction of evolution and the appearance and disappearance of forms are dictated internally from those behaviors, relationships, and circumstances presently extant, whatever the moment. We tend to regard later forms as more complex and intricate, but more often they are only different variations on a theme. Hence, popular illustrations showing a sequential series of changes in an isolated animal form—such as from mastodon to mammoth to African elephant, or, more radically, from monkey to ape to human—have little scientific merit and may be philosophically silly. The morphological evolution of a species should not be examined outside its ecological and psychological context.

Furthermore, East or West, evolution is a process without value. A more recently evolved form is not better than its predecessors. The organism simply must be able to survive under current situations. For all its massive size and intelligence, the mammalian elephant would have been dead meat in the age of reptilian dinosaurs; the few mammals at this time were small, scrawny, and obviously fleet-footed. In fact, the most ancient creatures, the bacteria, are also the most successful. They are ubiquitous and far outnumber all other life forms combined. Being the bottom links of the food chain and the chief atom recyclers, they are essential to all life. Bacteria were the first and certainly will be the last living organisms on this planet.

Despite the etymologies, development is functionally distinct from evolution, although it is certainly allied. The evolution of molecules and the evolution of biological forms to, and probably through, ourselves is the same continuing evolution; however, the development of planetary rings and the development of our representative elephant are only marginally united through physical and chemical laws that contribute to the behavior of atoms and molecules. *The development of each superior hierarchy contains elements of the development of the lower.* The arising of the elephant is thus influenced also by the development of cells and tissues. In traditional biological thought, development is genetically and exogenetically directed with little opportunity for the tricksters of randomness and chaos; indeed, it is repetitive for each new generation.

Development is cyclic. In contrast, evolution is open, unfixed, and serendipitous. Nevertheless, it is through conservative development that evolution occurs, which explains, in part, why evolution is such a slow and nearly invisible process. In this manner, the flow of development and evolution may be represented by a continuous series of branching loops.

We bring development under the banner of ontology, the embryotic origins of the individual organism, and discuss evolution as phylogeny, the origins of the kinds of organisms. In 1866, the embryologist Ernst Haeckel proclaimed, 'Ontongeny is the brief and rapid recapitulation of phylogeny.'[2]* This scientific slogan means that during its development, the embryo seems to undergo stages that mimic the progress of evolution, from a protozoan through a primitive metazoan to whatever species it belongs. He was wrong, but the scientific literature of today offers no such succinct catch phrase, no philosophically fundamental expression to replace it. The order, coordination, and mechanisms of embryonic development remain, after 100 years, a frontier science. We are burdened by ignorance. If every cell has the same genome, what makes one a kidney cell and another a muscle cell? Why are hands hands and feet feet?

Molecular biologists heady with the victories of reductionism and the informational power of the genetic code initially

---

*In 1916, Sigmund Freud adopted Haeckel's idea for his own frontier study: 'The psychic development of the individual is a short repetition of the course of development of the race.'[2]

thought that gene operations could provide the answers. 'The task of the molecular biologist,' declared Alfred Giere, 'is to analyze the embryonic development of a plant or animal into combinations of elementary processes that can be explained by the physicochemical properties of cells and molecules.[3] Captained by Sydney Brenner at the Laboratory of Molecular Biology of the Medical Research Council, England, they selected a tiny nematode worm with the imposing name of *Caenorhabditis elegans* as the subject of study.[4] This worm consists of only 959 cells of which 302 form the nervous system. The researchers traced the origin of every cell. They made note of every cellular connection to neural cells. They collected developmental mutants, because for analysts, exceptions do establish the rules. They then examined gene regulation. The worm has over 15,000 genes. However, they failed to find any genetic program. Instead, they are now seeking a higher order based on stereochemically specific interactions of gene products. In due course, I expect that approach will also fail to provide the definitive answer, and they will then need to consider even higher orders, but that would take them afield from molecular genetics and biochemistry.

In fact, they will find themselves in psychology, because new evidence shows that the worm is capable of learning.[5] It can become habituated to tapping, and, like Pavlov's dogs, can be conditioned. After learning to associate a chemical stimulus and its bacteria food, the worm will swim toward the chemical alone. The same chemical can elicit avoidance if it is associated with garlic extract. Treating an organism as a static form is always a serious error. The worm's nerve network is plastic.

Evolution is sloppy, full of inherited *ad hoc* modifications that defy customary machine logic.[6] Structures, even symmetrical units, are not assembled in a linear fashion; they arise from random aggregations of multiple cellular components and subassemblies. Brenner believes that 'molecular biology is the art of the inevitable. If you do it, it's inevitable you will find out how it works—in the end.'[4] Having discussed hierarchies, we can see this remark as chauvinistic. Biochemists, biophysicists, organicists, and gestaltists may claim the same after first substituting their own area of investigation as the starting point and pivot. As all the hierarchies of order are one circular flow, all the evolved scientific disciplines that examine them are more than interconnected.

We may find some basic clues to development and to individuality if we drop back from this simple undulating worm to the evolutionary origin of multicellular organisms, to the societies of bacteria and protozoa. As James Shapiro at the University of Chicago points out, we fellow bacteriologists wrongly treat bacteria in a given colony as if they were all nearly identical.[7,8] A bacterium in the top center of the mass is presumed to have the same biochemical characteristics as a cell along the periphery, and, therefore, activities of a colony are erroneously regarded as cumulative rather than synergistic. Shapiro has emphasized what many microbiologists have long known but nevertheless conveniently ignore: *based on their position, microbes within masses differentiate by function if not by form.*

Bacteria are usually grown in Petri dishes containing agar gel, where their colonies are often sufficiently distinctive for diagnostic use. Some surfaces are dull and rough; others are shiny and smooth. Colonies may be opaque or translucent, colorless or pigmented. Textural patterns may be concentric, radial, both circular and radial, or drably unvaried. Environmental colonies, usually far smaller in size, may appear on old food, rocks in water, shed leaves, fallen wood, and your teeth and skin. Scanning electron microscopy reveals a skin-like covering of most colonies, which may assist in intracolonial communication and attachment to solid surfaces and, like our own skin, retard dehydration. Shapiro, when using a special dye for detecting the presence of a certain enzyme, found that colonial concentricity may also occur in metabolism. The stained colonies of *E. coli* appeared as bull's-eye targets. Because bacterial growth extends outward, rings indicate temporal biological rhythms or pulses. Like certain urban primates, the social order of organization thus influences the metabolism of associated bacterial cells.

Furthermore, certain flagellated bacteria, classically of the genus *Proteus,* swimming outward in a process called *swarming,* also form concentric patterns on agar media. How they swarm is also evidence of social cooperation and differentiation. While most cells are short with few flagella, some long multiflagellated cells are generated. These variants move to the periphery of the colony. Coming together, groups set out with synchronated, resonance entrained flagella as an armada of Viking longboats. This coordination is a form of peer pressure, since a lone bacterium moving a little beyond the colony or veering away from the fleet will not proceed further on the journey. After a genetically determined period, they reach an open site along the radius, where they stop and divide into the smaller sedentary forms. The process repeats until the agar plate is confluent with terraced growth. When Shapiro cut out a trough at the side of the agar to block the progress of growth, the resulting pattern established that direction of expansion is dictated by the colony as a whole. Growth stopped in vicinity of the trough; the swarms did not flank the trough to form a tangental front. This means that the swarming direction is not merely a matter of swarms being channeled into a vacant nutrient-rich region free of self-competition, nor an escape to sites free of autotoxins. The explorer swarms are in communication with each other and with the home colony.

If a group of bacteria seem to alter behavior by social interactions, what is the information they share? How does the isolated motile cell respond to modified environments?

The discovery that motile microorganisms (and amoeboid white blood cells) follow optimal gradients toward growth-supporting molecules or away from toxic, growth-inhibiting substances (processes of chemotaxis) caused a stir among scientists of the nineteenth and early twentieth centuries. For them, bacteria and protozoa seemed to think or at least display awareness-mind. For instance, in 1889 Alfred Binet, the experimental psychologist whose scale of intelligence once was popular among educators, wrote a book entitled *The Psychic Life of Microorganisms* in which he stated, 'Cellular irritability can be considered the same as elementary psychic life.'[9] Here is introduced the radical notion of specific organismal behavior to chemical stimuli as mind, a microbe as a sentient being.

The idea was furthered by research teams led by Daniel Koshland, Jr. at the University of California, Berkeley,

Howard C. Berg, at the University of Colorado, and Julius Adler at the University of Wisconsin[10-12] By combining microscopy, strobes, and cinematography, they were able to examine the behavior of a single bacterium.

Like behavioral movements directed by light, heat, and magnetism, chemotaxis is a reflex. Koshland regards bacterial chemotaxis as 'a rudimentary pain and pleasure system' to regulate the direction of migration. Signals are relaid from receptors on the bacterial surface to flagella, which, despite the nomenclature, are not flexible whips but rigid wavy propellers. In broth or films where we can not speak of colonies, bacteria are pushed by counterclockwise rotating flagella. The cells continually change heading by reversing their flagella to clockwise rotation, thereby tumbling, and, upon recovery, proceed on a new course. Chemotaxis is actually a modification of tumbling frequency; tumblings are suppressed when the direction of movement is toward an attractant or away from a repellent, but are more frequent when toward the repellent or away from the attractant. Thus, chemotaxis is a net zig-zag movement. Bacteria act on smaller threshold concentrations of attractants than on repellents, which vary with each agent; tumbling frequency declines with stronger gradients. Even for bacteria, the carrot motivates better than the stick.

Koshland also noted that molecular gradients are sensed by temporal comparisons, not by simultaneous readings of environmental concentration at different receptor sites.[13] Bacteria have short-term memory! The mechanism is roughly analogous to how we determine the direction of a source of sound waves; because of the slight difference in distance the waves travel to reach each ear, the auditory signals are not simultaneous nor equally intense. The varying interval of impulse delay is perceived as a sound gradient.

Since in bacteria surface receptors are also involved in other metabolic pathways, as a switch connecting parallel railroad tracks, the hastenings or delays in a synthesis could induce indirect behavioral changes in motility. Furthermore, when Adler, expanding Wilhelm Pfeffer's original 1888 experiment, offered bacteria the 'choice' of moving into or avoiding a capillary tube filled with both an attractant and a repellent, he confirmed that the relative concentrations of the agents determine the outcome by tipping the cognitive scales.[14] While at this point we can not yet describe the signal for differentiation as chemical, the form and amount of diffusible chemicals do seem to alter the behavior of already differentiated cells.

In one of my studies of the interactions of bacteria and ringworm fungi on the skin, I mixed spores of fungi and micrococci and placed them on skin specimens.[15] After various periods of incubation, I then examined the samples by scanning electron microscopy. The series of photographs told a story: Upon germination, a threadlike hypha grows out of the spore. It then extends toward the growing colony of bacteria. With further growth, because this particular fungus synthesizes antibiotics, it kills the bacteria. I assumed that the fungus displayed positive chemotaxis along the gradient of diffusing nutrients produced by the bacterial colony. I am no longer so sure about the nature of the gradient.

Martin Dworkin at the University of Minnesota, studying on a video monitor the gliding movements on agar of a type of predatory slime bacteria, *Myxococcus*, observed a streaming mass or swarm make abrupt directional changes to move toward chemically inert latex or glass beads.[7] After reaching a bead, the group-organism proceeded on a new tack. Normally, if the lumps are edible bacteria, the aggregate of slime bacteria remain to feed. What then is the signal? How do slime bacteria detect the presence of the inedible inactive beads? Does the *Myxococcus* perceive a micro eddy in the surface film upon the the agar, or is it through a disturbance of the electromagnetic field by the dielectric?

Questions, questions—the food of science, the sighs of philosophy, and to the silence of religion, only babel. Concerned with such difficulties and versed in the congruent realms of differentiation and unity associated respectively with description and pre-thought wordlessness, a philosophical monk asked Zen Master Feng-hsueh (896-973), 'How can one transcend speech and silence?' The master cited an old poem: 'I shall always remember the scenery of Chiang Nan in

March. Partridges were calling amid fragrant flowers.'[16] How do you understand the Zen mind of Master Feng-hsueh?

As you reflect on this enigma, note how, in this discussion, we are so readily seduced by our limited senses and daily experiences to regard these bacteria and other biological organisms as fundamentally space occupying, clean-edged, and isolated objects in continuous linear time. While acknowledging these apparent features, we must also keep the perspective that the cells are of matter-mind and awareness-mind, of ever fluctuating, ever arising organizations and behaviors of ghostly molecules of wavy fuzzy atoms of non-localized no-thing-ness. We see individual unit organisms, but are beginning to discover that, being dependent on complexes of formless internal and external processes, they are essentially phantoms. We are dealing with mind-patterns as well as the patterns of our consciousness—mind. However, our task is not merely to recognize these two faces of reality. We still would be stuck in philosophical concepts. We need to realize them. Simultaneously.

The trek has hazards. A Korean Zen master residing in China once warned his students not to be attached either to oceanic structured formlessness or to the ordinary phenomena of the perceived world: Master Pa-Chiao (9th century) came to the assembly with his staff, a symbol which a teacher sometimes uses compassionately to strike erring students. (Today in the West, masters may simply state, 'I hit you'; it still hurts!) 'If you have a stick,' he told the monks, 'I shall give one to you. If you lack a stick, I shall take it away.'[16]

In this koan, to what stick is he referring? How can you avoid being struck by the master's stick? Once you break through this or any other koan, such barriers, which may seem like a covey of wrathful Odyssean jailers, are immediately transformed into compassionate guides that point the way.

If the above seems strange, let us continue to gather biological evidence. Science also can direct us along the path. Consider again the slime bacteria. In aquatic species that prey on other bacteria, millions of cells aggregate to form sponge-like spheres in whose protective and concentrating pores the entrapped bacteria are enzymatically dissolved and consumed.[7] While the vast majority of bacteria can exist as free single celled organisms (but typically do not), many myxobacteria are nearly obligate differentiated communities.[17] Terrestrial species reside on dung, bark, and decaying vegetation. When a cell strays from the mass, it soon returns. Of course, when there is no adjacent community, the cell manages adequately alone, dividing several generations to form its own colony.

As key nutrients become scarce, homogenous cells within the loosely arrayed mass begin to differentiate and the streamers migrate to a central area. The etiology of this environment-induced differentiation, yet to be elucidated, apparently is related, again, to the position of cells in the mass. Further differentiation divides cells into prestalk and prespore forms. The colony pulses as rivers of cells pile up in the center. There is no special tropism here; up is the path of least resistance. If there is a sufficient number of cells and the concentration of orthophosphate is adequate, the colony soon appears like a miniature yucca or a fruiting cactus: a central stalk mainly of hardened carbohydrate slime, sometimes branches, and one or more clusters of spores or of cysts. Sporulation is dependent on the side-by-side and end-to-end alignment of the cells.[18] The developmental sequence includes a massive (60% to 80%) dissolution (lysis) of vegetative cells in stalk formation and in conversion of spores or cysts, probably to provide crucial nutrients for the final stages of spore formation.

Cultural anthropologists have been fascinated with the seemingly independent development of unusual social features and artifacts among various peoples, such as the pyramids of Egypt and Mexico. Biologists find similar parallel forms, abilities, and behavior among widely diverse species, as the skin-adapting camouflage of prawn, flat fish, and chameleon. Myxobacteria have their almost exact counterpart among the eukaroytes, which, not merely a bridge of species, is a giant leap of kingdoms. These are the slime molds—a misnomer since they are protozoa.[19]

Like their junior analogue, these amoeboid cells can gather together to form a pronounced wandering coherent slug, and meet hard times by rising to a fruiting body on a single stem,

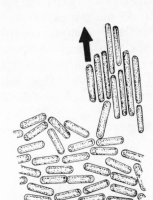

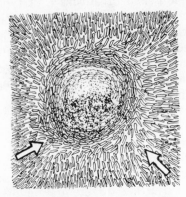

BACTERIAL COLONY
EXPANSION FLEET

MYXOBACTERIAL STALK SURGE

GEOMETRIC RESTRICTION AS AN AGENT OF DEVELOPMENT.

which is also composed of slime and debris of lysed cells. Phosphate figures in the development of this structure also, since cyclic adenosine monophosphate (cAMP), a hormone messenger in higher species, is the signal for aggregation and subsequent differentiation. It is enzymically blocked while the protozoans have plentiful food; but when key nutrients are insufficient, enyzme production falls, which consequently allows newly synthesized cAMP to act as tocsin. In a unique form of communication among identical cells—alike but for positional relationship—the concentration of cAMP oscillates as each cell, when stimulated, synthesizes its own cAMP. The leading edge of the concentric ripple, originating in the tip of the slug, provides a gradient that directs the position-designated stalk cells toward the center. After each wave passes, pre-movement is again somewhat random until a stalk arises after about 50 cycles. At this point, the cell is differentiated and, barring any tricks of the experimenter, can not return to its former state.

When cultured on agar media, the pattern of aggregation is remarkably akin to the previously mentioned self-organizing dissipative structures of the Belousov-Zhabotinsky oxidation reaction, a purely chemical process.[19,20] In another stunning case of parallelism indicative of deep order—in this case, of deep architecture—the reaction proceeds as regular pulsations with bursts of activity that prefer certain spatial direction, including concentric chemical waves, involutions, and spirals, patterns that occur with slime mold stalk development.

A particular bacterium or protozoan in a herd of bacteria or protozoa committing suicide for the good of the herd may seem altruistic for Dawkins, who wrote of defending 'kamikaze bees', but is it suicide?[21] And just what is the individual that makes the alleged sacrifice?

SPIRAL WAVES:
Is it chemistry (Belousov-Zhabotinskii reaction) or
is it biology (slime mold growth)?

First, the initiator of lysis is unknown. The high density of microorganisms, already a starved population with metabolism being directed to differentiation instead of cell division, may be killed by the concentration of their own toxic wastes.[22] Thus, death, while unintentional, is convenient for producing the stem and supplying remaining nutrients for spore formation. Also possible, since lysis occurs immediately before the maturation of spores, the developing spores may release products that kill their competitive clonal sisters. Now instead of suicide or accidental death, we find first-degree murder!

Second, what is dying? Genetically, all the cells are approximately alike, and most mutants (for instance, a clone of nonswarming myxobacteria) can produce spores, albeit sometimes inefficiently. Furthermore, prior to lysis and final spore development, all the cells have the capacity to replicate simply by dividing given a radical and favorable change in the environment. When the treshold of differentiation has been crossed, something amazing occurs; we can no longer speak of individual myxobacteria and mxyoprotozoa. We observe a complex plantlike unit organism.

Consider a true plant, an avocado tree: The attached fruit, the trunk, and the roots as well as the cells making up each are not separate and independent structures. Nor should we forget that the fruited avocado tree is an arbitrary stage of, well, avocadoing. Since the various avocado cells, each an organism, developed and differentiated from the zygote union of plant gametes, we can describe the process as *organismal fission*.

In contrast, development of the slime creatures is a process of cellular differentiation with concomitant *organismal fusion* and loss of both status and all semblance of cellular independence. Each special cell, of course, is important to the whole, but its separateness is fleeting. Its behavior is now regulated by the higher organism, which also determines its life and death. This reduces the lysis to the equivalent death and keratinization of epithelial cells in forming the external layers of mammalian skin. The death of slime stalk cells allows the development of a higher organization, which becomes the organism of record. *In the life cycle of these microorganisms, the one becomes the many; the many become the one; the one becomes the one.*

The often self-referential meta language of the Zen koan offers us a similar but far more basic and intrinsic relationship: A monk asked Master Chao-Chou (778-897), 'All things return to one, but where will one itself return to?' Chao-Chou answered, 'When I was in Tsing-Chou, I had a robe made that weighed seven chin.'[23] If you think that the robe is cited simply as an example of the differentiated many, where is the robe? Stop thinking!

Myxobacteria and slime molds are modern representatives of stages that may have led to true metazoans, multicellular organisms. From paleontological evidence, at the end of the Precambrian era nature experimented with pancake and ribbon-thin metazoa, but these forms, physiologically restricted by the relationship of surface area and mass, failed and became extinct.[24,25] A flat form of single-celled organisms, the very ancient archaebacteria, may have been the architectural template, since they are plates arranged as ribbons or as a quartet of postage stamps.[26] These organisms have survived by taking refuge in the harshest of environments: the boiling hot, sulfurous volcanic vents of land and the ocean floor, the ultra brine of evaporation ponds, and waters of extreme acidity or alkalinity.

Another contemporary intermediate form that makes good use of the third dimension is the spherical colony-organism called *Volvox*. Composed of thousands of flagellated cells (cousins of *Euglena*) conjoined facing outward in a single layer, the hollow ball behaves in a distinctly organized fashion. The flagella are coordinated, allowing the colony to move effectively. Moreover, it is a sphere with a front and back end, which is not a surprising condition when considering the polarity of Earth. The colony enlarges by cell division and replicates both asexually and sexually.

In the first and usual manner, a cell at the rear discards its twin flagella, drops into the protective hollow, and undergoes generations of divisions to form a smaller daughter sphere. Several such replicates can reside within the hollow until released by rupture of the parent. Indeed, the enclosed daughter colony can itself undergo replication, forming a self-contained three-generation system! When environmental conditions become unsupportive for growth, such as the drying of a pond, a cell within the ball may enlarge to form a nutrient-filled egg while another cell may divide repetitively without growing to yield small flagellated sperms. Union of these gametes from either different organisms or self-fertilization leads to a hardened cyst within which a colony develops awaiting a favorable environment to break free.

Thus, *Volvox* cells, with the exception of the sex cells, are fairly uniform in shape and activity, each capable under certain conditions of dividing and regenerating the colony. From this perspective its colonial attributes are readily apparent. However, when we regard the cytoplasmic network that links them, the cells are reduced to the regulated effectors of a higher organism which they themselves develop. The differentiated gametes are the sure sign of a multicellular organism, yet *Volvox*, like the slime molds, does not meet all the metazoan criteria of our contrived taxonomic categories. Life is a spectrum. It is easy to distinguish organisms whose patterns are poorly related, but the placement of separating walls between like biological patterns often generates scientific debates and reevaluations that move, demolish, or construct new dividers.[27]

One well-defined and noncontroversial invertebrate is the hydra. The hydra of Greek mythology, which Hercules faced as one of his twelve labors, was said to have nine serpent heads, each, when cut off, regenerating as two. (Science is like that: Solve one problem, discover two more!) Aptly named, the microscopic tentacled hydra has the capacity to regenerate lost tissue in a process probably regulated by the same agencies that govern development.

For those not familiar with this fresh-water denizen, the hydra consists of some 100,000 cells arranged in two adjacent layers, a folding through invagination. Besides the four to six or more tentacles extending longer than its trunk, the animal is composed of a mouth, a gastric cavity within its columnar body, and a sticky foot for attachment to rocks or aquatic plants. Although it is a simple organism, the types and distribution of differentiated cells are fairly complex: epithelio-muscular cells, stinging cells and other thread cells, sensory and other nerve cells (which form a network just beneath the surface layer), sperm and eggs, and phagocytic eating cells. The stinging cells, which after development from replicating stem cells migrate mainly to the tentacles, are specialized structures containing coiled barbed cytoplasmic threads that on discharge impale the victim and inject a toxin. Other thread cells are for adherence, one whose thread winds around the appendages of the prey like an Argentine bola. The hydra uniquely moves about its habitat by somersaulting!

The presence of gametes indicates sexual reproduction, but frequent asexual budding from the column is more common. As discovered in 1744 by the Swiss naturalist Abraham Trembley, if we were to chop the trunk into sections, each would develop into a new hydra.[28] This remarkable phenomenon was made even more astonishing by the experiment in 1935 of the Russian biologist M. P. Aisupiet. He strained hydral tissue through a fine mesh, and soon observed the aggregation, reorganization, and regeneration of living animals. If we were to examine closer the trunk slices, we would discover that each expresses polarity, as occurs when a bar magnet is cut into smaller units. Tentacles arise from the end that was originally oriented toward the head.

One explanation for this pattern is the graded concentration of a particular chemical, with the larger amount directed toward the head.[3] This is a plausible notion because if one were to sever the slug form of slime molds just behind the tip and graft the tip to another slug, introducing a new axis, a smaller slug would develop and then separate.[19] In the slime mold, the tip provides the initial signaling cAMP. In the hydra, because the nerve cell network of the mature animal is most concentrated around the head region and mouth and because nerve cells are among the first to differentiate from stem cells in the excised cross-sections, the morphogenetic chemical is probably derived from or acts mainly upon nerve cells. It may be a peptide or a hormone. Although gradients of development-associated chemicals have been determined and mathematical models support their plausibility, no one yet has discovered any morphogenic biochemical 'lodestone' nor the inducement of its production.[3]

However, another consideration is the electrical polarity of the hydra. The head is positively charged, and the tail, negatively. When this potential is overriden by introducing a reversed current to an excised section of the trunk, a tail regenerates where the head should develop, and head and tenticles arise where one would expect a tail.[28] The influence of electromagnetic fields on morphogenesis and the semiconductance of biological tissues has only recently been accepted. Biophysics is still unappreciated by biologists and physicists alike. Field-induced regeneration of lost tissues through cellular dedifferentiation is a medical frontier.

We see that development involves functional differentiation of cells, their distribution, and the physical and biophysical shapes of the higher social organism. Gerald M. Edelman, whose scientific eye has been trained on the molecular realm throughout his career, has made an unusual adjustment toward organism as holistic governor, although he remains entrenched in materialism. He regards topology (the properties of geometric forms that endure transformation) as a regulator of function, of differentiation, and thereby of morphological development. However, he has insightfully balanced higher order influences with an effecting mechanism built around three sorts of sticky molecules: cell-adhesion molecules, cell secreted substrate-adhesion molecules, and cell junctional molecules.[29,30]

Stereochemically complementary molecules or areas of molecules, which were introduced in discussions of enzyme activity, have become a profound biological and biochemical fundamental. In my own field of microbial ecology, medical bacteriologists and mycologists have fairly recently discovered what the molecular virologists had long ago recognized. As bacterial viruses bind specifically to bacterial cell walls or outer membranes, animal and plant viruses likewise find complementary receptors on the host cell. Now we know that adhesive molecules on the exterior of bacteria and fungi also bind to molecules embedded in the host cell membrane.[31,32]

This is also a specific process, since the bacterium *Staphylococcus aureus* adheres well to the cells lining the nasal vestibule, while *Escherichia coli* is unable to cling to this tissue but is superbly adherent to vaginal cells. Therefore, microorganisms are of, or secrete as an extracellular matrix, different adherent molecules that attach to different host cellular receptors. These host sites may also be corporal or extracellular material. Each microbe and host cell may include a variety of adhesion molecules, so that a microorganism may attach, for example, to a kidney cell with one adhesin and an intestinal cell with another. Likewise, a host cell may provide an attachment site for one kind of microorganism with one membrane molecule and another kind with a second molecule. The ecological principle of specific adherence helps establish the kind and number of normal flora in the flowing environments of mouth, shedding skin, or river and explains, in part, the ability of certain disease-initiating microorganisms to survive and home in on particular tissues, such as the colonization of *Streptococcus pyogenes* on your throat.

Edelman's functionally related *cell adhesion molecules* (CAM), which protrude from the cell membrane, are a kind of cell-to-cell one-shape Velcro®. The junctional molecules are more like cement.[29] CAM couple to each other, but they vary in type and specificity. All are long proteins with loops and a flexible hinge and a covalently joined carbohydrate group. Cells that are separate, spatially unorganized, and often migratory, such as mesenchymal cells, when experimentally induced to produce CAM, cohere and form a sheet of cells, an epithelium. Different CAM have characteristic numbers, distributions, and sequence-related appearances and disappearances. *These dynamics affect how cells cluster, which in turn influences gene regulation toward the progress of functional and morphological differentiation.* The resulting modification of surfaces leads to the expression of different CAM, and so forth. Edelman and his colleagues presently believe that adherent molecules regulate cellular movement, division, and even death during development of the organism, and that the linked arrangements of cell groups themselves activate developmental genetic expression compared to a similar group of unjoined cells.

Other investigators, focusing on the manner epithelial cells in an embryo become polarized and differentiated in form and function, have incorporated the lessons of CAM in a more inclusive analysis.[33] Before reviewing their important conclusions, we need to consider the structure of the cellular membrane, which is crucial to understanding the dynamics of development. The cellular skin, although pliable, is not a confluent plastic sheet. Instead, it is a fluid mosaic.[34,35]

Imagine one thousand ping-pong balls each affixed to a light-weight metallic rod placed in a pan of water whose surface area exactly accommodates them. The balls, representing hydrophilic protein groups, float covering the water; the rods, representing hydrophobic lipid groups, all face downward. Although the balls form a barrier sheet, they remain independent and are able to move about the crowd. The biological membrane is actually a double layer, the protein of the matched lipoprotein molecules facing outward to the environment and inward to the cytoplasm. We could place a mirror at the bottom of the pan to suggest this lower second layer. Now let us place among the balls various kinds of toy boats to represent membrane-bound proteins and glycoproteins that serve as CAM, receptors, enzymes, and other metabolic and sensory or signaling molecules. We can see how mobile these boats are, sailing the lipoprotein sea. Some embedded membrane molecules extend from the very exterior into the cytoplasm, as illustrated by the deep keel of the sailboats; others merely ride the surface layer as the rowboats. The reflected images in the mirror or, tangibly, the submerged toy submarine correspond to proteins that are located only in the inner cytoplasmic layer of the membrane.

Now, let us inspect a single free cell in solution. The distribution of the various proteins and glycoproteins in the membrane is random and somewhat homogenous in dynamic mixture. Let us make this cell a fertilized egg. As it divides several generations, the undifferentiated aggregate soon forms a hollow blastula, much like a *Vovlox*. With further divisions, the loosely connected spheroid cells are compressed and compacted, becoming cuboidal. *This changing architectural and physical arrangement, which includes piezoelectric* (voltage induced by compression of orderly crystal-like materials) *properties and a reduced exposed surface area, initiates a cascading series of anatomical and physiological alterations.*[29,33]

The reorganization of the cellular skeleton of microtubules and fibers, which apparently connect to CAM on the membrane, is instrumental in effecting changes in cell characteristics. Remarkably, when isolated in solution, tubulin subunits and guanosine triphosphate, an assembly cofactor, are all that are needed for developing cystoskeletal arrays.[36] *These self-assembling molecules are also self-depolymerizing,* their processes oscillating to yield traveling waves that resemble the Belousov-Zhabotinsky reaction.

Additional CAM are synthesized and move along the membrane to the sides of the cells, where a variety of sturdier, longer-lasting, and more specialized *junctional* structures are produced to hold the cells together for structural strength and intercellular communication. At the same time, the exposed exterior membranous region becomes convoluted in shape (increasing surface area) to permit nutrient and water uptake and secretions, as well as to provide protection.

Accordingly, the associated membrane proteins and glycoproteins passively congregate here. The basal or inner region takes on importance later in the formation of tissues and organs, and its contact with other cells and secretions influences gene expression. Also delayed are the specialized functions of the basal-lateral zones, which include hormone receptors, nerve connection sites, and other receptors for intraorganismal communications. The polarized epithelium is prerequisite to the invagination of the cellular ball forming a gastrula and inner, endodermal layer and subsequently the intestinal, neural, and branched tubes of the organs.

Edelman, who was honored with the Nobel Prize in Physiology or Medicine in 1972 for elucidating the structure of the antibody molecule, had left immunochemistry and immunology to investigate embryology, but soon found that he had gone full circle. He realized in delight that the cell adhesion molecules are part of a supergene family that includes free antibodies, bound histocompatibility antigens, nerve cell antigens, and a variety of cellular receptors that affect growth, morphology, and metabolism.[29,30] I will defer the discussion of this vast evolutionary network until we reach the particular labyrinth of immunology, the biological heart of self-identity.

Before leaving this chapter, we should recall Sheldrake's hypothesis of morphogenetic fields and morphic resonance as

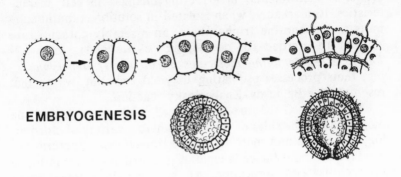

EMBRYOGENESIS

GEOMETRIC RESTRICTION AS AN AGENT OF DEVELOPMENT.

a metaphysic of development. When Edelman and others refer to an unspecific mechanism of higher spatio-temporal order that triggers genetic expression and development, we are left with a phenomenon—an organismal gestalt or unique pattern inducing lower order activity, which in turn alters the pattern. I have no problem accepting such a simple description, for even though we may someday be able to list virtually all the physical, chemical, and biological conditions comprising a given developmental pattern, it is awareness-mind that ultimately is the agency. Sheldrake gives the dynamic attributes of mind a convenient and provisional framework for apprehending the underlying principles of development and the regeneration of appendages, such as occur in amphibians. Developmental chreods and self-resonance in regeneration (filling in the phantom limb) that channel growth processes to conform with previous species experience should not yet be dismissed.

Especially noteworthy is the less abstract, measurable multi-dimensional electromagnetic vector system sketched by Robert O. Becker. In his scheme, differences in polarity, amperage, and voltage along a tissue arc between nerve and skin, the electric field around charged nerve cells, and the magnetic field around the current flow all pinpoint and physiologically influence each cell (or potential cell) of the body.[28] Here, there is no direct role for species history; the system operates homeostatically with relation to the whole organism. These propositions are useful models of higher order regulation. We have little else at this time.

In summary, science has found that reductionistic and materialistic concepts of molecular genetics and physico-chemistry as agency of development to be worthy, helpful, but exceedingly deficient. Chuang Tzu knew this long ago.[37]

> The disadvantage of regarding things in their separate parts is that when one begins to cut and and analyze, each one tries to be exhaustive.... One goes on deeper and deeper, forgetting to return, and sees a ghost—the externals of things only. Or one goes on and imagines he has got it, and what he has got is only a carcass....Only one who can image the formless in the formed can arrive at the truth.

Chuang Tzu does not tell us to refrain from seeking mechanisms of phenomenon within components; he only warns of the hazards. In fact, he encourages the pursuit:[37]

> The sage rests in the solution of things and is dissatisfied with what is not a solution. Common men are satisfied with what is not a solution and do not rest in what is a solution.

Development and regeneration, therefore, involve the entire system of organism-environment. It is an architecture- and sequence-dependent process regulated by intelligence gathering and comparative analysis. It is an operation by which an influence on one point affects all points. It is a coordinated network of activities, not objects. It is an ever-changing manifestation of form that is essentially insubstantial and illusory. It is yet a mystery.

We also have found that even cells are social creatures. With the exceptions of a small proportion of airborne or waterborne bacteria, amoebas, and many other but not all protozoa, a single cell in the natural environment is a rarity. Cells communicate among their kind, and this fact plus their cooperative or pathogenic behavior among other life forms challenge traditional notions of independence and organism. Just as a certain number of termites in a closed area can alter behavior to collective action, a gathering of clonal micro-organisms or a clustering and juxtaposition of embryonic cells can initiate structural and metabolic differentiation. *Community hence provides the seeds for biological uniqueness among the members.* 'Everything is different but inseparable,' Alan Watts told us. Indeed. Moreover, everything is the same but separable. Such is mind.

Chapter 9

FORMING A MORE PERFECT UNION

Ecology

Wherever man goes he is not alone.

Michael L.A. Andrews

Consider the following haiku by Basho:

My horse tramping
across the field, Ho!
I am in the picture!

We can imagine the scene: the poet and his tired steed
moving slowly across open terrain in the peaceful quiet of the
Japanese countryside unbroken even by the sound of the clop-
ping horse as it passes through the swishing grasses, scaring
up insects. Perhaps birds in song are also heard. Basho was
suddenly mindful not only of his surroundings, but also of his
place and role in it. He rarely referred to himself in his poetry,
but in this instance there was no separation of the poet and
the poem of nature. Horse, rider, earth, and sky were all
united in harmony of form and function. Basho experienced
Gaia. Scientists have a name for these relationships: ecology.

This is more than an empty word tossed about when speaking of air pollution, endangered species, and urban blight.
Understandably, it is difficult for most people to relate to the
plight of a heron returning to a marsh only to discover that
the refuge was filled and covered with concrete; it is equally
hard for ranchers to appreciate the predator function of eagles
and coyotes when their livestock become occasional victims.
But as living creatures in this planet (we live in atmosphere
as fish live in water), we can not escape ecology. We react to

our psychobiophysicochemical environment and our environment reacts to our presence. Some alterations of the ecology are minor and go nearly unnoticed, such as the clearing of a few acres of land at the edge of a forest; other changes are significant, lasting, and destructive, as the crater pocked terrain of a war zone or the burning of vast tracts of Amazon rain forest.

Unlike Basho and his fellow Tao- and Zen-inspired poets and artists, we become acutely aware of ecology only when our health (physical or mental) or our money (real or potential) is at stake. Hence, our ire is raised when unprocessed chemical wastes seep into the water supply or when land developers decide to build a major industrial park alongside our formerly quiet rural living room. Our interactions with the terrain and other organisms appear to be limited to the street, our fellow humans, the family pet, the flower garden, and the food on the table. Other creatures seem distant from us, the relationships indirect and indistinct. However, as will be discussed, the microscopic life forms (by population, the representatives of Earth's biology) are very much part of our lives. Indeed, *the lives of human and microbe intertwine, mutually supporting and co-evolving.*

The first Western idea of a functional balance or harmony among organisms, a natural economy, originated with the eighteenth-century Swedish naturalist and pioneer taxonomist, Carolus Linnaeus (Carl von Linne). Ernst Haeckel coined the term *ecology* in 1870, deriving it from the same Greek root as *economy*, i.e., house or household. His word showed an excellent insight into practical organization and management of a multitude of materials and operations necessary for maintaining the basic needs of life. Haeckel defined ecology as 'the body of knowledge concerning the economy of nature... the investigation of the total relations of the animal both to its inorganic and to its organic environment.'[1]

Despite Haeckel's slight of plant life, this biological science is holistic from the outset, so evident that New Zealand's godmother of skin microbiology, Mary Marples, observed, 'The interrelation of all living and non-living things is so profound that strictly speaking there is only one ecosystem on earth—the planet itself.'[1] James Lovelock would later fully develop and extend this principle as Gaia, the planetary living organism.[2] Emphasizing the geometry of the relational dynamics, Buckminster Fuller, the eclectic visionary of synergism, obtusely defined ecology as 'the world-around complex intercomplementation of all the biological species' regenerative intercyclings with nature's geological and meterological transformation recyclings.'[3] Perhaps the best description of ecology was provided by physicist and environmentalist Fritjof Capra: 'Like individual organisms, ecosystems are self-organizing and self-regulating systems in which animals, plants, microorganisms, and inanimate substances are linked through a complex web of inter-dependencies involving the exchange of matter and energy in continual cycles.'[4]

With Chinese and Japanese philosophies so steeped in the the unity and harmony of nature, ecology should have arisen as an Eastern science. One reason that it did not may have been the inability to achieve a distant perspective, as noted above. In contrast to the rich, clever, and poetic roots in Chinese equivalent expressions, previously encountered in earlier chapters, we instead find an atypically drab adaptation that refers ecology to the 'social relationships and behaviors of life forms.' However, in contrast to the thorough scientific descriptions given above, the concept of social behavior, which taps our bank of experiences, more readily imparts a feeling of the basis for such analysis.

Ecology was once an arcane word, known to but a small number of naturalists and field biologists and to an even smaller group of medical microbiologists and epidemiologists.[5] Then in 1962, Rachel Carson, a geneticist and zoologist, sounded the first public environmental warning in *Silent Spring*, which focused on the untoward effects of pesticides on the food chain.[6] Despite the popular success of the publication, its narrow scope failed to impact on, let alone stem, the toxic industrial tide. The book also fell short in that the principles of ecology were only indirectly related to human existence.

However, as a natural consequence of the American cultural revolution of the late 1960's, there arose an elementary but staunch holistic and ecological awareness. On April 22, 1970, the ecology movement was officially launched in a well-

ECOLOGY

reported nationwide teach-in.[7] Since then, the words *ecology* and *environment* have appeared almost daily in our newspapers as the litany of some Biblical prophet: holes in the protective atmospheric ozone layer over the poles; massive lethal oil spills along the shores; festering air pollution; toxic wastes of technology; the destruction of the forests; the increasing number of endangered and lost species; the greenhouse effect; the stress of urban commuting and crowding; and so forth and so on. Still, the public remains vague about ecological concepts. Furthermore, while humans are at last again regarded as part of nature, ecology is viewed as something we upset, something that comes back to haunt us. Dichotomies persist. We citizens, so dependent on science and technology as we face the twenty-first century, have yet to incorporate the ecological equation into the conduct of our lives, a deficiency which Rene Dubos, microbiologist and environmental philosopher, sought to remedy with the assistance of his slogan, 'Think globally, but act locally.'[8] We also remain ignorant of the ecosystems called humans, surely the most local of all.

In 1962, as *Silent Spring* was selling briskly, a quiet academic text was published that summarized the scattered information on the organisms gently residing on us, our normal flora; the book spurred new scientific thinking about our dependence on them. This seminal review was Theodore Rosebury's *Microorganisms Indigenous to Man*.[9] Next, a more specialized treatise boldly grasped the essential relationship and presented the microbes' perspective of us; the book was provocatively entitled*The Ecology of the Human Skin*.[1] We see that two divergent but complementary paths of science were developing at this time, the tidal flow of reductionist molecular genetics and the countercurrent of holistic ecology, including medical microbial ecology. *Thus, to understand the basics of ecology we need not look further than ourselves.*

This chapter has two objectives. The first is lead you on a tour of the microbial habitats of your own body, providing some appreciation of the science of ecology. The second is to show that the web of life is like Indra's net of jewels, each node, each multifaceted gem reflecting another. Therefore, by focusing on the example of these limited ecosystems of tiny creatures on miniature territories, we may gain some sense of the way of every other ecosystem, however large, and, more important, the manner in which we are that web.

To begin, are the mouth and intestine inside or outside the body? This is a trick question, which may be answered by remembering Lao Tzu's teaching on the unity of form and space. Guarded by the valves of the throat epiglottis and anal sphincter, the hollow of our alimentary passageway is external, a continuum of the atmosphere in which we live. So, too, the culs-de-sac of lungs, vagina, ears, nasal sinuses, and bladder are both of and outside the body.

The skin and mucosal surfaces of our body, which border the microbe-laden atmosphere, are microcosms, nourishing or harboring over one hundred trillion microorganisms. The vast majority reside in the gut, yet a trillion flourish on the skin and about ten billion can be found in the mouth.

Lest these facts initiate revulsion followed by an urge to shower with a deodorant soap, gargle with mouthwash, and purge the body with laxatives and antibiotics, I assure you that almost all of these normally harmless microorganims are important in maintaining health and natural resistance to infectious disease. Even if you had followed the above regimen, the treatments would have had little and only temporary effect in reducing, not eliminating, the population of indigenous microbes. It might even have placed your well-being in jeopardy. Stretching the point to the limit, the normal flora is almost an appendage of ourselves, their patterns of distribution, composition, and density reflecting our individuality.

To further abate any distress, the horrific mental image of the astronomically large number of microorganisms, mentioned above, can be tamed by discovering that when one focuses down on a one square centimeter area of skin, one finds only a few hundred microscopic creatures. If that fails, then recall that every cell of your body necessarily contains vestigial bacteria and that some varieties of white blood cells strongly resemble amoebae. Furthermore, *in the continuum of life you are evolved bacteria. They are kin.*

The reverence for life by strict adherents of Jainism in India is so extreme that as they walk, they gently sweep the path ahead with a broom to prevent their inadvertent stepping on insects and cover their mouth so not to swallow any flying creature. They are not aware that they daily kill millions of their own microbes whenever they eat or wash. A similar quasi-religious practice that seems hypocritical in light of scientific knowledge is the eschewal of all animal tissue and products in the diet by certain zealous vegetarians, as if animals were more worthy than plants and more primitive life forms. Whitman, the 'deep ecologist', valued animal, vegetable, and mineral equally within the whole cosmic fabric in a passage introduced earlier: 'I believe a leaf of grass is no less than the journeywork of the stars, And the pismire is equally perfect, and a grain of sand, and the egg of the wren.' Through their experience of radically different environments, city folk spending some time alone in the wilderness may come to apprehend as well as appreciate the poet's conclusion. The selective dietary 'pro-lifers', however, are unaware not only of the many microorganisms, mites, and tiny insects in their food, but also of their very own mammalian epithelial and white blood cells (about 100 grams) that are consumed every day. It thus would be wiser if such practitioners focused on the spiritual merit of intention and choice rather than on that which in fact are impossibilities.

The study of human microbial ecology is not a new science; it is as old as microbiology itself.[10,11] In September 1683, Antony van Leeuwenhoek, a highly accomplished and clever Dutch amateur microscopist and cloth merchant, rubbed his teeth with salt and cloth, as was his morning custom, and, spotting some matter between his teeth, decided to inspect it under his self-built single-lens microscope.[12] He discovered the major forms of bacteria—rods, spheres, and spirals—and observed motility. Leeuwenhoek's curiosity led him to expand his survey and then to experiment, which was still unusual for scientists at this time.

For three days he abstained from cleaning his teeth, and removing some accumulated matter around his front gums, observed with satisfaction large numbers of his heretofore unknown 'animalcules'. He later encountered an old man who avoided tobacco and brandy, but who asserted a life-long neglect of even simple dental hygiene. Leeuwenhoek was surprised to find the man's saliva free of microorganisms, but the material collected from the teeth was teeming with bacteria. Leeuwenhoek's next approach was to convince another man who regulary drank brandy in the morning and wine in the afternoon to submit to dental probing. Leeuwenhoek was disappointed to find no difference in the saliva of the abstainer and the drinker, and just a few microbes on the drinker's few remaining teeth. However, the material between the front teeth again yielded a multitude of bacteria. Leeuwenhoek next experimented on himself. He swirled vinegar in his mouth, but still found living microorganisms, mainly around his molars. This contrasted with the apparent death of the microbes when he had placed some of the white matter in a solution of vinegar-water. He concluded that vinegar can not penetrate this material if it is lodged between the teeth, and that only those organisms located on the outermost edge are susceptible to the detrimental effects of the liquid.

Nine years later he again investigated his own flora. Frustrated by recent repeated failures to detect moving organisms from his teeth, Leeuwenhoek finally realized his new habit of drinking hot coffee was killing his intended specimens. Only by obtaining material from the back molars, where the heat could not pervade, could he satisfy himself of the vitality of his animalcules. It is remarkable and a credit to Leeuwenhoek's inquisitive, analytical consciousness-mind that his 300-year-old approach of surveys and alterations of the environment (testing the effects of acid, alcohol, and heat in this instance) is still standard operating procedure for ecological investigations of the normal flora.

As noted above, economy and ecology are related. Therefore, it is not surprising, particularly to Chinese philosophers, that interrelationships within the community of normal flora bear a resemblance to human social behavior. In a society, many are lone, independent residents with no care for the welfare of others, but most are communal and committed to mutual benefit. While all will exploit any advantage afforded them, a small proportion are ruthless competitors, thieves, and murderers. Others are charitable, anonymously providing goods and services to the needy in the neighborhood, and a few are totally dependent on the kindness of strangers. In the social ecology of microorganisms, these economic aspects are transformed into physiological terms. A given microorganism is subject to a variety of interactions with its neighbors.[13]

Neutralism among the flora is not like the nonpartiality of Switzerland; it is the very lack of interactions. Such a relationship is rare, but when it occurs, it is either at or shortly after birth, when microorganisms are acquired for the first time, typically from the mother, medical staff, and hospital environment. Thinking of the future and expanding the principle to larger domains, we will find temporary neutralism on establishing agricultural settlements on Mars or other distant orb. *The common denominator is virgin territory.* In this hypothetical colony, the species of microorganisms will be few, their populations low, nutrients abundant, and functional and spatial niches vacant. With crowding of the habitat, the same microorganisms will no longer enjoy unrestricted or uninfluenced growth, but will suffer or perhaps thrive in the consequences of interactions. Of course, when considering our own micro-habitats, microbial colonization is hardly neutral.

Commensalism occurs when one microorganism benefits from another without reciprocation of any kind. This is not always charity; it may be simply a tramp finding something useful in your discarded trash. Advantages may be obtained in several ways: (1) a useless chemical substrate may be processed by the associate in such a manner that it becomes a nutrient for the first microbe, as an artist makes use of findings; (2) the partner secretes a growth factor, often a vitamin, whose effects may be observed on Petri dish cultures as enlarged colonies of one type surrounding a colony of a different type—a phenomenon called *satellitism;* (3) the commensal assistant can block the action of toxins or host-derived inhibitory molecules; (4) the benefactor can alter the physicochemical environment, such as acidity, presence of free oxygen, or degree of osmotic pressure, to favor the proliferation of its companion; and (5) one microbe may provide its own surface for the attachment of another, as in the case of a remora, the sucker fish, which rides below the mouth of a shark to share in the spoils of the kill.

This last means is uncommon, but it has been observed in dental plaque, the relentless and tenacious film that defies our best hygienic habits. This noxious material is composed primarily of bacteria, salivary glycoprotein, and cement of microbial origin. Food is not a significant component. Tartar or calculus, which is found on some teeth, especially the back of the lower incisors, is simply calcified plaque. Early plaque is disorganized, but with increased thickness, the microorganisms align themselves in parallel columns. Palisades of spherical cocci are sandwiched between chains of filamentous bacilli. At the surface of mature plaque are found unique structures that bear striking resemblance to corn cobs. The cores are filamentous bacteria and the kernels are cocci.[14,15]

The oral cavity also provides the example where oxygen-loving aerobic species consume available gaseous oxygen, permitting the colonization and dominance of anaerobes for which free oxygen is toxic. The series of replacements of one species in a habitat by another, whether they be bacteria within gums or trees in a forest, is called *succession*. A climax community is the final pattern in the series; however, we must recognize that ultimately a major change in the environment, such as prolonged drought or widespread fire storm, will wipe the slate clean and allow a new series to commence.

Microorganisms interacting positively defines *protocooperation*, and when this relationship is of total reliance, the association is known as *mutualism*. But, oh, to prove it! If two organisms were dependent on each other and especially needed to be in proximity, their separation, as occurs in routine bacteriological methods, would not permit growth and detection of either. Sometimes a nutrient-rich, complex isolation medium will provide all that is necessary for survival and replication, but mutualistic relationships still would not be perceived. Hence, mutualism, as found in fungus-alga lichens or in bees and flowers (at a distance through the agency of pollen), has not been described among the human indigenous flora. Protocooperation, nevertheless, has been noted in mixed broth cultures and in *synergistic* infections, where the neighboring organisms yield a greater or more intense result than the combination of their separate responses. Despite the paucity of evidence, mutualism is highly probable in a nutrient-limited habitat that supports a diverse microbiota. The interacting partners need not comprise new species; they could be defective mutant strains of common microbes.

Because there is no Utopian economy, we should not be surprised in our survey of ecological relationships to find the opposites of altruism and partnerships. Within the harmful activities of *antagonism* or *interference* are the categories of competition, amensalism, predation, and parasitism.

Need I explain *competition?* We are continually bombarded with this practical, successful, but twisted motivative tenet of capitalism, and recognize it as a sign of ego insecurity. I will note, nevertheless, that when microbes vie for a nutrient, they suffer metabolic inefficiency to some extent. *Interference*, which is when a member of one species blocks the colonization or infective processes of another member, seems to be a result of competition.[16,17]

Examples of *amensalism* (the word refers to denial of the food table) are those microorganisms that release toxic molecules, antibiotics, or bacteriocins to the detriment of their neighbors, without receiving direct gain. However, the elimination of competitors provides a significant indirect advantage. In Petri dish cultures, the colony of an antibiotic-producing microorganism is detected by a clear circular zone on a lawn of susceptible organisms.

Predation may be found in the intestine and sometimes in the vagina, where transient protozoa feast on bacteria, or in hair follicules, where the mite *Demodex folliculorum* also devour bacteria.[1] Bacteriophages could represent *parasitism*, if you still feel comfortable with viruses as organisms perhaps as superimposed systems. As far as is known, the familiar interactions of parasitism and predation, one organism feeding on another for survival either insidiously or overtly (to say the least!), do not occur among bacteria or fungi on the human body. Some soil bacteria and fungi of marine and soil environments do live in this way.

These categories of relationships among the constituents of the normal floras can be applied to all ecosystems, be it a stately and ancient redwood forest or a churning Pacific atoll. On first inspection, the human being as ecosystem, or even several ecosystems, seems highly questionable, since the body must be regarded both as territory for microbial life and as an organism interacting with its microbial load and the environment at large. However, this ecological organization is not that unusual. Except for experimental arrangements, ecosystems are not entirely closed, not even a desert pond. Since living organisms are hierarchically organized as loops, their interactions with environments, substrates, and life forms above, below, and alongside may be described as ecological; hence, *ecosystems are themselves hierarchial.* How then would the ecological web be affected if a major level were removed? What particularly would happen to us if the normal flora were eliminated?

A world without microorganisms would be as barren as Mars seems to be. All life forms today are their descendents. Microbes recycle the elements, help provide our food, dispose of wastes, and create new chemicals.[18,19] They are found everywhere from ocean to soil to atmosphere, from plants to insects to humans. As Strickland Gillilan plainly put it, 'Adam Had'em.'

Is germfree life then possible? Pasteur hypothesized that it is not, but he left the problem to others to resolve. At the turn of the century, researchers attained germfree plants and insects, which appeared to live normally. Because eggs are easily isolated and maintained, germfree amphibians and chickens soon followed. Generations of germfree birds and rodents were raised. However, with microorganisms in and on everything, the methods and technology to achieve and maintain a sterile environment were slow to develop. Nonetheless, scientists were able to establish that advanced life forms do not require microorganims to live.[20] But their life is as sterile as the environment in which they live.

Once microorganisms inhabit the body, sterilization by antibiotics and chemicals is virtually impossible; therefore, it is best to have the animal born in a germfree area. In the instance of mammals, the infant animal (historically we must include the human baby with combined immune deficiency) is delivered by Caesarean section and placed immediately into a sterilized chamber, which will be its home.[20,21] The creature must rely on researchers outside the isolation chamber to provide all food and remove wastes. Food and water must be sterile, as well as the air that enters the gloved-compartment.

In some studies the food has to be reduced to defined chemical nutrients to exclude influences of more complex microbe-specific products. The technology being mechanically clumsy and procedures exacting, microorganisms frequently intrude. For example, a tiny puncture in a glove, which serves also as environmental membrane, is sufficient to introduce contaminants. Such an occurrence may be lethal.

Researchers studying rodents have established that the *absence of a flora profoundly affects the anatomy, physiology, growth, and even life-span of the animal.*[20] The cecum is enlarged and the intestinal contents are more liquid, more alkaline, and more oxidative. Germfree animals have a lower metabolic rate. Higher amounts of cholesterol are found in the blood and in the liver. Since microorganisms produce vitamin K and pantothenic acid of the B vitamin complex, germfree rodents require these nutrients in their diets. Normally, they would absorb these microbial vitamins through eating of their feces. Germfree animals also have a smaller heart and reduced blood volume but, in compensation, more red blood cells with higher hemoglobin levels. The alveolar walls of the lung are two-thirds as thin as that of conventional animals. The entire immune system is sluggish from lack of stimulation, and there are fewer white blood cells in surface regions. Some evidence suggests that germfree animals live longer than their germ-laden siblings, probably because of and despite their poorer nutrition. Undernourished, starved conventional animals generally live longer, too. In the absence of bacteria, dental caries and body odor do not exist, establishing their etiological relationship. The most serious problem is nutrition: the cause of death is usually associated with the enlarged cecum and impaired intestinal movement.

Germfree existence is an artificial condition entirely dependent on a germ-interrelating world. Such imprisoned animals have demonstrated the role of normal flora in maintaining an active and efficient physiology. Taken together, microbes living on us are not commensals, they are cooperative. The humblest and the most advanced life forms are joined as a team, each benefitting the other. With their antagonistic properties, the normal flora should be included as part of our defense system against alien pathogens, as the microorganisms of Earth in H.G. Wells' *The War of the Worlds* were the downfall of the Martian invaders. We should also not forget the less distinct evolutionary functions of microorganisms in gene transfer and selection. As minute factories, they are cornerstones of biotechnology and the further development of our civilization.

Korean Zen Master Seung Sahn tells us that it is through our practice of 'correct situation, correct relationship, and correct function (action)' that we attain enlightenment. *These three fundamental components may be ascribed to all phenomena as well as to mind.* All three are required for existence. Recognizing a situation is easy; understanding the involved relationships is fairly simple; grasping the fundamental activity is difficult. This is why the various Zen koans and verbal exchanges between master and student seem nonsensical when taken linearly and superficially.

For example, a monk asked, 'What is the one word (the marrow) of Zen?' Master Chao-Chou responded, 'What did you say?' 'What is the one word?' the monk repeated. 'You make it two' was Chao-Chou's reproval.[22] If you attain this koan, everything becomes clear and unobstructed.

Ecology, hence, is more than the defining *relationships* listed above. Let us now look at the *situations* among the various ecosystems of the human body.

Being a skin microbiologist, I shall begin with this largest of the organs (comprising 10% of the body weight) and the most obvious ecological surface. Furthermore, skin is the traditional boundary of self and other, but it is the edge only perceived through the eye. When our hand drifts above the skin from foot to head, through our sense of touch, we can feel the thermal differences. Electronic sensors can detect our magnetic field.[23,24] When we concentrate on smell, do we not detect odors emanating from different areas of the skin? Also, the air around us is filled with shed fragments of skin, squames, many of which are floating rafts of attached microorganisms.[25,26] Some 10 billion squames are cast off each day. House dust is composed chiefly of such debris; the heavier coating on furniture near the bed is due to the extended period in which we frequent that spot. Likewise, when another person hears us speak or sees us, or reciprocally we hear or see that person, does not something of ourselves extend beyond our skin? Upon my death, the pages of this book will not represent the author, but the thoughts contained within will. Although from the strict and limited perspective of the senses, the skin is not the true boundary of our perceived bodies and certainly not of our selves (we extend well beyond it, beyond ordinary three-dimensional space), the organ, nevertheless, is a divider, a semi-permeable screen and base of diverse microbial habitats.

The reason I use the plural is that the skin is far from homogeneous. The distribution of sweat glands, coarse hair, and sebaceous glands differ dramatically. Several environmentally distinct regions may be readily found on cursory self-examination. Our toewebs are bogs, the forearms and legs are sparse savannahs, the cheeks are warm tar fields, and the armpits, groin, beard, and scalp are steaming jungles and rain forests.[1]

This variation translates into humidity, and for any microbe one region of the body can be a paradise while a nearby area will offer certain death. Exposed skin is largely dry, the external layers being composed of dead flat cells. While concentrated water vapor exists over sweat pores and hair follicules, much escapes the body through the intercellular matrix. Relative humidity over the horny layer is slightly over 90%, which is close to the threshold of 85% humidity below which most microbes desiccate and die. *Thus, the general insufficiency of moisture is a selective influence on the kinds of microorganisms able to colonize the tissue.* Hair and the closeness of toes, as any skin fold, holds moisture; relative humidity here will reach 100%.

As fruit trees could grow in a desert if the farmer were to irrigate sufficiently, so, too, could microorganisms thrive if sufficient water vapor and liquid were to accumulate. Two days of experimental occlusion by a plastic cover on the forearm will elevate the population density of normal flora 1,000 to 10,000 fold and provide an environment suitable for those microbes normally unable to survive on the otherwise arid surface.[27] From the clinical viewpoint, occlusive dressings, which are applied to protect catheters and wounds from hostile pathogens and opportunists, may actually create hazard-ous conditions for patients. The use of antiseptics and microporous plastics has eliminated the risky alternative of repeated aeration and exposure to pathogenic microbes.

Other physical features include acidity, temperature, and oxygen and carbon dioxide tensions.[27] Skin is somewhat acidic, roughly pH 5.0 to 6.5, depending on location, sex, and age. With puberty, the armpit may become slightly alkaline, up to pH 7.9, and the uro-gentital regions may be close to neutral, pH 7.0. Since most microbes grow poorly at pH 5.5 and are almost completely retarded at pH 5.0, the major expanses of human skin present formidable selective environments. So, too, are Bohemia's once lush meadows and forests now destroyed by acid rain, no longer hospitable to human and bird.

We are familiar with body temperature being 37° C (98.6° F.), but this is the internal temperature recorded under the tongue. Skin, being exposed to the heat of the summer and cold of winter, is substantially lower and variable, with the exceptions of groin and armpits. In old age, skin temperature of the hands can fall as low as 24° C. Heat rises; hence, toes are the coldest sites of the body, usually only 30° C. Toes are the first sites to suffer frostbite on mountaineering and polar expeditions. The cooler temperatures of the skin surface do not prevent most infectious bacteria from residing there, but since 37° C. is optimal, skin temperature slows growth and alters metabolism. A particular enzyme may be synthesized at 30° C. but not at 37° C, or the reverse may occur. *A change of temperature, thus, can shift the ecological balance to eliminate or support transients or pathogens*, as the occasional displacement of warm, tropical ocean currents northward brings the great white shark to the Northern California and Oregon coast and its plentiful seal population.

Despite its ubiquitous presence, oxygen becomes critically important in skin ecology when we consider hair follicles associated with sebaceous glands. The reduced oxygen tension in the deep pits, plus other conditions, support the growth of anaerobic bacterial species. It is interesting to note that the 100% oxygen atmosphere in which astronauts operate their space vessels eliminate these anaerobic microorganisms from their skin.[28] Carbon dioxide normally diffuses through the skin, but, like water vapor, it concentrates under occlusive dressings, clothing, or skin folds. This is important because its presence favors the growth of some bacteria and supports the pathological processes of certain microorganisms, such as the ringworm fungi.

We know that life forms will evolve to use almost any seemingly improbable material as nutrient source. Some bacteria digest oil and toxic industrial wastes. Cyanobacter and certain plants manage to live on water, atmospheric nitrogen, carbon dioxide, and little else. For bacteria encountering the skin, a treasure of proteins, fats, sugars, and minerals awaits. Still, the distribution, concentration, and variety do not meet the optimal conditions of laboratory growth media and, indeed, they may not support the more fastidious microbe. Moreover, particular skin molecules are inhibitory to many microorganisms. These include lipids (fatty acids and sphingosines) and an iron-binding protein, transferrin.[29]

If skin can be considered a harsh temperate desert, hair follicles and their associated sebaceous gland are oases. Scanning electron microscopy has provided photographs of bacteria clustered around these openings as a herd of wildebeest and zebra gathered around some African watering hole. The hospitable follicule provides a well-insulated, humid shelter, and a ceaseless flow of nutrients. Its closeness to a rich blood supply; a partial lining of active, living cells; the accumulation of cellular debris; a warmer, more stable temperature; and energy-rich sebaceous lipids are a boon for microbial growth. The depth of the follicle also affords microorganisms protection from wash water, soap, and the many chemicals we apply to the skin. In contrast, microscopy shows the openings of eccrine sweat glands devoid of microbial visitors, except after prolonged occlusion when the sweat gland may be temporarily arrested from releasing its fluid.

A sheltered nook in a granite mountain may seem a stable habitat for a fern, but rock cracks, crumbles, and erodes under forces of rain, wind, and extreme temperature cycles. Skin likewise is an unsecure habitat. As epithelial cells rise from the germinal layer to the surface, the outermost layer is continually shed, subject to cycles of flooding, abrasion, and

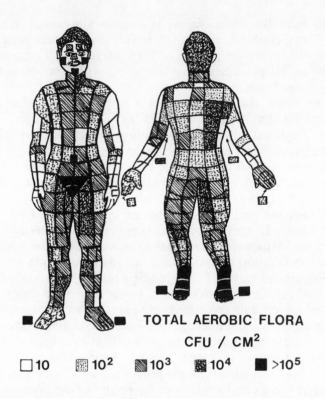

TOTAL AEROBIC FLORA

CFU / CM^2

☐ 10   ▨ 10^2 ▨ 10^3 ▨ 10^4 ■ >10^5

HUMAN AND MICROBES:
Different but inseparable by mutual influence
and dependence.

drying. We abuse our skin, certainly an extraordinarily resilient shield, as if it were made of steel armor.

Successful microbial colonization depends on replication and movement to new skin cells. The transfer may not be as rapid and critical as the slave Eliza, in *Uncle Tom's Cabin,* escaping the pursuit of bounty hunters by stepping across flowing sheets of ice to reach the other side of the Ohio River, but it comes close. Those microbes that do not relocate are carried off into the air as survivors on a life raft. Unlike soil, which may become depleted of particular nutrients, skin continually replenishes itself as does the sea, and just as the sea is subject to tides, the skin is influenced by circadian rhythms in cell division, sebum secretion, temperature, and so forth.

Skin differs as people differ. It may be smooth or rough, and either oily, moist, or dry. In addition, sex, age, race, family, and diet, as well as systemic disease or therapy, influence the ultimate pattern of normal flora. I have encountered some individuals with such a distinctive normal skin flora, characterized by the shape, color, and variety of colonies, that I could easily identify their culture from a large set of Petri dish specimens. The patterns of flora among people are not as unique as fingerprints, but they may fall into various analytically useful types.

Each of the other ecosystems of the body provide similar but more complex situations. The brief descriptions, through additional similes, may also reinforce the mystical view and experience of oneself as the world, as one self.

As the gateway of a fortress is inherently the weakness of its defense, the mouth surely provides direct access between the skin bulwarks to the more susceptible interior of the body. Microorganisms can reach the orifice by spreading along the facial skin, by being ingested along with food, or by being inhaled in aerosols or in dust particles. The mouth comprises numerous, rather diverse habitats, although all can be described as wet.[30,31]

Would you not expect oxygen, which is about 21% of the atmosphere, to be plentiful in the mouth even after 30 seconds of nasal breathing? Experiments have shown that such is not the case. Only 12% oxygen is found over the back of the tongue. Within the tight pockets formed by teeth and cheeks or lips, where little gas exchange can occur, researchers have detected a mere 0.4% oxygen. Anaerobic microorganisms thrive under these environmental conditions, while obligate aerobes suffocate.

Except when we bathe, skin cells face the gentle flow of wind; cells of the mouth, however, are continually flooded with circadian-regulated saliva, secreted under the tongue, along the jaw and the molar groove, and from cheeks, lips, and palate. Saliva supports the functioning of taste buds, acts as a lubricant, neutralizes chemicals that might injure exposed tissues, prevents desiccation by breathing, and washes away debris and foreign material. Of neutral pH, saliva is a mixed bag of molecules that can support or inhibit microorganisms, depending on species. Adherence is a crucial mechanism of survival here. The situation is like hanging on to a rock in the middle of a stream that leads to a large, long waterfall. Many species of bacteria and fungi take the plunge.

There are rocks in the mouth, of course. Like barren granite mountain peaks, the outer surface of teeth is composed of the hardest material of the body, hydroxyapatite. The crystals, organized into enamel, are salts of calcium and phosphate. Although smooth to the touch, the enamel surface upon magnification presents a lunar-like landscape with bumps, depressions, pits, and confluent craters. These hollows provide stagnation zones, entrap debris, and offer attachment sites for microorganisms.

The muscular tongue is a lush lawn of nipplelike papillae on a flat or grooved base. Resembling a spongy clump of moss, it provides protected channels where microbes can find refuge and nutrients. Needless to say, the food that we chew and drink is shared by the microorganisms of the mouth and the rest of the alimentary tract.

At the back of the mouth, the upper region of the throat, is a hub called the pharynx. It communicates also with the ears and the nose. Dermatobiologists also study the nose, particularly the vestibule of the nostrils. This organ is not simply the protrusion of the face; it includes the larger, twisted cavernous passages over the mouth and the sinuses behind the cheek bone, whose presence is painfully recognized when we combat a cold virus and lose. Air flowing rapidly through narrow passages has a cooling effect on the walls. Thus, the nose is lined with a thick mucous membrane that warms and moistens the inhaled air in addition to entrapping dust particles and microorganisms. While temperature reaches about 32° C., relative humidity approaches 100% by the time air reaches the pharynx. On each exhalation, however, the tissues are warmed with an airflow of increased carbon dioxide. The situation is not very different from the coming and going of waves along shoreline habitats. Interspersed with the mucous-producing cells are ciliated cells, which screen the air of fine particles, conveying it back to the pharynx for swallowing. Nearly all of the microorganisms dwelling in the nose reside near the opening, the population density rivaling a Manhattan office building.

Air from the nose continues passed the pharynx into the trachea, bronchials, and lungs. The lungs are typically free of microorganisms for mainly physical reasons. Aerosols have been examined intensively since they are considered one of the primary means of transmitting infections from person to person. The size of the airborne particle is crucial, determining whether the microorganism will be stopped in the nose and throat or will penetrate into the lungs. Almost all bodies over 20 micrometers in diameter are retained in the nose. Depending on whether breathing is through the nose or mouth, some 50% to 80% of particles two micrometers in diameter enter the lung. Because of aerodynamics and oscillation of air flow, particles of 0.5 micrometers, the size of small bacteria, are not deposited among the ten million alveolar air sacs but, upon exhalation, are pushed up to the bronchioles. A wind tunnel is not a suitable environment for human or beast. If some microbe or foreign particle does become lodged in an alveolus, it generally is engulfed by specialized white blood cells. Tubercle bacilli depend on it, and the bacteria of pneumonia have a slippery capsule by which to avoid it.

Microorganisms fare much better down the other tube of the throat. There is a significant obstacle, however: the stomach. This churning digestive organ secretes potent protein- and lipid-digesting enzymes and, because of hydrochloric acid, the pH of stomach fluid is about 1 to 2. Despite the unfriendly conditions, many microorganisms are able to pass through the stomach unharmed by their lodgment in unaffected solid food or by their being liquid-borne, for fluids are not retained long nor do they stimulate as well the caustic gastric secretions.

The intestines provide the most complex microbial ecosystem of the body.[32,33] The environment of the small intestine gradually alters along the 20- to 30-foot long canal, despite the uniformity of temperature and the constant 100% humidity. As digestion progresses, more processesd nutrients are available and intestinal motility is reduced, factors that promote microbial expansion. Furthermore, the atmosphere becomes reduced to support anaerobic species. The large intestine can best be described as a cesspool. The accumulation of debris, cells, secretions, and other nutrients coupled with poor motility, warm temperature, and fluid offer favorable conditions for massive microbial growth. Whereas the small intestine has a large surface area and plentiful sites for microbial attachment, the colon is basically a smooth-walled tube. Here, microorganims grow mainly in the sludge.

The last microbial habitats to be discussed are the vagina and cervix.[31] Like the oral cavity, an assortment of environments and tissues abound. The occlusive folds and caverns present a hospitable zone of moist, warm surfaces. The labia have sebaceous and sweat glands. However, no glands are located on the rugose vaginal wall, and lubrication is provided by secretions from the cervix. The depth of the organ and the many folds contribute to an anaerobic atmosphere. Pregnancy and the monthly rhythm of hormones in menstruation have a profound influence on vaginal habitat, altering secretions and cellular activity. Levels of glycogen vary, and pH is in constant flux within a moderately acidity of pH 4 to 5. Monthly cycles also influence the number of receptor sites on epithelial cells for microbial adherence.[33]

Within this short survey of terrain and climate—a geography of the human body—we have examined the great diversity of environments in which different microorganisms can flourish. Yet only a small proportion of the thousands of Earth's microbial species can survive somewhere in humans (the indigenous flora), and an even smaller number can be routinely isolated (the normal flora). Clearly, *ecology can not be reduced to single survival factors.* Interrelationships among microbes and between host and microbe are multifaceted, and the highly variable and yet incompletely defined environmental situation would strain the credibility of mathematical modeling, systems that now may need to include chaos theory.[35,36]

Having described situations and relationships, we are ready for the third aspect of phenomenon, *action*. A vivid work by the poet Ransetsu (1653-1707) may help provide the manner it is integrated:[37]

Above the pilgrims,
chanting on a misty road,
wild geese are flying.

Choosing but one representative, let us follow the activities
of a notorious indigenous bacterium, opportunist extraordinary, under various ecological circumstances: *Staphylococcus
aureus* in the best of times, the worst of times.

Some 20% of a healthy population, approximately 90% of
patients with the skin condition atopic dermatitis, and about
50% of men having acquired immune difficiency syndrome
carry this bacterium in the vestibule of their nares. No one
knows why. It is known, however, that carriers have more
staphylococcus binding sites on their mucosal cells, suggesting
that increased adherence may be a leading contributor to the
microorganism's survival.[38] For whatever reasons, the nose is
a reservoir for *S. aureus*. But it has neighbors.

S. aureus usually comprise less than 50% of the population
of the nostrils. It shares this unique habitat with club-shaped
coryneforms, chains of streptococci, other grape-cluster
staphylococci, and, with some people, motile rods more at
home in the intestine. Nothing is static. Each microbe has its
own rate of replication, and the nasal cells have their own
metabolic cycles. Mucous production and flow vary over the
day. With each inhalation new microorganisms enter the
habitat, perchance to colonize and interact; and with every
sneeze, every forceful utterance, microbe-borne cells are
loosened and expelled. Through antagonistic interactions, the
microorganisms die also at different rates. This is a complex
dynamic system that is nevertheless orderly. Scientists can
predict trends, but never exact numbers.

Approximately a million bacteria colonize the nasal
surface. The population varies often ten-fold from day to day.
Also the proportions of each species or strain of microorganism vary over time. The coryneforms, the bacteriologist's
equivalent of the miner's canary, are the most sensitive to
environmental change, taking full advantage of moist surfaces
but as weak competitors retreating to minimal survival populations. As *S. aureus* or its cousin *S. epidermidis* fall in

numbers, the coryneforms return. Therefore, when proportionally large numbers of coryneforms are isolated from a habitat, the clinical researcher can be confident that for the moment at least there is comparative environmental stability and health. The two staphylococcal species themselves also have a reciprocal relationship. While the nasal epithelium may support several different strains of *S. epidermidis* (accepting the current taxonomic schemes), rarely are detected more than one strain of *S. aureus*. This interference is the basis of substitution therapy in ridding the habitat of a particular hazardous strain of *S. aureus*.[39]

Let us suppose that doing what comes naturally, we touch our nose and then stroke our cheek and chin and, in doing so, let a cellular raft supporting *S. aureus* be transferred. Jumping ship to the new shore, the microbe encounters a new environment, a less kind habitat, and new competitors. Adherence is weaker on skin with far fewer binding sites, but it manages to find a safe haven. It may neutralize the grease of inhibitory lipids with enzymes or depend on other flora to supply the antidote. Still, replication can not keep pace with the climatic, biological, and chemical forces restricting growth. Except for the depths of hair follicles and the sebaceous pores on the nose, where anaerobic bacteria are densely packed, facial skin supports far fewer bacteria, only 10^3 to 10^4 colony-forming units per square centimeter. The variety of normal species is more restricted. So similar to *S. epidermidis*, the ubiquitous microorganism of skin, *S. aureus*, nevertheless, is unable to colonize the stratum corneum for long and is soon eliminated. Again the reasons are obscure. Perhaps its endowment of so many virulent pathogenic factors is a burden. One would not expect an oak to endure the Mojave desert; with fewer needs, *S. epidermidis* is the cactus of the normal floras, able to grow in a variety of habitats.

If, however, *S. aureus*, during its brief sojourn on the face, is introduced into a minor nick made by a razor, or sundry scratches, or an ingrown hair, or an occluced follicle, or an existing inflammed lesion, then its arsenal of exploitive and defensive enzymes is no longer an onus, but the key to the candy store.[40] Free from microbial competitors and antagonists and able for a while to overcome our cellular and humoral defenses, *S. aureus* will induce a variety of diseases from minor follicle inflammation and pimples to boils, carbuncles, bullous impetigo, and occasionally to the infection of blood. Certain toxin-producing strains of *S. aureus* (actually products of incorporated bacteriophage DNA or extrachromosomal plasmids) are also associated with scalded skin syndrome, toxic shock syndrome, and food poisoning. Upon certain circumstances, the microbe will induce pneumonia, bladder infection, or abscesses in any other body system.

None of these insults can be tolerated. Thus, we developed drugs and agents to prevent, but more often to treat, them. In doing so, we find that there are always unforeseen detrimental effects, as when the pesticide DDT leads to the fragility of brown pelican eggs. Antibiotics are not magic bullets specifically targeted for a beligerent microbe; sometimes an innocent party is hit. The normal flora is always altered whether the antibiotic is applied locally or taken systemically. Some antibiotics have such an extensive effect on microorganisms that, to fit the analogy, the weapon should be a shotgun, since all body habits are usually affected.

From antimicrobial investigations, universal ecological phenomena are recognized.[41-43] *Antibiotics exert a selective influence on the indigenous flora.* Those microbes that are uniformly susceptible and have no capacity to alter their status quickly—foremost the target pathogens—are eliminated outright. Within a second microbial population are typically a few mutants, which are inherently resistant to the antibiotics. These strains are able to flourish in the demise of their sensitive relatives. A third group of bacteria are resistant to the antibiotic at the outset. *With the void created by the eradication of the first category of microorganisms, resistant species that can fill the vacant niche can expand in population,* as the shooting of wolves has permitted the deer population to increase beyond available food reserves. If there is no other species available for the niche, as the loss of anaerobic skin bacteria, the total population decreases, for skin obligate aerobes can not increase or survive at the depths of the follicle. *An empty niche or habitat, of course, is an open invitation for pathogens,* as occurs when a European or Asian insect reaches the fields of California. Remarkably, once the antibiotic stimulus is removed, the sensitive strains return from occult, dormant, weakened, or extraneous sources. The reasons for this reversal are unknown. *Because of intracacies of interrelationships, an ecological network is characterized by its flexibility to fluctuation.*

Antibiotics are not the only substances that are directed against microorganisms. Almost everyone uses soaps, and in developed nations these soaps are mainly antimicrobial, deodorant varieties. Indeed, deodorant soaps are used by over half the American public. Since these soaps are designed to influence the composition of skin flora, one wonders what the realistic definition of normal skin flora is. The decrease in population density is the primary effect, but composition is also considerably modified.[44,45] Antimicrobial soaps also simplify the composition of skin flora to a smaller variety of types than what exists in the truly normal state. In addition to soaps, the normal floras can be altered by such factors as diet, malnutrition, emotional stress, sex, age, prolonged water immersion, and so forth. We are our flora, our flora is us.

By now you should have attained a good appreciation of how one can play the harp web of ecology, more often than not attaining discord. Plucking one strand, be it bear, birch, or bacillus, causes the entire net to react or sound, changing conditions and resonating in distant unexpected regions. I have reviewed human microbial ecology only as an example, but consider that in an ever increasing network, all nodes penetrate and depend on each other; there is no middle, no edge. Basho, master of the haiku, penetrated the music of this resonating web. Let his words resonate in us:

The fading temple bell
Carried on by blossom scents—
Evening.

Chapter 10

A SENSE OF THE WHOLE

Psychoneuroimmunology

*Only by seeing biology in its broadest evolutionary,
genetic and developmental perspectives while pursuing
specialized research can one connect what may first
appear to be unrelated matters into a whole that is both
organic and intellectually satisfying.*

Gerald M. Edelman

Know thyself.

Inscription at the Delphic Oracle

One of my favorite cartoons by Sidney Harris, who special-
izes brilliantly in the humor of science and its hallowed institutions, depicts two researchers before a chalkboard. The
board is covered with lines of a long and complex equation—the archetypical mathematical scrawl in the center of
which are the words 'Then a miracle occurs'. The critic says
to his colleague, 'I think you should be more explicit here in
step 2.' For the scientist, a miracle is not some divine or
supernatural event, but, as the root indicates, a wonder, a
curiosity piece, a stimulus for thought and investigation.

Something extraordinary took place some 500 million years
ago: vertebrates began to swim the oceans. How these spinal
creatures with internal growing skeletons came about is poorly
understood; it is prime evidence for the concept of macro-
evolution. However, their physical or metaphysical origins do
not matter in this particular discussion. What is important is
that with these biological novelties there arose primitive
consciousness-mind and a crude but true adaptive immune
system. The two marvels are not separate, and with the succession of new life orders from fish through amphibians and

reptiles to mammals and us, both of these conventional mental and material aspects increased their complexity and strengthened their apparent union, mind minding itself. The ancient waters gave birth to individuality, to volition, thought, and psychological and physiological self-awareness.

Various functions have been ascribed to the immune system over the past 100 years, but the notion of its serving as an *internal sense, having regulatory capacity, being associated with consciousness-mind, and hence contributing to ego formation* is a significant departure from the simplistic concept of defense against infectious disease, which we readily acknowledge whenever we not so readily face the vaccinating syringe. In fact, few scientists and philosophers have considered it. I expect the situation to change in the coming decade with the growth of noetic and neurosciences and the realization, now ripening among the deans of immunology, that *immunity is a collective net quantitative process, not a categorical condition.* Therefore, a distillation of the historical development of this still radical and unorthodox idea would be worthwhile.[1,2]

The term *immunity* means exempt, and was applied to conscription and taxes as well as to disease. The equivalent Chinese phrase refers to avoiding or escaping pestilence.

The first recognition of inherent and acquired states of immunity surely occurred among Neolithic peoples. An epidemic would race through the tribe while some individuals would remain healthy, thereby able to tend the ill with impunity. If the same infectious disease returned, the previous survivors would resist the onslaught, but they would remain susceptible to a different disease. Of course, knowledge of contagion and subclinical infection was nonexistent and would remain so for thousands of years. However, the bite of a poisonous snake or the eating of known toxic plants had a clear causative association. Survivors would have the power to overcome subsequent encounters with the poison, a trick soon acquired by the shaman and, later, palace plotters.

While in modern usage *virus* describes a class of infectious microorganisms, it means noxious slime, such as a poison. However, for many years it was applied to any unseen disease agent. Until the World Health Organization accomplished its

IMMUNITY

goal in 1980 of removing the smallpox virus from circulation through a massive vaccination campaign, a notable exception to prevention of genocide, it was for thousands of years the internationally feared contagion and occasional weapon of war. The successful preventive measure, developed by Edward Jenner in 1798, was the injection of a weak cousin of the smallpox virus. Because of shared antigens (configurations of chemical structures that elicit complementary antibodies and activate immune cells), immunity to the vaccinia virus rendered resistance to the smallpox virus.

However, Jenner's vaccine was not the first approach to fight smallpox. Probably at the end of the tenth century, Taoist healers in Szechuan, China, using fire to fight fire, discovered a method to attenuate the smallpox virus in aged and heated pulverized scabs taken from infected children (in hindsight, reducing the number of active viral units).[3] They then introduced the preparation into the body of their patient by blowing a measured portion of the material into the nose. The practice, which induced in most people a mild infection, spread along the caravan and sea routes by Arab and Turkish merchants, and was later modified by applying some of the powder into an open cut in the skin. Variolation reached Europe and the American colonies in the early 1700s.

Such are the empirical beginnings of immunology; the scientific origin was the work of Louis Pasteur after he, Robert Koch, and Joseph Lister had made the germ theory of disease plausible, if not yet acceptable to the medical establishment. In 1880, Pasteur developed a vaccine to a known, microscopically visible infectious agent, the bacterium of fowl cholera. His economically important anthrax vaccine was successfully tested the following year in a bold but shrewd public demonstration. (Technology and scientific ideas must be effectively marketed then and now.) Both vaccines employed living, low virulent strains of bacteria. However, no one had yet determined the mechanisms of disease resolution and immunity within the human or animal body. Pasteur himself only guessed from test tube experiments that the attenuated infectious bacterium depletes an essential nutrient, not knowing that the body replenishes its fluids and tissues. By the end of the century, the protection afforded by preparations of killed typhoid, cholera, and plague bacteria as well as the studies on vaccines to snake toxins blasted apart the nutrient-exhaustion hypothesis.

The origin of immunity as a biological activity rather than as an ill-defined quality of blood is the early research of Elie Metchnikoff, then an invertebrate zoologist and comparative embryologist.[4,5] This Russian, like many other biologists, was well-acquainted with the wandering amoeboid cells in the blood and tissues, which have the capacity to engulf introduced foreign particles, including bacteria. Almost everyone else, however, thought that these cells are either passive transporters of microorganisms or their food. Metchnikoff, who approached the amoeboid cells from the perspective of embryology and evolution, traced their ancestral function to both a possible source of the lower and middle layers of the metazoan embryo and, through intracellular digestion, the organism's means of nutrition. Thus, instead of the cells being food for invading microbes, bacteria are food for the cells. Furthermore, he observed that these eating cells are involved in removing atrophied tissues in embryonic development and in metamorphosis of tadpoles into frogs.

The amoeboid cells, according to Metchnikoff, provide integrity to the developing organism by regulating disharmonious constitutents. Therefore, rather than being a damaging force, inflammation is a healing and uniting process, and rather than a dictate of the organism of the whole, immunity is a fortuitous net activity of quasi-independent amoeboid cells. It was particularly Metchnikoff's picturesque description of combat between fungi and amoeboid white cells in infected water fleas — with a variety of outcomes — that established immunity as a dynamic interactive process. He provided a scientific description of infectious disease and recovery based on the individual abilities or characters of white cells, microbe, and environment, but his theory, which underwent another twenty years of development and modification, was weak in explaining immunity to subsequent attacks and its specificity. What was the source of immunological memory? The major point for us to remember is that Metchnikoff did not designate *phagocytes* (as he called these wandering white cells) as protectors against germs;

instead, they are digestive inflammatory cells directed toward the ideal of organismal harmony and order.[4] Their function was not limited to infectious disease.

The question of immunity to snake and microbial toxins was first tackled in 1886 by Henry Sewall in the United States and in 1890 by Emil von Behring and Shibasaburo Kitasato in Germany. The European workers first attributed immunity to a changed quality of the blood fluid, and showed that the antiserum, when transferred to a susceptible animal, could render that animal immune. Temporarily. Soon researchers in Italy discovered that the responsible immune factors in sera are chemical substances, *antibodies*. Others observed the destruction of certain bacteria in cell-free serum.

A long and often bitter polemic ensued between the French camp of cellular immunologists led by Metchnikoff, who by then had emigrated to Paris to work at the Pasteur Institute, and the Austrio-German humoralists. Metchnikoff soon acknowledged antibodies and their associated blood-borne cofactors, declaring, however, that their origin is lymphoid white cells, probably the phagocytes called macrophages (in opposition to the microphages, known today as neutrophils), and that the phagocytes, at the end, are the necessary eliminators of the microbial menace. The debate then became a matter of emphasis.

The humoral immunologists had no special biological philosophy until Paul Ehrlich, an innovative German laboratory physician, chemotherapist, and father of immunochemistry, described immunity again in terms of nutrition and cells. In 1900 he postulated that antibodies were initially nutrient receptors sticking through cell membranes that when coupled with the food stuff, signal the synthesis of new receptors. Over-compensation, regarded as normal, would then lead to the secretion of excess antibody into the surrounding fluid. Specificity of immunity would be correlated with unique receptors. Borrowing the simile proposed by the chemist Emil Fischer, Ehrlich envisioned the coupling of food/antigen and receptor as a lock-and-key arrangement of atomic groups and recognized that different atomic groups on each substance have their own biochemical roles. Since no one knew the exact structure of any of these chemicals, Ehrlich was far ahead of his time.

Immunology took a philosophical leap from these conceptual derivations of food processing when, during World War II, tissue transplantation was attempted to treat burn patients. Unless taken from the affected individual, the donated skin was incorporated for a while and then shed in an inflammatory reaction. Second attempts failed even more rapidly, but a fresh trial with a different donor endured as long as the very first transplant. There was something unique about an individual's tissue. The rejection of transplants was deemed an immune response. From the flames of war came a radically new concept of immunity: the immune system is the biological basis of individuality.[6-8]

Earlier, Karl Landsteiner in Vienna had discovered blood groups. Blood is a tissue, and transfusion could be described as a liquid form of transplantation. However, there are only four major blood groups, types O, A, B, and AB, and several minor blood groups of clinical significance. Red blood cells, which in humans lack a nucleus, do not reflect individuality as do skin and other organs.

The incompatibility of tissues is observable in invertebrates as well, but rejection is usually between species, not between individuals.[9,10] If two varieties of sponge or hydra are disintegrated through a sieve and mixed, the cells will segregate themselves to reconstitute the differing organisms. Cells from the same species do not show such differentiation. However, if grafts on intact animals are involved, rejection of the tissue from another member of the same species may occur, depending on taxonomic order. In this instance, phagocytosis and, in more complex animals, the induced release from blood of toxic, nonspecific coating agents remove the foreign tissue. This limited inherent immunity is very different from the adaptive form found in vertebrates. Cells from different tissues within the same individual vertebrate, such as kidney, liver, or muscle, when likewise dispersed and intermingled, will organize themselves into their respective types.

Both situations probably involve in part structurally different cell adhesion molecules (CAM). It would be like trying to form a zipper with two rows of teeth differing in size and spacing. There is a further nongenetic consideration: If the mixed cells were of two sponges, hydras, or other invertebrate of the same species that were raised in different surroundings, they would then segregate, indicating that even at this primitive level *environment influences individuality*. In passing, I should also mention that higher plants have nonspecific means for resisting microbial intrusion; these range from sealing off the diseased tissue to releasing inhibitory chemical agents.

The doctrine of immunology today is that it is the science of self-nonself discrimination.[11-13] Aha!, you might exclaim, at last we have found a scientifically precise description of self, of true separateness and distinction. Not quite. This naked philosophical conceit, so atypical in the biological sciences, obligates the wiser immunologist to place quotation marks around the word 'self' when introducing it, for immunological self is not equivalent to the psychological self we love so dearly.

Even with this qualification, I do not accept this sharp-edged and specious definition. Do I then contradict myself after having referred to the rise of individuality? Self and individuality, while allied, are not synonymous. Self is a value-laden term, indicating the separate identity of the individual and the associated subjective experience. However, the choice of words is not the basis of my disapproval. Recasting immunology as the science of individual-nonindividual discrimination is no improvement.

As this book is attempting to convey, *both* self and individuality are elusive and illusive. *The self, the individual is not an object nor a stable state of existence.* Immunologists can refer to unique individual sets of features, but there is no single chemical marker that is equivalent to either self or individuality, as Macfarlane Burnet, the Nobel-distinguished Australian microbiologist and immunological theoretician, and his associate Frank Fenner proposed in the biochemical and genetic innocence of 1949.[14] *Nor can the specific set of biochemical structures by themselves be said to constitute self.*

What today is regarded as immunological 'self', much like the psychological description, is conceptual shorthand, a convenient symbolic transformation of a range of patterns within a vast dynamic process. The distinction is clear, since *immu-*

nological self does not include some tissues that are clearly of the body, such as the cornea, sperm, and brain. Furthermore, *what is considered self may include obvious foreign material,* such as certain bacteria. In addition, the immunological system and operation that deem a certain antigen as *self paradoxically include molecular configurations that mimic nonself or alien antigens.* The biochemical structures of self and nonself are strictly nonsense; however, the gestalts or integrated patterns of those immunological processes that recognize molecular forms do provide uniqueness.

Concretizing phenomena, I admit, is practical in performing experiments and discussing results among initiated members of the scientific profession, but it should not extend beyond laboratory application, certainly not without qualification to the responsibilities of public education and student training. Because of the numerous popular accounts of 'new physics' over the past fifteen years, the public (meaning those people who would read books such as this) has begun to accept the flux and immateriality of matter and its weird quantum behavior. The schism today between the neo-Pythagorean and Heraclitean philosophies of physics and the residual materialism of the biological sciences is more a result of the consensus of stodgy biologists than the contested phenomena. Moreover, so-called self-nonself discrimination, like defense against microbial intrusion, is an ancillary function. Immunology at its core is more than the science of discriminating ghosts and shadows.

Immunobiology was beyond the ken of the Zen monks of ancient China, of course. Although Taoist philosophy influenced Zen and perfused medical practice with the concepts of energy opposites, flow, cycles, and balance and the therapeutic pursuit of harmony, monks themselves were trained to avoid philosophical discourse and speculation. The role of the Zen Master was and remains to help students toward their personal discovery of Tao, of mind, of their face before their parents were born.

(In the following exchange, the reader should know that, despite its metaphysical use as, in part, The Way of Nature, *Tao* simply means way, path, road, or street.) A monk asked Chao-Chou, 'What is Tao?' The Zen Master replied, 'That beyond the fence.' 'No, Master,' said the monk, 'I was not referring to that.' Chao-Chou, knowing that he had hooked a fish, pressed onward: 'What Tao to you mean?' 'The Great Way,' answered the monk. Chao-Chou then responded, 'The Great Way leads to the capital.' If you understand this episode only as a comedy of puns, then Chao-Chou has caught another fish. Perhaps insight into the story can be gained with other examples. Another monk asked Chao-Chou, 'What is Zen?' The Master declared, 'The cypress tree in the courtyard.' Was that any help? Then consider what Chao-Chou's own teacher, Master Nan-Ch'uan, replied when he himself asked about Tao: 'Ordinary mind is Tao.' Nan-Ch'uan was not referring to our normally confused and conditioned consciousness-mind. The Zen Master pointed to the unimpeded activity and intelligence of nature, such as eating when hungry and sleeping when tired, or in the words of a scientist-poet:,

Even more wondrous
among smooth purple and green:
the withered brown blooms!

In order to discuss the developing new immunological principle and the inherent intelligence of gathering intelligence, we first need to know more about the fundamentals of immunological structures and processes. Immunology is still an explosive science, and although the shock wave is slowing and dissipating, researchers are continually making refinements in the scheme, generally describing subsets, subunits, and subfunctions. Every day additional strands and knots are being woven into the network. Like molecular genetics, in which immunogenetics forms a unique case, immunology is an incredibly and increasingly complicated body of knowledge. The immune system, like one of Charles Dickens' novels, is elaborate, interwoven, and replete with numerous quirky characters, mainly peripheral to the plot, yet each important, even essential by contributing to the tone and flavor of the entire work. Immunity is also like a Shakespearean comedy in which at least one female character assumes a guise of the opposite sex to produce a strange informational feedback loop with the hero.

Alas, to demonstrate such sweet intricacies would require a tome far greater than this. I trust that the brief description of major components and pathways will suffice in suggesting the wonder beyond.

Immunity involves complementary stereochemical relationships of atomic groups in molecules, as nearly everything else we have encountered. I mentioned that cell adhesion molecules may have a role in the quasi-immune process by which invertebrates tend to accept cells of their own species while shunning those of other varieties. Gerald Edelman proposed, quite rightly, that the codons for these CAM are the ancestors of a gene superfamily whose many diverse but structurally similar molecules are responsible for antigen recognition, immune regulation, the induction of cellular growth and division, proper nerve function, and developmental anatomy.[15] The common evolutionary principle is the regulation of shape through direct cell-to-cell contact and the communication of soluble chemical agents between distant cells.

This extremely broad spectrum of relationships virtually defines *an inward inspecting sense* that monitors the state of the organism and effectuates and influences its dynamic organization. As in other sensory functions, self-nonself concepts are meaningless. The very moment when you hear a fire engine siren, there is just the siren warble; when you see a red apple, there is but the red orb; and when you taste salt on the tongue, it is only salty. Alastair J. Cunningham, who has taken a systems approach to immunology while maintaining the pretense of self-nonself distinctions, compared the informational processes of the immune system with that of the nervous system, noting their mutual adaptiveness, memory, and tolerance (habituation).[16,17] In 1985, at the close of his career and shortly before his death, Burnet reflected, 'I still prefer to think of immune regulatory processes broadly as complex homeostatic and self-monitoring functions....The immune system exists primarily to maintain the structural and chemical integrity of the body.'[18] But what is the template?

While I am lobbing philosophical stones upon the concept of immunological self, Francisco J. Varela and his associates

SELF VS. NONSELF

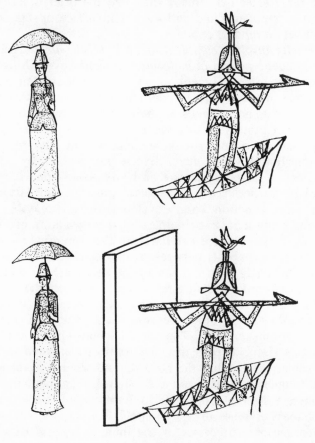

SELF VS. NON-SENSE

THE FURTHER EVOLUTION OF IMMUNOLOGY

in France and Brazil are undermining the façade through the mathematics of their specialty, cognitive system science. They have reached similar conclusions: 'The only valid imunological self is the one defined by the dynamics of the network itself. What does not enter into the cognitive domain is ignored (i.e., it is non-sense)...That which is foreign is only so because it is similar to (or only slightly different from) self.'[19] Such a informational network, which laces every cell, every organ, and every system, is certainly awareness-mind. But it is more so. The net envelops consciousness-mind as well.

It is time we get to specifics, but where is the boundary of the immune system? Immunology of 1885 was the phagocyte. By 1900 it was two types of phagocytes, an assortment of blood-borne antibodies with different functions, and accessory *complement*, which we know now as a cascade of structural and enzymic proteins. In 1970 the immune system also included the nonphagocytic white blood cells called lymphocytes and the lymphoid organs, such as lymph nodes, spleen, and thymus, 'self' markers on tissues, and a small number of mediating immunochemicals. The immunology of 1985 had expanded to natural killer cells, to a great variety of chemical mediators that conjoin the traditionally and falsely delimited immune, hormonal, and nervous systems, and to consciousness-mind. What will be the immunology of 2020? Alan S. Perelson at Los Alamos National Laboratory, who foresees our thorough understanding of all the components of the immune system but general ignorance of higher level algorithmic functions, anticipates the field of computational immunology.[20] The diploma on my wall states that I trained in immunology; I am no longer confident what that science is!

Since, tissue transplantation is an artificial situation, let us begin with the most frequent natural introduction of foreign material, excluding food: the invasion of a bacterium through a break in the skin barrier. Let us further suppose that this microbe is flagellated, has never been encountered before, and is moderately virulent. After the neutrophil phagocytes—the U.S. Marines of the body—enter the tissues from adjacent capillary highways in response to released complement and other alterations of the internal environment, they may effectively retard the advance of the bacterium and further the inflammatory cascade. During the melee, flagella as debris come in contact with *B cell lymphocytes* (so-called because their initial avian source is the bursa; fetal bone-marrow is the equivalent in mammals.). The B cell and its fully developed form, the plasma cell, are distinguished by their ability to produce antibody. Indeed, particular classes of antibody are located on its membrane as signal receptor, as Ehrlich foresaw. Our imaginary flagellar protein passes along the B cells in blood, lymph nodes, and spleen until it binds to one with the correct antibody specificity.

We need to pause for some explanations. What precisely are antibodies? How can there be a B cell with the right specificity when the bacterium was not previously encountered?

Antibodies, the legendary invisible guided missiles of blood, finally were realized in the mid 1960s as a bilaterally symmetrical four-chained protein (two inner long chains and two outer short chains). Its shape is a twisted Y. Each claw, composed of a short and long chain, forms the antigen receptor; the tail has its own binding capacity, but only to certain cells and complement. Antibodies were soon organized into five classes, two of which differ appreciably in configuration. The exceptions are immunoglobulin M (IgM), which is secreted as a star of five Y's with conjoined tail, and IgA, which as perimeter sentry is secreted into the intestine, tears, saliva, milk, and nasal mucous with the aid of a secretory component. The remaining classes include IgE, which is chiefly found attached by its tail to tissue mast cells and blood basophils (the notorious allergy and inflammatory cells that release histamine), IgG, the typical antibody of blood, and IgD, which is mainly the antigen receptor on B cells.

Any given B cell produces antibody of only one specificity, but an individual may include hundreds of millions of different B cells. *The collection is an immense contingency bank too extensive to be encoded by genes alone.* The specificities are generated in immature cells by a combination of genetic endowment, selection from a series of minigenes, mutation, and chance recombination. *The antibody thus is a composite.* Once the dice have been rolled, the cell is commited to antibodies of that specificity, but not of class. The first antibodies to be secreted to antigenic stimulus are IgM, followed by IgG and then others. This sequence may be a phylogenic recapitulation, since the first evolved antibodies were probably similar to IgM, as suggested by the protoantibody in the most rudimentary vertebrate currently existing, the hagfish.

In addition to specificity, *affinity* is a defining attribute of antigenic binding. It is a measure of the strength of fitness. This quality may be visualized as several keys capable of entering a lock *(specificity)* but only one or two sufficiently complementary to turn the tumblers, the one with the strongest affinity being the easiest to turn. In terms of molecular kinetics, the antibody-antigen union with the greatest affinity has the least potential to break apart. Thus, a simple antigen with one combining atomic configuration *(an epitope)*, such as the polymeric protein of our bacterial flagellum, may, nevertheless, unite with more than one clone of B cells. IgM is usually of low affinity, a weakness perhaps offset by the componding strength of its ten-armed arrangement.

Another relationship of variance in complementary coupling is *cross-reactivity*, which refers to a given antibody able to bind to different antigens with similar epitopes. The operation is analogous to a shark attacking a human swimmer whose shape from below resembles a seal, the shark's special meal.

Returning to our B cell, we discover that the signal for antibody production is not given. The signal from membrane receptors of whatever stripe seems to follow a rule of two. At least two receptor molecules need to be spanned or otherwise brought together to induce a change in their cytoplasmic configuration. (Also the first component of the complement cascade needs to bridge the ends of two IgG molecules or one IgM to initiate the complement series.) Soon the linear flagellum swings across to another receptor, and the lymphocyte undergoes activation and replication, and in due course molecules of IgM and then IgG are released in large numbers.

The immunoglobulins reach the site of microbial growth where they combine with the flagella, entangling them and immobilizing the bacteria. Tissue macrophages and blood monocytes, which by now have arrived to engulf the debris of tissues, neutrophils, and bacteria, are potent killers of bacteria. The coating of the bacterial cell wall by a serum complement protein enhances phagocytosis, because macrophages have receptors for this protein. If the macrophage has difficulty engulfing the bacteria, the presence of IgG will help, because macrophages also have receptors for the tail of the immunoglobulin. The coating of microorganisms in order to promote phagocytosis was dubbed 'opsonization' by Sir Almroth Wright, a friend and intellectual sparring partner of George Bernard Shaw; the writer made this process the scientific vehicle in his play *The Doctor's Dilemma:* 'Opsonin is what you butter the disease germs with to make your white blood corpuscles eat them.'21

Let us assume that the microorganisms are eliminated by the altered environment of inflammation and the direct killing by phagocytes. If later the organism is infected again by the bacterium, antibody is already present in blood and lymph, and an expanded and distributed B cell clone awaits in blood, lymph nodes, and other lymphoid tissues. The secondary IgG response will be more rapid and enhanced with antibodies of greater affinity. Of course, there is the small problem of lymphocyte turnover, since B cells in lymphoid organs live only up to a few months and those in blood perish within days. We shall later take up the question of memory.

This path of immunity, considered the norm in 1967, is now known to be one of the exceptions. From our present day perspective it is also the most direct. Immunity is a far more complex phenomenon, whose difficulty challenges even the specialist in the field. Therefore, the following relatively simplified descriptions should be sipped like bitter medicine. After all, when we discuss immunology, we are referring to our very health and well-being.

All biology, as society, is governed by checks and balances. Antibody formation and immune reactivity to most antigens require the cooperation of other types of lymphocytes, all varieties of *T cells* (for thymus-processed). These include the *helper and suppressor,* which regulate antibody production, and the *cytotoxic cell,* which secretes membrane-disrupting proteins against viral infected, cancer, or other aberrant cells. Antigen-presenting cells, such as macrophages, are also involved. These various cells interact through membrane molecules coded by the major histocompatibility complex of genes.24

Histocompatibility molecules are Burnet and Fenner's 'self' markers. Related to CAM and immunoglobulins, they have been organized into two classes. Class I membrane antigens are carried on nearly every adult cell, and are particularly plentiful on lymphocytes and macrophages. Class II antigens are generally confined to the immunological cells.

In the practice of transplantation the antigens differ in their induction of immunological respones. Twins, of course, are perfect matches for transplantation, but nonidentical siblings have an excellent 1:4 chance of tissue matching. Within a relatively homogeneous population, such as the Japanese, the opportunity for compatible tissues is good. Still, the odds are better than 1:20,000 that a suitable match can be found in the heterogeneous population of the United States. Considering the four billion humans dwelling on this planet and the odds for compatible tissues among them, *the concept of immunological individuality based solely on transplantation is faulty.* There is also the matter of hamsters. These animals are special because they carry only one kind of class I antigen, allowing prolonged survival of tissue transplants.[22] Their class II antigens, therefore, become more important in this regard.

The very term *histocompatibility antigen,* biased by medical application, tells us nothing of its natural purpose. Short of a sweeping regard for its assumed role in evolution and protection against microorganisms, the need for such a large variety of molecules is yet unknown. However, certain antigens of the major histocompatibility complex have been associated with predisposition to a variety of disorders, such as juvenile diabetes, rheumatoid arthritis, ankylosing spondylitis, and psoriasis. They also have been linked to individualistic odors and pheromones important in animal mating selection and behavior.[23] Like features of the immune system, receptors of olfactory nerve endings have the ability to distinguish chemicals of different shapes.[25]

Because transplantation is not a natural operation, what is the role of class I histocompatibility molecules? They involve the recognition of altered tissue, be it from normal degeneration, cancer, or viral infection. Either the aberrant cell or a macrophage or other antigen-presenting cell brings together the cancer-specific or viral antigen and the class I protein.

This complex is encompassed by the receptor of the cytotoxic T cell, which then releases its deadly products. Tumor cells are destroyed by lymphocytes, natural killer cells and macrophages armed with antibody.

Thus far, the immune response seems cellular: macrophages, T cells, and B cells engaged in close encounters to release antibodies or cytotoxin. What regulates this apparatus? First, there are the antibodies secreted against a given antigen. In a process of feedback inhibition in antibody excess, their very combining with the epitope blocks further stimulation of the B cell clone; but if the antigen has several epitopes, then other B cells may still be activated.

The second means of regulation is the release of T cell *lymphokines*. The first one discovered inhibits macrophage migration to keep them in the vicinity. Others activate or enhance macrophages and draw them into an inflamed site. *Interferon*, a nonspecific communicative anti-viral protein produced by various tissue cells, has a unique lymphocyte variation. Other immunocyte regulators, called *interleukins*, are secreted by both macrophages and lymphocytes to influence their respective partners of the immune triad. These mediators induce the synthesis of growth factor receptors, the production and removal of histocompatibility antigens, and the switching of classes and types of immunoglobulins, for example, from IgG3 to IgG2a to IgE. Interleukins also can affect other tissues and systems, inducing fever, promoting liver metabolism, aiding the growth of connective tissue, and controlling muscle wasting and bone reabsorption.

A third regulator provides the fine tuning of the immune system and probably its memory. *It is a self-referential system within a system based on the strange loop of an antibody being itself an antigen!*[26] Immunoglobulins consist of constant and variable regions. For instance, all the IgG molecules have common sequences of amino acids describing their class and sequences shared with IgM and other immunoglobulins. The variable region is called an *idiotype*, the molecular configurations or antigens arising from it being *idiotopes*. The more restricted antigen-combining site within the variable region is called a *paratope*. Antibodies to an individual's own immunoglobulins are directed against the idiotopes, including those of the paratope.

What ensues can be readily understood by an Air Force missile strategist or a sculptor casting bronzes; others, however, may need to go slow, mainly because of the unfamiliar terms. The original antigen, say a viral peptide, selects and induces an antibody whose receptor (paratope) is complementary in shape. This antibody induces an anti-antibody (antiparatope), whose own antigen combining site is an *internal image* of the original peptide epitope: 'The enemy of my enemy is my friend.' Such an anti-antibody can block the coupling of the primary antibody and the peptide, damping the immune response. On the other hand, anti-idiotope antibodies, when binding to B cell antigen receptors, can stimulate antibody synthesis. Receptors on helper and suppressor T cells may also be idiotype-specific. As in an insane arms race (a tautology?), anti-anti-idiotopes are also possible; and now it

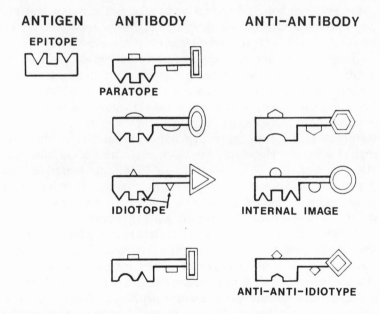

ANTIGEN   ANTIBODY   ANTI-ANTIBODY

EPITOPE

PARATOPE

IDIOTOPE   INTERNAL IMAGE

ANTI-ANTI-IDIOTYPE

IDIOTYPIC NETWORK: Where nonself is self.

it has been reported that, like a puppy chasing its tail, an antibody can have a paratope combining site for its own idiotope![27] The tricksters in this jumbled switchboard are the paratopes that have enzymic and hormonal activities.[28-30] As mentioned, the combining site of the antiparatope-antibody is similar in configuration to our example viral peptide. Such a relationship did not escape the attention of vaccinators. The injection of anti-antibodies, whose antigenic sites mimic a microbial product, could be used instead of the microorganism.[31,32] This tactic would eliminate the hazards of attenuated microbes reverting to virulent forms or of inadequate inactivation in 'killed' microbial vaccines.

The shape of the external being yet the internal is reminiscent of a painting by Paul Klee, entitled *Chosen Site*. He used overlapping geometrics and rectangular towers to suggest a cityscape. In harmony and as counterpoint, a full moon is nearby; however, the oval is itself constructed of the same geometrics and pastels. Do we cast our urban concepts onto the moon, symbolic of primal nature, or is the moon and the city extrapolations of the same form? *In the immune system, antiself is still self, together yielding a sense of itself.*

The father of the amazing and powerful network theory of idiotypes is Niels K. Jerne, a Danish immunologist whose theories have dramatically altered the science.[1] The Nobel Prize is customarily given for a breakthrough or a body of research that significantly expands the scientific frontiers. Rarely does a theory merit this honor, especially in the biological sciences. However, the work of Jerne was so honored. His proposal, formally presented in 1974, was tentative, but it provided a framework for testing, one of the marks of a good theory. That it proved to be correct and even more inclusive than expected makes it a great theory.

Jerne, I should add, was not the first to consider regulatory anti-antibodies; it was Ehrlich 70 years earlier.[2] In writing a research paper, scientists are obligated by convention to include a brief historical introduction to provide the reader with a background of the experimental problem. History to most investigators, it seems, begins about 15 years prior to the experiment. Since history may be conceived as a growing self-resonating helix, what insights could a researcher attain by reading the much earlier and now unfortunately ignored major works of the pioneers, the giants, of the discipline?

In the immunological network, cognition arises from the complementary interactions of the entire system of spatial patterns. As Varela and associates stipulated, when new paratopes of immunoglobulins come into existence, they need to be incorporated into the system by connecting with complementary forms and by boosting through internal images, else be lost or remain immunologically inert.[19] Cross- reactivity of foreign materials and fully integrated antibodies may be the only agency that renders the introduced molecules antigenic, capable of recognition. Since the system from birth is ever changing in the scope of cognition, *immunological self varies each moment,* hardly the secure measure of individuality.

Computer models of the immune network demonstrate that oscillations of variable components may be built into the system and that tiers or subsets of idiotypes serve as buffers against the overall flux. Accordingly, *memory of spatial patterns lies in the levels or depth of the dynamic web* rather than in a particular cell, messenger RNA, or other molecule. Of course, the long lifespan and replication of the cellular and chemical nodes of the web are crucial. Likewise, our mental memories are stored holistically and nonlocally within the relationships of the nervous system, if not the entire organism. Since memories are not things, even immunological memories of molecular shapes, it would be ridiculous to seek them as independent biochemical structures. There have been many ridiculous scientists lost in a haze of reductionism.

The models indicate that the immune system is fundamentally self-referential, which is to say functional without the introduction of outside antigens. If germfree animals, as discussed earlier, are also fed a defined diet of simple chemicals not recognized as antigens, and thus are fairly antigenfree by traditional standards, their immune systems, although somewhat sluggish, are active with the production and circulation of IgM and immunocompetent lymphocytes. *Immunity, hence, is autosensory, the boundary of self expanding with each new encounter of a system-permitted antigen. Nonself antigens are immunologically invisible, and, therefore, the immune system does not differentiate self from nonself.* As an internal image of anti-self immunoglobulins, relative nonself (seen from an outside observer), is self. There is no paradox, but there are logical knots!

With millions of B cell specificities, what prevents the organism from producing antibodies against its own tissues? How are self antigens accepted? These are the questions of *immunological tolerance* or, as Ehrlich first formulated it, *horror autotoxicus*. The reader by now can guess the answer: antibodies are indeed made against constitutive tissues and tolerance is a dynamic balancing act. But in 1971 on the eve of Jerne's network theory, Raphael H. Levey at Harvard Medical School pondered 'the problem of whether or not there now exists or could be formulated a unitary theory or general law which would explain natural tolerance, induced cellular chimerism, low-zone and high-zone paralysis to foreign proteins, the inhibitory effect of antibody on antibody formation, partial tolerance, recovery from unresponsiveness, adaptation, and especially enhancement.'[34]

The last phenomenon refers to the enhanced growth of tumors or prolonged graft survival in animals immunized with tumor or donor antigens. Paralysis is unresponsiveness due to insufficient number of antigenic molecules for recognition or a swamping of the antigen processing cells by a vast surplus of antigen. Cellular chimerism pertains to the sharing of cells by animal embryos having connected circulatory systems, a normal circumstance among fraternal twins of cattle. Such animals as adults will tolerate each other's grafts.

In 1953 the British team of Rupert E. Billingham, Leslie Brent, and Peter Medawar experimentally induced graft tolerance among mice by injecting the foreign tissue into embryos.[1] Burnet considered this in describing his theory of clonal selection of antibody-forming cells, whose specificity was predetermended by random generation: 'Self-not-self recognition means simply that all those clones which would recognize (that is, produce antibody against) a self component have been eliminated in embryonic life. All the rest are retained.'[1] However, Medawar's conclusion that 'the conferment of tolerance is not of an all-or-nothing character' was conveniently discounted or ignored by Burnet.

For decades investigators supposed that the related B cells were eliminated during fetal development. They were wrong. It is the immature T cell in the fetal thymus that is expunged from the repertoire; the B cells are put into limbo.[34] One possibility of how all the myriad self antigens, including those synthesized at different stages of life, are presented to T cells at this time is that within the population of lymphoid cells a small number of molecules of most of the genome products— whether muscle, epithelial, endocrinal, or so on—are randomly expressed.[35] There is some experimental evidence for this. The authors of the idea, Richard Linsk, Max Gottesman, and Benvenuto Pernis at Columbia University, define immunological self as 'what you have a gene for.' Also, some anti-self T cells with low affinity can escape clonal abortion and migrate to other tissues.

Tolerance also seems to be induced by suppressor cells, which may be anti-anti-self. Furthermore, unless the given peptide can associate with the major histocompatibility molecule, it is not recognized. Of course, mechanical exclusion or hiding of an antigen by tissue barriers also renders it nonsense.

In 1971 the suggested mechanisms of tolerance were far more simple, generally based on cross-reactivity of antibody-antigen complexes.[33] However, some researchers had already accepted the unity of tolerance and immunity, seeing it as a delicate dynamic balance. Twenty years later the shift from absolutes and steady states is now nearly complete.

A break in tolerance leads to pathologic autoimmune reactions.[36] When the attacked tissue is the myelin sheath around nerves, multiple sclerosis develops. The target in myasthenia gravis is the cellular receptor for acetylcholine, a neurotransmitter. In systemic lupus erythematosis, DNA, blood vessels, skin, and kidneys are affected. There are many autoimmune diseases. I will not take the time to delve further into this subject, except for noting that cross-reactivity to microbial antigens may effectively alter the balance of the regulatory network. For instance, rheumatic fever, an acute inflammatory disease of heart, joints, and the nervous system, is associated with streptococcal infections. Antibodies to one of the bacterial cell proteins will bind heart tissue. Also, antibodies to the idiotype of antimicrobial antibodies may be cross-reactive to tissues.

Of course, an internal physiological etiology is equally possible, since there is a fair chance for the development of a defect in such a vast network sufficient to overcome fail-safe redundancies. Alan Perelson observed that the dynamic idiotypic informational network provides both immune memory and, being subject to the gain and loss of system altering clones, immune forgetting.[20]

The concept of immunological self is directly confronted in pregnancy.[37] Is there one self or two? A mother and fetus have juxtaposed circulatory systems. They share plasma and an occasional transferred blood cell. IgG crosses over into the placenta, and a newborn child will have its mother's antibodies as a temporary shield as its own immune system matures and expands. Although the fetus carries some of the histocompatibility antigens of its mother, the paternal contribution seemingly would pose a hazard. A fetal cell or soluble antigen, coming in contact with the mother's immune system, would induce antibodies that would attack the developing child. With its immunogenetic differences, similiar to a foreign graft, how does the fetus survive?

The solution to this problem has not yet been achieved. We know that the embryo is surrounded by a protective wall formed by the massive fusion of trophoblastic cells. Because this wall is deficient in class II major histocompatibility antigens, it is immunologically invisible. The placenta, which carries paternal class I molecules, serves as a sponge for corresponding maternal antibodies. Adding to the barrier is an antigen-masking layer of mucoproteins and mucopolysaccharides. Local suppressor T cells and low-dose tolerance help further retard any untoward effect. Oddly, as I shall soon discuss, an immunological response of some order may be necessary.

However, the paternal Rh antigen of fetal blood cells could initiate in the Rh negative mother (usually in the second or third pregnancy) antibodies leading to potentially lethal hemolytic disease of the fetus. To prevent such occurrences, anti-Rh antibodies are injected into the mother within three days of each delivery, beginning with the first.[38] To prevent antibodies, provide antibodies? This seems to be another koan! The reason is that during birth a small amount of the baby's blood can enter the mother's circulation. These prophylactic antibodies, blocking contact of any of the child's red blood cells with the mother's lymphocytes, keep the specific B cell clone unstimulated. A subsequent pregancy would not have the risk of Rh antigen memory and the enhanced immunological response. Of course, the introduced antibodies would be eliminated by then.

Having acquired an excellent understanding of the traditional and modern immune system, we are ready for the avante-garde perspective. Earlier I mentioned interleukins and immunological mediators. Evidence is now substantial that these agents and their receptors are shared with other body systems.[39] The boundaries of the neurological, endocrinological, and immunological systems are crumbling, and a new field appropriately called *neuroendocrinoimmunology* came into being. For a moment. That synthesis was only a short-lived interim stop, for science has at last faced the *placebo effect*, stress, and the role of psychological conditioning be it externally or willfully induced. *Psychoneuroimmunology* (short for the proper but most awkward psychoneuroendocrinoimmunology) is now a recognized specialty.[40,41] But even this label is fast becoming obsolete. Researchers now refer to particular axes of function across tissues, organs, and systems, as a traveler plots a route across the network of highways. The next step is a return to integrated organismic biology. Let us look at the basis for this extraordinary paradigm shift in science.

Macrophage Interleukin-1 acts upon liver, neural, and pituitary cells. The lymphokine inhibits the release of insulin, but aids the secretion of adrenocorticotropic hormone, luteinizing hormone, growth hormone, and thyroid-stimlating hormone.[42] The endocrine-gland secreted glucocorticoid hormones in turn inhibit IL-1 production, forming a feedback loop.[43] Estrogens have been associated with enhancement of antibody production perhaps by suppressing the suppressor T cell, and it seems that the epithelial matrix of the thymus, which itself provides a T cell maturing hormone, thymosin, carries receptors for the sex hormones.[44] In pregnancy, the level of sex hormones increases substantially; concomitantly, the cellular immune responses are depressed, prolonging the survival of grafts and perhaps protecting the fetus. However, this course of activity is also circular, since lymphocytes produce gonadotropins. With respect to the nervous system, macrophages and lymphoctes have receptors for neuropeptides, while these cells also produce neural mediators. Pain-controlling endorphins modulate lymphocytes, yet lymphocytes themselves secrete them.[45] Other neuropeptides regulate mast cells. Furthermore, the thymus, lymph nodes, bone marrow, and spleen are innervated with nerve endings selectively located among the regulating T cells rather than the antibody-forming B cells.[46] T cells were found to secrete a neuronal growth factor, neuroleukin, which also regulates B cell activation.[47]

My presenting this flurry of recently discovered materialistic feedback loops is the cart before the horse. Scientists would not have sought them if clinical and experimental animal studies had not challenged them and if reductionism had not failed to provide a simple answer. These pathfinding investigations have a long history of fits and starts because there was and still remains fear and loathing among biochemists and cell biologists of embracing higher order psychological etiologies. Unless one was a psychologist or a philosopher, research on the mind/brain problem would jeopardize a young scientific career in biology or biophysics. Now, again, psychobiology is a hot field!

In 1891 Metchnikoff presented at the Pasteur Institute and later published a series of lectures on comparative inflammation, which painted the medical science of immunology and the role of phagocytes on the canvas of zoology and evolution. Broad in scope and deep in evidence, the work is a medical milestone. At the end of his last lecture, Metchnikoff offered his insight on the connection of inflammatory, neurological, and noetic systems:[1]

The defense of the organism against deleterious agencies, which is at first confined to the phagocytic mechanisms and the somatic system of nerves, by and by spreads to and is undertaken by the psychial nervous apparatus. With the nervous cells, which direct the contraction and dilation of the vessles, become associated other cells that control thought and voluntary actions.... The application of agents which set up inflammation...is the conscious continuation of the defensive measures which have been unconsciously evolved by the long series of animals in their struggle for existence.

He nor anyone else looked into the network for 30 years. The experimental foundations of psychology and immunology were still shaky. Today on solid ground, Ed Blalock at the University of Alabama observed, 'It's as if the immune system is just a bunch of miniature, floating pituitary glands,' and suggested that the immune system is that sixth sense that informs us when we are undergoing an infection before symptoms appear.[48] Michael Ruff at the National Institutes of Health would agree. Noting that macrophages synthesize neuropeptides, he speculated that the phagocytes may serve as free-moving nerve cells in communication with the brain.[49] The motion was seconded by Hugo Besedovsky at the Swiss Research Institute, who discovered that the activity of neurons is altered during immune responses.[50] Metchnikoff would have been pleased.

It is appropriate that one of Metchnikoff's many students, Serge Metalnikov, was sufficiently alert to Ivan Pavlov's research on the conditioned reflex and sufficiently curious to test the principle on the immune system.[1,51] As reported in his 1926 article, he injected either tapioca, anthrax bacilli, or staphylococcal filtrates into the abdominal cavity of guinea pigs followed by scratching or application of a heated plate to their skin. After a series of such procedures to condition the animals and a period of rest, he stimulated them with the cue. The assay was the number and kinds of white blood cells in their peritoneal cavity before injection, after injection and stimulus, and after stimulus alone. Metalnikov found a similar cellular response to the cue as with the injection of foreign material. He put the conditioned animals to a grave test: they were stimulated and then injected with what should have been a lethal dose of cholera. Indeed, the control, unconditioned animals died. However, the conditioned guinea pigs, having initiated a cellular response prior to the cholera injection, were able to resist the infection.

Metalnikov published his monograph on the role of psychological factors in immunity in 1934 at a time when psychoanalysis and psychotherapy were in full flower. Soon the bloom wilted in inconsistencies and failures and the absence of adequate controls and quantitative assays. Instead, the growing sciences of biochemistry and physiology offered the safety of the tangible, the isolatable, the measurable. Mind studies were too dependent on interpretation and prone to deceit and quackery, but who would dispute charted peaks of globulins upon serum electrophoresis? And so the trees rather than the forest were examined, classified, and used to interpret nature.

In the 1950s came consumer television and the vogue of hypnotism, a linkage if not then, then certainly now. Having been a child of the Golden Age of TV, I recall several programs discussing and showing the powers of hypnosis. A bright light of English immunology, John Humphrey at the Medical Institute of Medical Research, watched similar demostrations and wondered if hypnotic suggestion could alter the immune system. Hypnosis certainly seemed to induce people to do some extraordinary things in social behavior and in muscle control. In a carefully controlled study, Humphrey's research team discovered that *a posthypnotic suggestion could indeed inhibit both the clinical manifestations of immediate allergic reactions and the positive delayed tuberculin reaction in allergic volunteers.*[52] Microscopic histological examination did show that the immune cells had reacted to the antigen; however, the inflammatory fluid swelling was absent.

The United States' own rising star, Robert A. Good, was conducting similar experiments at the same time.[53] He injected both forearms of nonallergic volunteers with serum from a highly allergic donor. In the usual Prausnitz-Kustner test, the challenge of an antigen would react with the passively acquired antibodies and induce an inflammatory response. In Good's trial, before the antigen was inoculated into both forearms, the volunteers were given the hypnotic suggestion that one of the arms would not show the reaction. The result was minimal response in the designated arm and full response in the other.

Soon psychiatrists and immunologists established that *people with multiple personality disorder may present person- ages with differing ability to manifest immune reactions, such as allergy to food or fur.*[54,55] Although this fact reached a mass audience long ago through an old *Perry Mason* television episode, the scientific establishment continued to shy away from probing the association of immunology and conscious- ness-mind. All conclusions of mind/brain explorations must ultimately relate to such cases. These composite people especially urge answers to questions of self and individuality.

Even more exciting is the report of willful, fully conscious modulation of a cutaneous immunological response to a viral antigen.[56] The subject was an experienced meditator, who used Tibetan-style *visualization techniques.* As black-body radiation was the wound in classical physics that would not heal until the development of quantum mechanics, the regula- tory powers of consciousness—mind, as displayed in hypnosis, multiple personality disorder, and meditation, is overthrow- ing dualistic and, especially, strict materialistic paradigms.

Today, immunological conditioning is a well-documented fact. In a procedure much like Metalnikov's, Novera Herbert Spector, leading a team at the University of Alabama, trained mice to respond to the aroma of camphor as cue to enhance the activity of cancer-attacking natural killer cells.[57] Using flashing lights and the noise of loud fans as conditioning clues and egg albumin as immunological sensitizer, Glenda MacQueen's research group at McMaster University in Ontario, Canada, induced rats to release inflammatory media- tors from their mucosal mast cells by audiovisual clues alone.[58] Such activity has inspired people to attempt willful positive conditioning through visualization techniques or self- hypnosis. The court of scientific opinion on their success is still in session. However, sincere belief, when cued by sugar pill placebo or 'faith healer', can boost the immune system.[59] In determining the effectiveness of a therapeutic drug or pre- ventive vaccine in humans, scientists must allow for a placebo effect of up to 30% of subjects cured or protected.

The most powerful stimulus for altering immune responses is stress, the leading dis-ease of our time. As everyone knows, stress comes in many forms. Sudden loss of spouse, home, or job induces physiological havoc. Malnutrition; poverty; crowding and its opposite, isolation; noise; worry; the pressure of final exams or poor work situations; and other agents of emotional investment lay one open to infection, cancer, tension headaches, ulcers, and, at the extreme, the loss of the will to live. 'All existence is dukkha (dissatisfaction/suffering),' said the Buddha. *Psychological depression is materially translated as immunological depression.*

Reflecting on how consciousness-mind alters the human condition, John Milton wrote in *Paradise Lost,* 'The mind is its own place, and in itself can make a Heav'n of Hell, a Hell of Heav'n.' One thousand years earlier in Korea, the monk Won Hyo was trying to cross a desert on his journey to China. At nightfall he reached a site where there were some trees and water and fell asleep. Awaking in thirst in the midnight black of a moonless, overcast sky, he groped along the ground for some water, and was relieved to feel a vessel with liquid. Drinking from it, he found the contents delicious and quenching, and fell asleep contented. When he awoke in the morning, he discovered that his fortuitous cup was a shattered skull, blood-caked and with shreds of flesh, and that the water was foul with insects and soil. As Won Hyo began to vomit in repugnance—ZAP!—he was enlightened.[60]

In a 1983 issue of the journal *Science* a fascinating study by Mark L. Laudenslager and colleagues at the University of Colorado appeared that demonstrated the subtleness of stress-influenced immune responses, as well as the consciousness-mind of rats.[61] The stress was an electric shock. Rats were divided into three groups. One set received a series of escapable shocks that could be terminated by movement of a wheel; the second group had no escape presented to them; the last group, serving as controls, were free of any shock. Testing the ability of T cells to replicate in response to plant mitogens, they found reduced lymphocyte activity only among the rats subjected to inescapable shocks. The wise general who is surrounding an enemy, Sun Tzu tells us in *The Art of War,* should leave a gap to relax their determination to fight.[62] Even the reasonable chance of escape will reduce the stress response.

In this chapter we sought the biological basis of self through immunology, but instead found the encompassing sense of the organism and its afferent and efferent operations through awareness- and consciousness-mind. However, this organism has no set immunological boundary, and its realm, so dependent on space and shape, is itself outside space-time.

Candace Pert, one of the discovers of endorphins and opiate receptors and a leading reseacher in psychoneuroimmunology at the National Institute of Mental Health, recognizes that emotions are not a characteristic of the brain, but are of the entire body.[63,64] There is no nervous system, no endocrine system, no immunological system. Such divisions are obsolete. The macrophage, which is the founding member and core of immunology, has proved to be a jack-of-all-trades, a *de facto* nerve and endocrine cell. The various neuropeptides are the currency of biological regulation between cells; Pert has preliminary evidence that all neuropeptide receptors are the same flexible linear polypeptide molecule differing only in conformation.[64] Although this sounds like biochemical heresy, we should remember that, albeit larger and two-chained, the class II histocompatibility protein can adjust its shape to accommodate a select variety of processed peptides.

Jesse Roth and associates, taking a page from Metchnikoff, examined the evolutionary origins of these neuropeptides and were delighted to find molecules strongly resembling most neuropeptides, including endorphins and insulin, and their receptors in the protozoan *Tetrahymena* and in *E. coli* and other bacteria.[65] Spinach and wheat also have neuropeptide-like molecules. Do these precursors serve similar duty as intercellular regulators? Probably. The researchers further suggested that an immune response to one of these bacterial peptides could cross-react with the host's receptor to thyroid-stimulating hormone and initiate an autoimmune disease.

Plant and animal pheromones in the wind and water and cousin neuropeptide hormones in the fluids of blood and pond unite apparently separated cells and organisms in a telecommunicative system, a cognitive sensory network. Some science fiction stories are based on such a premise. The problem with visionary sci-fi is that reality catches up!

Mind is treated in this book as the process of pattern recognition based upon complementary forms, which includes shapes and actions. Pert, having become incapable of scientifically distinguishing brain and body, is still anchored to these materials and dualism, offering the view of 'mind and consciousness as an emanation of emotional information processing,...independent of brain and body.'[64] We differ in that, for me, processing of information or patterns is itself mind. Awareness-mind and conscious-mind are particular network processes. Body is no different than mind, because atoms, molecules, cells, tissues, and the composite are all such activities. The body is no thing. The body is also inseparable from the environment, which penetrates it as internal images and information. Our sense of self, our knowledge of self, our image of self, which the psychoneuroimmunological network (which is to say, body/mind) helps provide, are illusions, constructions of consciousness-mind.

Ch'eng Kuan (738-839), a master of Hua Yen Buddhism, described phenomena and things as manifestations of mind, adding that nothing has a definite or fixed form or quality, that all are mutually dependent and interpenetrate, and that all are like phantoms and dreams, reflections or images.[66] A visitor to the Exploratorium in San Francisco, a hands-on participatory science museum, can attain some feeling for these interpretations by entering a chamber whose walls are mirrors. The visitor is completely surrounded by reflections, and reflections of reflections, as in the metaphor of Indra's jeweled net. The subject's awareness- and consciousness-mind react to the images, which react immediately (ignoring the speed of light) to the subject and to each other. The sense of spatial boundaries is quickly distorted and lost. Next, ego vanishes concomitant with the mounting joy and absorption in the wonder. The visitor is everywhere and nowhere. Master Fa Tsang (643-717) prepared such a room (adding mirrors to floor and ceiling for full psychedelic effect) to explain Hua Yen for the Empress Wu of the T'ang Dynasty.[66] 'How marvelous!' she cried.

Chapter 11

SINGING THE BODY ELECTRIC

Neuroscience/Consciousness

The following sentence is false.
The preceding sentence is true.
Douglas R. Hofstadter

Dogen (1200-1253), the most philosophic of Japanese Zen masters, wrote in his major treatise, *Shobogenzo* (Treasury of the True Dharma Eye),[1,2]

> To model yourself after the way of the Buddhas is to model yourself after yourself. To model yourself after yourself is to forget your self. To forget your self is to be authenticated by all things. To be authenticated by all things is to effect the molting of body/mind, both yours and others.

With our review of immunology, we have crossed the jagged threshold into psychology and consciousness-mind, a frontier junction where the sciences and humanities have often glared at each other in fascination and anxious respect. At one entrance to the fog-settled labyrinthine forest, the scientist ponders whether within the amorphous shade lies, at last, the limit of the self-assured intellectual and experimental pursuit of truth.[3,4] Nearby, the religious philosopher of transcendence remains certain that the modern institution of science, if not the scientist, indeed can not survive the passage, since the objects of inquiry are but illusive mind-processes. Nevertheless, this cleric-guru wonders whether his own time-honored training programs and supporting organizations leading to the great yogic experience may eventually be replaced by a drug, some laboratory-synthesized indigenous body opiate, consumed under scientifically defined efficacious conditions. Of course, when the scientist and the mystic are the same individual, there is no conflict and nothing to defend. When asked what is Buddha, Master Yun-men (862-949) replied, 'Dried shit-stick [the equivalent of used toilet paper].'

Despite the long history of psychedelics as significant tools in mystic or transpersonal traditions, all religious systems deny that chemicals alone can provide instant beatitude or nirvana.[5] These botanical agents in the best of circumstances allow only a glimpse behind the screen, which is still sufficient to be a salutary experience, particularly after the user has developed a strong philosophical or religious foundation.* For instance, the scholar John Blofeld, who had spent decades traveling in the Far East in study of Taoism, Zen, and Tibetan Buddhism, had his first satori much later, after having experimentally consumed mescaline in Bangkok. His experience was in 1964 just prior to the hysteria of both conservative and young hippie zealots, in the brief era when psychedelics were being investigated firsthand (a time-honored scientific tradition) by psychologists, anthropologists, philosophers, and other intellectual adventurers and malcontents. The orthodox view centers on the difference between knowledge and wisdom.

----

* For there to be drug abuse there must be drug use. These ancient sacred agents should not be confused with the physiologically addictive and lethal numbing drugs, such as the opiates, or the various stimulatory or tranquilizing drugs, all of which are properly and legally restricted to medical and dental applications. It is scientifically, philosophically, and religiously improper to deny legal status to awareness-expanding, psychotherapeutically useful psychedelics. The illogic is even more extreme when we note that nicotine smoke and alcoholic beverages are socially supported.

There are some 20 traditional ritualistic psychedelics. We are most familiar with those derived from mushrooms (psilocybin], from the peyote cactus (mescaline), from the hemp plant (cannabis), and from Amazonian trees of *Virola* species. LSD, which is derived from ergot, a fungus that infects rye, became a modern ritualistic hallucinogen.

Having engaged in introspective meditative explorations with and without the use of psychedelics, I must concur. However, should science—as I hope—be allowed to attempt the improbable enterprise (which means governmental permission through lifting of both legal and funding barriers), any fruits of discovery would again, inanely, be banned as taboo.

The problem lies, in part, with the vested secular and ecclesiastical parties of major social institutions, who fear losing their control over individuals. For instance, on December 14, 1989, the Vatican issued a 25-page document that warned Roman Catholics about engaging in Eastern meditative practices. The authorities worried that Zen Buddhist and Hindu yogic meditation might 'alter fundamental elements of our faith' and might lead to 'psychic disturbances', 'moral deviations', and 'syncretism, the merging of different religious practices.' The reactionaries seemed oblivious to the 'fundamental' experience shared by all religions and to the history of imported customs and practices adopted by Christianity, including the repeated recitation (mantra) of the rosary tracked by a string of beads (mala). In more worldly affairs, the practicing mystic is the joker of the deck, free and impervious to political power games even while participating in the economy.

The forest mystery concerns the relationships and source of self, the identification of consciousness-mind and its delusive separation from univeral mind. We are content with our self-awareness and enjoy being unquestionably distinct individuals. But are we independent individuals? I do not refer to the bond of economics and livelihood or the sometime psychological need for social interactions, including the sharing and feedback of friendship. Nor am I alluding to the profound cultural influences of society on personal cravings, scope of knowledge, and philosophical and religious comforts. Moreover, we all acknowledge that as units within a society—be the organization as large as a nation or as small as an isolated family in some wilderness—individual humans, at least for the first decade of life, are functionally dependent on other humans and are always dependent on other life forms. Although our modern food may sometimes taste like it, we do not eat plastic. The question is whether we are independent

selves, truly separate egos and consciousness-minds. It is consciousness-mind, after all, that allows the identification of *we*.
At this point in our trek we have come to realize how
interconnected every form, every organism is in conventional
material aspects, however ghostly it may be when probed.
Despite the mild uneasiness of suspecting yet another trap, we
are satisfied that in the realm of consciousness-mind our
memories, our learning, our experiences, all that of which we
build our ego must stand in isolation. Interactions with people
may have contributed to the shape of our selves, but we are
confident that no one shares the complex pattern. It is as if
each of us concretizes the myth concerning the birth of
Buddha, who, on leaving the womb, proclaims to the startled
attendants, 'In heaven and on earth I alone am honored.' (But
what *I* is there with that first cry?) One of the significant
experiences of my life was when as a young child I suddenly
realized that other people not only act and speak, but think
and imagine and have their own fears and desires. I had
recognized *self* in others, and felt diminished and separated—
a closed gate, the loss of innocence, the commencement of an
ego fortress. Before sealing the axiom of existential insulation,
we need to discuss the major challenge to our smug complacency: identical twins.

Environmental behaviorists and behavioral geneticists, who
have long disputed the relative roles of upbringing and
heredity in the development of personality and idiosyncracy
of character, have examined twins to help solve the problem.
Such studies have brought new insights; although they have
eliminated the extreme positions, they have also led to far
more perplexing questions. No one faults the assumption that
a supportive home and social environment will help children
develop their personality to its full potential, while depriva-
tion and abuse will retard it. Police records are ample evidence. What is sought are clear scientifically controlled situations where environment is uniform but the children's genetic
endowment differs and, conversely, where there are identical
genes (twins) but differing environments. The first circumstance is provided by fraternal twins whose like age eliminates
environment-altering age-dominance among siblings. The
latter situation is exceptional, since for study purposes

identical twins must have been separated at a young age so as to live in unique settings. Nevertheless, more than 350 pairs of such twins have been located and examined. To appreciate the rarity, consider that in the United States alone twins number some 2.5 million.

Thomas Bouchard, a psychologist at the University of Minnesota, is leading a large team of medical and scientific specialists into the ancient mystery of twins and identity.[6-10] Among the sets of doubles he has encountered are two men born of a Trinidad Jewish father and German Catholic mother. After the children were born in 1933, the mother took one twin back to Germany, where the boy was raised by his grandmother as a Catholic and Nazi; the other child remained with his father and later resided in an Israeli kibbutz. Not surprising, the two families were estranged, and like many twins in the study, they had not seen or communicated with each other until visiting the research center. Such environmental differences in upbringing would be an excellent test for the role of genetics, but the researchers were not prepared for the amazing shared idiosyncracies of these and of other separated twins.

Both men arrived at the airport wearing a two-pocket shirt with epaulets and carrying wire-rimmed glasses. Both had mustaches. After extensive interviews, observation, and standardized medical and psychological examinations (some 15,000 questions) the researchers learned that both twins were fond of spicy foods and sweet liqueurs, flushed the toilet before use, stored rubber bands on the wrist, dipped buttered toast in their coffee, and impishly sneezed among strangers in an elevator.

Another set of twins, separated and adopted as infants in Ohio, chose law enforcement as their career. They had the same pastime of carpentry and mechanical drawing, vacationed in Florida on the same beach (but at different times), drove the same make and color of automobile, named their dogs Toy, married and divorced women named Linda and remarried women named Betty, and named their sons James Allan and James Alan.

A third set of twins, this time women, who until the study never met after their separation during World War II, came to the university wearing seven rings on their fingers and a bracelet on each wrist. The children of one are Richard Andrew and Karen Louise; the children of the other are named Andrew Richard and Catherine Louise.

Despite the astronomical odds, most researchers assign the numerous matches of such personal quirks as statistical coincidence or rationalize them as logical consequences of, for instance, physical appearance. Another explanation is only whispered.[8,11] There are powerful sociological considerations within the conduct of science, and I regard such equivocation as conservatism at its worst and a fearful sign of peer pressure against unorthodoxy. The bugaboo is variously called ESP (extrasensory perception), psi, paranormal, and in Sanskrit (since for some 2,000 years it has been recognized as a by-product of meditative practices) siddhis.[12,13]

In 1969 after a long struggle, the Parapsychological Association was admitted, over protests, into the scientific establishment, the American Association for the Advancement of Science. Nevertheless, the vast majority of scientists refuse to acknowledge the existence of such well-documented, probably related phenomena as telepathy, remote viewing, and precognition, and you will not find such research articles in the AAAS journal.[14,15]

A coincidence involves unrelated events, for instance, the San Francisco Giants winning a baseball game on one's birthday. The sudden remembrance of an old, almost forgotten friend shortly before he telephones is not a coincidence. The standard argument that only the agreements of cue and event are cited over the many unmatched is hollow and hypocritical, because the numerous failed trials in conventional laboratory experiments are not publically presented either. A paper in a research journal reports findings after the experimental conditions have been properly adjusted and in harmony. These optimal requirements are always in reference to the hypothesis being tested; some biological or chemical behaviors will occur only under narrow limits of reagent concentration, temperature, acidity, or other variable. (Even then, researchers do not expect 100% successful results.) So, too, must the far more complex psychological circumstances be correct for permitting cognition of atypically conveyed information.

Actually, once the methods and conditions were discovered, remote viewing and precognition were easily tested and validated.[14],[15] I participated in such experiments as both subject and later tester, and I must admit that they profoundly altered my world view.* However, I am merely suggesting, not claiming, that the reason that both men in the second case of twins mentioned earlier named their dogs Toy is subconsciousness-mind communication through mental resonance, one echoing the other. My only purpose here is to urge a forthright appreciation and testing of such intertwin powers.

Twins living together or remaining in frequent contact do aver such communication.[8],[11] They separately may choose the same birthday card and gift or select the same clothing. Twins may successfully signal each other from afar, and often know what the other is thinking. They may also feel each other's sudden physical pain or anguish. However, such empathic resonance is not restricted to twins; married couples, close siblings, devoted friends or, in respect to a patient, a similarly caring psychoanalyst may likewise from afar sense distress in the other. If science were to conclude that genetics is the fundamental explanation, I would not disagree, but just as such proponents would state that higher order genetic expression predisposes twins to a given behavior, I would still give credence to predisposed direct communication. Because of their genetic compatibility, twins meet a basic parapsychological gestaltic prerequisite, a resonance. While not necessarily a correlation, one of the Minnesota investigators confirmed that within normal variation the electroencephalographic (ECG) patterns of brain waves of twins are much alike.[6],[10] I shall return to this subject.

Less controversial are the similarities of physical and medical condition, which are strong indicators of gene-derived behavior.[8],[9] The mentioned second set of twins chew their fingernails, have hemorrhoids, and manifest identical blood

---

* As I sat remembering these studies, the apt 1960s expression, 'blew my mind', popped up. The comical image is much older. Inside a major Korean Buddhist temple (Hae In Sah) is a picture of a monk in walking meditation whose head has literally exploded as the fountain gush of a volcanic eruption!

pressure, pulse, sleep patterns, and headache syndrome. Other separated twins share phobias and the compulsive behavior of counting objects—dispelling Freudian explanations—and have nearly identical styles of handwriting. Twins have the same distortions of vision, whether they wear glasses or not. Also IQ of twins are similar. At the Gregor Mendel Institute in Rome, Luigi Gedda observed that twins will suffer the same noninfectious illness about the same time and that female twins often menstruate simultaneously. The biological clocks of twins are generally synchronous. Other studies have shown concordance of walk, speech, mannerisms, electrocardiograms, arteriosclerosis, lumbago, irregular menstruation, and miscarriages.

While the mutual occurrence of hives, eczema, and hay fever suggest a similar immune system, it may be limited to IgE responses; too much somatic mutation occurs to permit complete identity. However, no one has carefully sought immunological distinction among twins by, for instance, investigating their capacity to react against a battery of chemically defined antigens. However, differences in the inward-looking immunological sense, as any variation in hearing or smelling, would not induce feelings of ego separateness.

From the twin studies of Bouchard and others around the world, we have learned that the genetic influence apparently includes the traits of leadership, social and political attitudes, vulnerability to alienation, phobias, depression, alcoholism, and shyness. Some of the medical conditions have been linked to specific biochemical imbalances, confirming their genetic origin, while the social environment has a stronger correlate in the aggression, achievement, and orderliness of the individual. On the other hand, success is due to geduld, geschick, geld, und glück—patience, talent, money, and luck—according to the successful medical scientist Paul Ehrlich.

Identical twins, of course, are not truly identical. We have seen how mutation, chance recombination, and alterable somatic expression arise to differentiate units of a genetic clone. Therefore, twins have slightly different fingerprints, patterns of small skin growths, blood chemistries, heights, weights, presumably immunoglobulin specificities, and similar measurements. Nevertheless, these minor distinctions, which among nontwins contribute little if any to self-identification, do not alter the strong force of mutual identity in young twins. Individuality needs to be encouraged by parents or by the twins themselves.[11] Twins may attempt to accentuate psychological differences, one becoming somewhat more aggressive, independent, or extroverted, the other a little more passive, dependent, or introverted. Eventually, as they become adults with their own jobs, environments, and experiences, individuality is less forced. It comes of itself. Although overlapping, learning, conditioning, and memories (the references of ego) become unique but not entirely independent.

A psychiatrist interested in the nature of self-identity described some of his most disturbed patients as 'profoundly torn between an overwhelming yearning to return to a symbiotic state of existence and an equally compelling urge to assert their separateness as individuals....Symbiosis implied to them a ceasing to be, a dissolution of their reality as persons. Individual separateness, on the other hand, doomed them to total isolation, as if they were suspended in the void.'[16] Twins chronically face this dilemma.[11] However, any pathology would be in their extreme behavior, because, as described by Einstein, these insatiable tugs are part of the human condition: 'The individual feels the futility of human desires and aims and the sublimity and marvelous order which reveal themselves both in nature and in the world of thought. Individual existence impresses him as sort of prison and he wants to experience the universe as a single significant whole.'[17]

Mystics confronting the simultaneous realities of cosmic unity and separate ego, sometimes show the trauma and mental anguish seen in the patients.[18] Mahayana Buddhist training not only propels the student into realizing through experience the interpenetrating ego domains, but as an ancient system of psychotherapy, cuts the student's attachments to either extreme and transforms any conflicts into play and zestful sport. Hindus and Buddhists describe the common world as *maya*, meaning creative self-imposed illusion; the Latin root of illusion means to play.

As each twin acquires different experiences and knowledge, developing a sense of self, the brain likewise and simultaneously becomes unique. If you believe that the brain is hard-wired as some personal computer and that the unique information is equivalent to software, you are mistaken. As will be described, *nerve cells and their connections are structurally and biochemically altered on organismal learning.* Processes of consciousness-mind are converted into new patterns of the biophysicochemical structures of awareness-mind. Psychokinesis is not always a dubious paranormal power; here it is intrinsic to the mental development of the individual!

This operative linkage, as Hofstadter informed us, is also a bizarre strange loop worthy of the sportive surrealists, M.C. Escher and Rene Magritte.[19] I particularly refer to Escher's sly drawing of two hands emerging out of a flat blank paper by drawing each other, a variation of lifting oneself up by the bootstraps. Creative activity is like that. *Patterns grow out of emptiness, influencing each other to differentiate further from mythic Chaos while remaining rooted to it as fingers to a hand*

It is time we explore some outer meadows of the neuro-psychological woods, leaving the interior mists for the next generations. Human individual identity is an organismal psychoneuroimmunological property, not exclusively a brain function. Thus, when people debate the brain/mind question, whatever their position, they have already lost. However, the cortex of the brain is the major site of consciousness-mind processing. Be careful; I did not say that consciousness-mind is located here. Before we become acquainted with a few features of this region, a basic description of the lower order material components and activities is first required.

We begin with the textbook average nerve cell. Because no other cell resembles it in form or function, it is instantly recognizable. Here certainly, unlike the individual motile macrophage or an artifically isolated liver cell, no neuron can act alone. It exists solely as part of a network. The cell's main features are multibranched rootlike structures called *dendrites*, numbering up to 1,000 filamentous ends, the nearby pyrimidal or spherical cell body of nucleus and mitochondria, and a long (up to a meter!) sliver slim, 10-20 micrometer diameter tubular stem called the *axon*, which terminates in a large number of button-tipped branches, the neural flowers.[20] Because neurons have the largest ratio of surface area to cell mass and also ex-

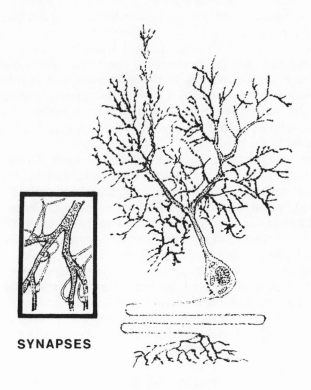

SYNAPSES

NO NEURON IS AN ISLAND OF ITSELF.

tend over greater stretches of territory, they have excellent environmental sensitivity.

The axon stem usually wears a jacket, either a simple covering or multiple layers of the myelin sheath formed by the spirally rolled membrane of *Schwann cells.* An enveloping membrane suggests that these cells may be another instance of Metchnikoff's hypothesis of immunological modification, especially since on artifical culture the Schwann cells transform into phagocytes. Surrounding cells physically support, protect, insulate, and feed the nerve cell. Adjacent Schwann cells, which fuse through pores in juxtaposed membranes to form a supercell are also semi-conductors responsible for a slow wave, low potential direct electrical current and thereby a magnetic field.[21] This extraneural bioelectromagnetic network regulates the electrochemical function of nerve cells and may have additional roles in the generation and processes of consciousness-mind. When a neuron is quiescent, these surrounding connective cells remain active. Another type of neural support is the *glial cell*, which fills the interneural spaces of brain tissue.

Just what does a nerve cell do? Nothing much. The minimal neurological activity requires at least two neurons. An axon terminal conveys an impulse to a dendrite or sometimes to the cell body of an adjacent cell across a exceedingly narrow gap called a *synaptic cleft*. Synapse means 'touching together'. This term seems contradictory, since the membranes do not actually touch; however, the space is spanned by biochemical transmitters and an electrical field. A neuron may connect with 10,000 other neurons, and the brain may consist of 10^{14} synapses. Let me emphasize that: 100,000,000,000,000 synapses! Interaxon and interdendrite synapses also occur. Such a defyingly intricate network provides us with our unique processes of analogical, nonlinear thinking.

Electromagnetic forces, which define the cosmos and organize the behavior of chemicals, are no more conspicuous in biology than it is in the nervous system. In its resting state, the neural membrane is charged -70 millivolts to its exterior.[20] The electrical potential arises from the selective membrane transport of potassium ions into the cell and the removal of sodium ions. For every three sodium ions expelled, the membrane ion pump pulls in two potassium ions. Also within the membrane are proteins that serve as selective potassium and sodium channels. Normally, these ion gates are closed. If at one site on the membrane the potential is reduced to about -50 millivolts, the sodium channel temporarily opens by the realignment of the proteins in the altered electric field, allowing ions to pass unrestricted toward concentration equilibrium. The membrane potential then reaches about +50 millivolts. After the gate shuts, the potassium channel is activated, again reversing the charge.

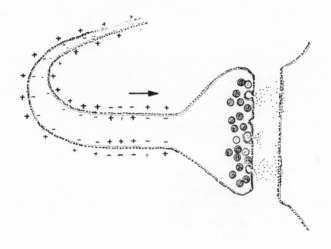

THE CAPACITOR OF CONSCIOUSNESS-MIND:
A Psychoquantum trigger?

This dynamic homeostatic pulse takes place in about a millisecond, a snail's pace compared to the cheetah-swift electronic computer. The immediate effect of the local reversals in polarity is to influence adjacent membrane sites to undergo the same process. A spreading wave ensues. Thus a signal may be transmitted along the length of the axon to the presynaptic terminals. Because the membrane is exposed to the exterior ionic environment only at the junction of Schwann cells (they are still connected internally at common pores), myelinated nerve fibers conduct impules faster than unmyelinated neurons, which comprise the bulk of brain cells.

What happens at the synaptic cleft? How is the signal transferred to the next neuron? Along the axon membrane are myriad membraneous vesicles containing some 10,000 molecules of a neurotransmitter (usually acetylcholine at neuromuscular junctions, but one of a variety in the brain). These globules are attracted to the altered cellular membrane and fuse with it, creating an invagination whereby the molecules are suddenly externalized. At the opposite side of the cleft on a dendrite or the cell body are specific protein receptors, which are also ion gates. When at least two molecules of diffusing acetylcholine combine with the receptor, the gate is mechanically open for a sufficient duration to permit an influx of potassium and sodium ions that neutralize the membrane potential. Acetylcholine rapidly dissociates and is removed enzymically from the channel. An impulse thus is generated along the recipient neuron. *However, the signal varies according to the nature of the synapse.* Some neurotransmitter receptors are selective for the passage of positive ions, inducing excitatory potentials; some select for the removal of potassium ions, damping the voltage impulse. The neuron receiving mixed signals for inhibition and transmission spatially and temporally (cumulatively) weighs them for a net response. This integration determines the frequency of 'firing' that transmits the impulse to the next neurons in series. To complicate the picture, dendrites in the brain often link with other dendrites, some of which form a feedback loop by connecting with the first neuron.

Not only is the cognitive nerve network temporally responsive, dependent on *frequency modulation* of neuronal firing and impulse transmission, some forms of learning apparently involve *amplitude modulation.* (These are the characteristics of radio, a device which, as will be discussed below, is serving as a metaphysical metaphor in noetic studies.) Wave propagation also occurs in certain cultured paraneural cells, which may be responsible for long-range signaling.[22] Nerve cells can be conditioned for enhanced and moderately persistent efficiency, strengthening the intensity of firing; here, reinforcement is due to to the feedback of nitric oxide released by the impluse receiving cell.[23]

The increased concentration of calcium ions in neurons has been correlated with the effect, but too much ion is hazardous. Calcium metabolism alters in aging, increasing the ion in nerve cells to possibly toxic levels. A happy side-effect was discovered to a drug used to treat the elderly with cerebrovascular disorders: improved learning.[24] Nimodipine blocks calcium channels in the nerve membrane, decreasing the concentration of calcium in the cell. Optimal physiological performance is like walking a mile-long tightrope.

However complex neurophysiology and neuroanatomy may be, these fields are simple and approachable compared with higher orders of the nervous system. The 100 trillion synapses that form the direct neural circuitry combined with the neuropeptide mediators that are synthesized by immunological cells added to the electromagnetic influences of the Schwann and glial cells equals a staggering yet incomprehensible network. This vast, intricate system allows you to read and understand these words, form an opinion, and induce an emotion. Science in the 1970s was a blossoming of immunology and ecology, and in the 1980s it was an explosion of genetic and biological engineering; the 1990s will bring a tidal wave of psychoneuroscience. Researchers are gearing up for a combined multidisciplinary crusade to make sense of the senses, to think about thinking, to investigate the investigator. Will we be successful like Escher's graphic hands, which drew themselves? Will consciousness-mind truly be able to explain itself? Ha! But we will gain a wealth of knowledge and perhaps some wisdom about what we are and how we act.

The Chinese, who knew about the circulation of blood some years before William Harvey, also had an even earlier appreciation of viscerocutaneous reflexes, referred pain, and nerve-like circuits: the acupuncture meridians.[25] Many acupuncture points, empirically determined two thousand years ago, have been found physiologically significant by their influence of the psychoneuroimmunological network. Remarkably, these cutaneous foci are conductors of current that flow into the central nervous system.[21] The strength of the current undergoes 15-minute cycles. In addition, the electric field surrounding each acupuncture point has a characteristic shape.

Nerve is represented in Chinese by a two character phrase. The first is composed of two radicals, meaning *to show, make known, set forth, explain, and extend.* The entire character indicates divine, miraculous, wonderful, mysterious, and mystical; appearance and expression; and mind. The second character is a complex, which refers to regulation and management by internal body channels. The nervous system is thus a marvelous manager of mind expression.

NERVE

For instance, to the delight of scientists, much of the developing brain—other than that controlling life-support systems—actually is an omnipotent tabula rasa. The patterns of experiences do select or 'impress' neural pathways sometimes at the expense of others. We all know that an infant makes an amazing variety of sounds. Born with the potential to speak any language, a child learns the sounds of the indigenous culture while losing sensitivity to others. Experimentally, researchers have concentrated on the more accessible visual pathway to examine microscopically the plasticity of nerve nets and the role of degeneration. The cat is used in experiments because its binocular vision resembles that of humans.

Photons focused on the retina stimulate light-sensitive cells. The image is split in two. The activities from the left side of both eyes are relaid to the left hemisphere of the brain; those of the right are passed to the right hemisphere. Anatomically the connection is more complicated. Retinal neurons bundle into a cable called the optic nerve, which is divided into left and right clusters corresponding to the left and right side of the retina. The left cluster from the left eye and the right group from the right eye crossover at the optic chiasm, each joining with its counterpart of the opposite eye to enter a hemisphere of the brain at a well-defined area in the thalamus under the cerebral cortex. However, the nerve pathways from each matched retinal cluster remain segregated in alternating bands that lead to the primary visual cortex at the back of the brain. The signals later move to other areas of the cortex where they are integrated and processed for what we call sight. Since peripheral impulses may come from one eye only, binocular depth perception arises, in part, from the different angles by which reflected light reaches each retina and from the stimulation of matched retinal sectors.

Newborn kittens have neurons that respond to impulses from both eyes. In one experiemnt, when these animals had one eye sutured shut for several months, there was a loss of large numbers of the neurons in the cortex that would otherwise become dedicated to process the impulses from the closed eye.[26] Neural bands stimulated by the active eye expanded into the vacated space. When the sutures were later removed, vision remained monocular. Although retinal and optic nerves of the formerly closed eye still responded to photo stimulation, the eye was perceptively blind. If suturing is delayed for several months, the visual cortex is sufficiently developed to maintain binocular vision during closure. Furthermore, if kittens were born and reared in darkness, the critical developmental period could be delayed for years; subsequent exposure to light would commence the *experience-dependent* wiring process. Even several hours of light exposure followed by a return to darkness would be sufficient to initiate the operation, suggesting a biochemical mediator.

Similarly, humans who were born blind but later had their sight restored are for many months unable to perceive and distinguish visual patterns. Psychologists describe this incapacity to a lack of visual memory for comparisons and subsequent interpretations; neuroscientists reduce it to undeveloped nerve circuitry. A mathematical model based on the competition of stimulatory patterns from the two eyes has been developed to demonstrate the production of alternating occular columns.[27]

These studies showed that constructive neural wiring occurs in the young mammal. Regressive processes are also normal during the development of the nervous system.[28] This activity is a biological editing, for those extensions and connections of some 10^{12} nerve cells that are misdirected, undirected, provisional, or redundant are eliminated. Such fine tuning is no small matter. In some regions, up to 75% of neural cells die and are removed.

There is probably no single guidance system for embryonic and neonatal neural growth, and no one has been able to explain fully how any extending nerve finds its appropriate target and establish synapses.[29] If you have ever observed a pea tendril elongating and gyrating in search of a support, then you may have an appreciation of the problem.

A scaffolding of CAM or other adhesive molecules on glial cells lends support but offers little clue for direction. However, the lack of a suitable matrix or the presence of inhibitory molecules will passively direct the axon tip elsewhere. If trailblazing neurons have already moved into an area, secondary axons can bundle with the pioneer axons.

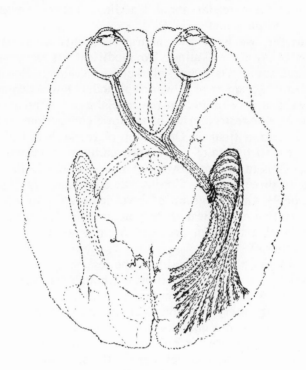

THE VISUAL PATHWAY

Chemotaxis to and away from diffusible molecules is another consideration. Most scientists who take things apart to see how they work forget that the organism itself regulates. As Jane Dodd, a neurophysiologist at Columbia University has pointed out, 'Current approaches to defining adhesion and recognition molecules are heavily reliant on in vitro assays, and in few cases is there clear evidence that these molecules operate in the same way in vivo.'[29] Virtually ignored by molecular neuroscientists is the larger scale influence of site-specific electromagnetic fields.[21] However, electrical waves of synchronously firing retinal ganglion cells may guide neural connections long before photoreceptor maturity.[30] I should also remind the reader about Waddington's and Sheldrake's ideas of morphogenetic fields.

Thus far, we have seen neural flexibility as a maturing process of awareness-mind. Do modifications occur in the cognizant adult? Data are yet sketchy, although researchers confidently accept it as a working model. Early demonstrations were largely limited to the special cases of regeneration after injury or restructuring of synaptic connections to transplanted nervous tissue.[31] One group of researchers has monitored the distribution of presynaptic endings on normal mouse ganglial cells (a micro network of neurons outside the brain) for up to three weeks, finding a continual but gradual alteration.[32] Another group of investigators found a massive reorganization of cortical sensory neurons in macaques whose nerves leading from an arm had been severed some twelve years earlier.[33]

Considering the complexity of the research target, psychoneuroscience is still very crude. Although we know much about our psychological framework, as indicated by the vast, well-ordered purely psychological literature of the East and West, and despite our good knowledge of neurophysiology, the union of the sciences is still in its infancy. As the interdisciplinary science matures, it will need to develop a common jargon, for psychological structures may or may not have correlative counterparts in material systems.

Let us look at an example of this necessary fusion. What are the neurological foundations of optical illusions, such as illusory contours, the perception of bright geometrics with well-defined edges that are not actually drawn? *The illusion depends on the entire configuration of the inducing diagram.* In studies involving monkeys as subjects, neurons of the visual cortex were stimulated by the illusory contrasts even if the retinal focus was not on the apparent contour.[34,35] *The entire retinal image is coordinated and analyzed (or misanalyzed) as a synergistic activity of consciousness-mind.* It would not be such a far leap from this example to discover that the whole perceived universe is another sort of optical illusion, particularly when regarded from transcendence.

ILLUSIONS OF CONSCIOUSNESS—MIND:
A. OPTICAL. The bright contours are not perceived.
B. CONCEPTUAL. This is not a pipe.

Similarly, the expression 'focusing attention' has a psycho-physiological basis.[36] Have you ever noticed that when you concentrate on a narrow area of a visual field, a tunneling occurs? The peripheral objects blur, darken, and fade while the attended zone brightens. After visual impulses pass the striated zone, they are directed to the temporal cortex, where object color, orientation, texture, and shape are separately regarded, and to the posterior parietal cortex, which involves spatial attention and perception and visuomuscular coordination. Although target objects in the visual field induce an enhanced neural response in the parietal cortex, *consciously* ignored objects stimulate poorly, if at all, the corresponding neurons. Meanwhile, impulses in the temporal cortex lead onward to brain areas where the shrinking of the receptive field occurs. There the strength and frequency of discharge increase in nerve cells corresponding to attended stimuli. Selectivity and sharpening gradually intensify with the degree of attention.

We find similar powers with other senses. Our friend Basho demonstrated the spotlight effect in a haiku:

Quietly, quietly,
Yellow mountain roses fall—
Roar of rapids.

Concentration can lead to absorption, as in another of his vignettes:

The crisp sound
Reaches the Big Dipper:
Someone pounding cloth.

Because of such holistic phenomena, we must be cautious in evaluating data acquired from people who suffered brain injury or were neurosurgically altered. Clutching this warning, let us now examine what occurred in 1953 to a man whose hippocampus and structures of the medial temperal lobes were removed in an attempt to treat his severe epilepsy.[37-39]
The surgery helped control the violent seizures, but it destroyed his ability to form long-term memories. His memories prior to the operation remains intact, but every moment thereafter is viewed afresh. Living moment-to-moment unfettered by worries of the past or projections of the future may sound like good advice, but this poor gentleman is obliged to carry it to the extreme. If he reads a newspaper article, minutes later he not only remembers nothing about it, he does not even recall having looked at it. He could meet a person every day for a week, but the next day fail to recognize the visitor. Because experience is both teacher and guide, the inability to learn has arrested his mental development. *Thus, through his experiences, we linked the processing of long-term memory, so crucial to self-distinction, with particular areas of the brain: the hippocampus, amygdala, and adjacent tissues.*
Bilateral symmetry is the uniform characteristic of vertebrates, and while it may not extend to all the digestive organs, this arrangement includes the brain. However, the hemispheres are united at the forebrain commissures. That the left-brain and right-brain have specific functions has become popular knowledge, although they are no longer as clean edged as reported initially. This funtional separation contrasts with the redundancies of kidney, ovary, and hand. The left hemi-

sphere is said to be linearly logical, intellectual, and responsible for syntax in language, music, mathematics, and in other symbolic operations. The right brain appears to dominate analogical, pattern cognitive, poetic, artistic, and similar creative processes. In early studies of left brain injury of patients (many a result of war, some of stroke) most psychologists concluded the right side was mute and symbolically blind, and thus gave the left hemisphere the kingdom of higher level consciousness-mind. Roger Sperry, professor in psychobiology at California Institute of Technology, recognized the flaw in their assumptions; these previous examinations were lacking holistic appreciation.[40]

What these investigators were dealing with was a defective unit brain, and left or right hemisphere activities could not be isolated from their relationship to the entire brain. A faulty preamplifier may block the function of a stereo, but if the defective semi-independent component were by-passed, then a listener could still enjoy the equipment, although its performance would be somewhat diminished. Likewise, if the hemispheres were surgically split, then instead of one defective brain, there would be two brain units; the healthy left unit, no longer chained to the injured right, would thereby be free to be analyzed for its intrinsic attributes.

Again, epileptics provided new insights. Severe epilepsy has been successfully treated by severing the connections between the two hemispheres. Although left and right brain regions can no longer communicate directly, these patients experience no untoward effect, and unless they are observed for a long duration, no one can detect anything unusual.

Experimentally, monkeys and cats have been valuable subjects for split-brain studies, but these investigations are limited by their being unable to provide information on symbolic language, arts, and other uniquely human traits.[41] The visual pathway is the major testing system for both human and beast, for objects presented to one side of the retina are recognized by only one hemisphere. Other tests designed for patients involve the tactile sense of either hand, whose neurons lead to opposite hemispheres. Soon, researchers established that the right brain, while unable to speak or write, can at moderate proficiency read and comprehend spoken words.

The implications are profound. *Each hemisphere appears to have its own perception, memory, and learning, its own associations, images, and ideas.* It is as if every individual consisted of two personas, a mathematician and an artist of Abstract Expressionism, who regarded each event and object in different ways. The polarities—on the right—of analysis and symbolic pattern recognition and—on the left—of synthesis and spatial pattern recognition along with intercommunicative channels or functional interpenetrations make the brain a living Taoist yin-yang symbol!

Despite their split brain, patients experience unity. Sperry discovered that each of the separated right and left hemispheres has an ego sense. Although they recognize name and photographic image of the individual, of kin, and of possessions, I wonder if it is precisely the same ego. The situation goes beyond that of identical twins because of the different attributes. However, Sperry and others also speculated that information in the right half leaks through the undivided brain stem in the form of emotional clues sufficient for the left brain to make inferences and seek causal relationships. Ego, of course, is the ultimate possession and therefore is anchored by the greatest emotional investment.

The distinct complementary features of the hemispheres have provided the impetus to organize the brain as a coordinated interactive collection of functional modules.[42] This arrangement is much like the breakdown of visual physical information into color, shape, position, and motion for separate but later integrated processing. It includes the abstract language components of semantics, grammar, association, and comprehension, the left hemisphere serving as senior interpreter.

In one related experiment, researchers simultaneously flashed a picture of a chicken claw to the left brain of a patient and a picture of a snowy landscape to the right hemisphere. The volunteer was then presented with a variety of images in full view, which included drawings of a chicken and a shovel, and asked to select those associated with the first pictures. After choosing the chicken with the right hand (via the left hemisphere) and the shovel with the left, he was asked why. Recalling that only the left brain can speak or write, the patient replied was, 'The chicken claw goes with the chicken, and you need a shovel to clean out the chicken shed.'

When one uses the 'mind's eye' to visualize a form, such as a letter of the alphabet, the entire image does not appear at exactly the same moment. Instead, the sequential process occurs in about a tenth of a second, depending on complexity. When retrieved from memory, the appearance of the letter duplicates the hands-on way in which it is drawn, line by line.[43]* How the brain achieves this assembly is unknown. Not only are we ignorant of where memory is located, we have not yet fathomed its form and arrangement. Are parts in or only processed at one location, and are the rules of spatial (or temporal) relationships in or only accessed at another? While both sides of the brain share the same abilities (there being no all-or-nothing effects) and both are involved in imagery, they do differ by functional dominance. Again, the left hemisphere seems to be the major contractor responsible for the correct arrangement of the parts *(categorical memory)* that are brought forward chiefly by the right hemisphere *(coordinate memory)*.

Further evidence of modular processing, the functional division of feature detection and pattern recognition, has come from positron emission tomography, the PET scan. This instrument, which inspects a focal plane of the brain, detects, through radioactive tracers, especially active metabolic centers and the changes in cerebral blood flow during particular cognitive operations. The relationship arises from the requirement of activated nerves for more blood-borne nutrients and the response of regulatory neuromuscular cells around nearby capillaries.

Michael I. Posner and associates at Washington University in St. Louis followed the blood patterns of volunteers while

---

*Reading may likewise retrace writing steps. Acquisition from storage or external stimuli may require active personal repetition, as when we silently and immediately echo the words somewone speaks to us. Watch the lips of listeners. Also note the synchronous 'dance' between listener and speaker.[44]

they silently read words, vocalized words, and concentrated on word associations.[37,45] All detected brain activity associated with visually attended words took place in the lower, rear (occipital) lobes as far foward as the temporal boundary; auditory words activated other areas, particularly the left middle brain region. A third area (the left prefrontal cortex) was activated by both visual and auditory stimuli, indicating a general language processing center.

I have often referred to consciousness-mind, but this is a general category. Several levels may be described, not all of which are recognized by Western psychologists: transcendent consciousness; the fully attentive, single-pointed consciousness by which associative thinking and self do not occur; linear-thinking, ego-enforcing consciousness; the various levels of subconsciousness, as in linear-processing hypnosis and analogical, parallel-processing dreaming; and the unconsciousness of unattended perceptions and processes of information retrieval not yet brought to attention. John F. Kihlstrom, a psychologist at the University of Arizona, also describes nonconsciousness, which agreeably includes unaccessed long-term memories but also operative features that I consider awareness-mind, their being primarily neurophysiological.[46] The term *a-consciousness,* meaning toward consciousness, is probably more appropriate, the prefix *non* being too broad. He also notes the favorable revision of short-term or primary memory as working memory, which seems correct since retrieved long-term memories need a structure for utilization. The working memory is also the potter's table for dreams.

Of course, *all major levels are engaged simultaneously,* allowing us to converse while subconsciously a-thinking of the 'right word', consciously remembering a 10-year-old event, and unconsciously keeping track of time through the biological clock, located conveniently in the hypothalamus. Furthermore, *the levels interpenetrate.* One dramatic example, mentioned in Chapter 7, is lucid dreaming, our ability to be a conscious critic, director and editor of our own dreams while asleep.[47] Meditation is another instance of bringing higher levels of attentive consciousness into certain areas of subconscious-mind.

This sort of abstraction is a good indicator of our sorry state. These mechanical interpretations are much ado about no-thing. Arguments have raged on such empty structures, winning and losing careers. The countless psychological experiments and clinical studies do indeed point to certain mental activities and organizations, or their shadows, but they distill down to guesswork. Until the neuroscientists and cognitive systems analysts can provide more than imaginative maps of the mind, we should neither be a firm believer nor a zealous skeptic. Instead, we may want to consider accepting such classifications lightheartedly and artistically, for are they not blocks of clay to fashion and reshape, perhaps to dispose of, perhaps one day to display? But likewise, we should remain cautious about joining the consciousness-as-brain advocates, who find the neural pathways sufficient, although our comprehension of consciousness-mind has yet to go beyond the rudimentary awareness-mind neural networks of invertebrates. Joseph Campbell, mythologist and teacher, continually reminded us of the danger in concretizing the metaphor, in focusing on the symbol rather than the essence.

For instance, many of us are able to drive on automatic pilot. That is, we drive across a too familiar terrain absorbed in our thoughts and fantasies to the point of substituting the images of our mind's eye for the roadway ahead. Suppose at the beginning of the trip we want to turn off at an exit not part of our usual route. As soon as we mistakenly pass it, our distraction is broken. Also, let any serious abnormality occur, such as a car cutting in too close or a ball bouncing onto the highway, and we are quick to turn our attention to the event, usually responding before fully cognizant. After cursing ourselves for daydreaming, we wonder how we managed to drive the car.

Are you familiar with the story of the millipede, which upon being asked how it coordinated its many feet when walking, thought about the problem and found itself unable to move? Apparently, there exists an operational limit to the number of activities that can receive our attention. In fact, the capacity is small. If you listen intently to music while concentrating on viewing an object, you will experience a tug-of-war. The sound will become slightly less sharp as the image becomes more distinct; the instruments are readily differentiated at the expense of vision. *Generally, we live lives of attentive compromise.*

These automatic processes, inherently developed or acquired, fall within subconsciousness-mind and unconsciousness-mind, which, therefore, must have a huge capacity. Subliminial perception, notorious for its potential exploitation in advertising and other forms of 'brainwashing', is the subconscious recognition of meaningful patterns flashed before the viewer for 1 to 5 milliseconds, a duration too brief to stimulate the attention of consciousness-mind, unless, perhaps, the subject is in deep meditation.[46] Their influence on behavior would probably depend on physiological or emotional needs and the interval after presentation. If not hungry, one is not affected by the suggestion of popcorn, and by the time one does crave food, the stimulus of the word 'popcorn' is no longer active. No one knows the mechanisms of hypnosis, but they seem to involve the subconscious as well, although through different and more extensive processes.

Where among this maze of neurons and inferred mental structures is self? Is self itself modular, as suggested by those suffering multiple personality disorder? For that matter, why is there a self at all? Questions of Where?, What?, When?, and How? are so much easier to approach than that hopeless shrug of Why? Echoing Carl Jung, Kihlstrom writes, [I]n order for ongoing experience, thought, and action to become conscious, a link must be made between its mental representation and some mental representation of the self as agent or experiencer—as well, perhaps, as some representation of the environment in which these events take place. These episodic representations of the self and context reside in working memory, but apparently the links are neither automatic nor permanent, and must be actively forged.'[46]

Except for his error in requiring experience to be ego-identified in order to achieve conscious attention, I am in agreement. While practicing, master meditators may be supremely attentive, but dwell in working memory before ego is involved. The metaphor for meditation is the mirror. Therefore, the meditator reflects whatever perceptions, feelings, impulses, and subconsciousness—delivered memories that may bubble up and dissolve in ceaseless series. The experience may include timelessness and spacelessness or a confluency of time-space. This practice is a creative fount. By remaining in moderate concentration, consciousness-mind can interrupt the parade; however, like trying to remember a dream upon awakening, paper and pen had better be at hand to record the information before it fades from working memory.

Who is experiencing the experience? No one. There is only the experience and sometimes we can speak not of experience but of attainment.. Because no associations are made to link these events, ego is absent, breaking a viscious cycle. Normally, ego connects the condition-moments as a string unites the beads in a necklace. This process leads to thought and karmic investment (mental momentum), which produce further thought associations and ego-actions, and so on. Ego appears and is reinforced from memory-referenced comparisons of one's own form and behavior with those of other organisms and the environment, explaining in part why twins at first share self-identity. In other words, *your thinking creates your self, which in turn induces your thinking about yourself.* The importance of seeing our true nature, the situational patterns, relationships, and processes behind and beyond the occlusive and conditioned hungry self, is why Zen masters urge us to regain beginner's mind, to live in the Unborn, and to demonstrate the mind before our parents were born.[48,49]

We make ego, but it is nowhere to be found. To declare that it appears and disappears in working memory accomplishes little because memory has no body location. Before you challenge that remark with the postulate that memory, thoughts, all creative abstractions, and willful attention of consciousness-mind are mathematical patterns of switches in brain circuitry, as the memory of a computer lies within its electrical components, where then is the site of those incessant silent sexless whispers of self-dialogue? How do twins sometimes communicate from afar merely by thinking? Oh, how we become so enchanted by tangible tissues, measurable entities, and those activities of perception within time-space, and forget that these biological structures are behavioral patterns of awareness-mind! Nerve tissues are of ghost-atoms and their electromagnetic and chemical behaviors are nonlocally connected. Ethereal thoughts and memories of consciousness-mind are nowhere and perhaps everywhere. Again, we must not confuse the map for the territory, or as is traditionally said in the Far East, the moon-pointing finger for the moon.

There are many scientists who accept the idea of thought and stored memories emerging through bioelectric codes of the brain. If so, into what does consciousness-mind emerge? This question is much like asking, Into what is the universe expanding? Because form is dependent on background emptiness and emptiness is inseparable from form, we must answer, 'Itself'.

Karl H. Pribram, a neurosurgeon and neurobiologist formerly at Stanford University, was at a loss to find an explanatory model for an apparent paradox of memory. Brain injury and even the excision of large amounts of brain tissue do not seem to eliminate memories. Instead, these assaults may prevent the input of information into storage or the proper retrieval of memory, as in amnesia. Memory itself is largely intact and seems to be distributed holistically over wide areas of the brain. When Pribram then came across a description of a laser hologram, he was captivated by its properties and the way they could be utilized in consciousness studies.[50] Other investigators saw the connection also, but Pribram has publicly become the central authority.

Photons and brainwaves are both electromagnetic waves, and both are subject to interference. In holography the incidental beam and the reflected beam bouncing off an object interfere on a plate, which stores information about the object. The brainwaves of memory and perception may possibly interfere as patterns of consciousness. If a hologram should break, each fragment, as a jewel of Indra's net, yet holds the whole, albeit somewhat fuzzier. Accordingly, the removal of damaged brain tissue would not eliminate memories. Indeed, the removal of diseased tissue may improve memory processing. Therefore, the brain in this model, as far as memories are concerned, is holographic. Moreover, consciousness-mind here is *organized* in the body, particularly in the brain.

There are other scientists and philosophers who gladly regard the brain as processor of information and ascribe to it the simile of the most familiar and ubiquitous electronic devices. David H. Hubel, who is a pioneer in the study of visual pathways, likened the brain to 'the circuit of a radio or a television set, or perhaps hundreds or thousands of such circuits in series and in parallel, richly cross-linked.'[51] Hubel may not have recognized the richness of his analogy, because radios and televisions are transformation devices that convert externally delivered information in the form of invisible and intangible electromagnetic fields into audible airwaves and, if TV, into photons as well. The representation of a radio has been adopted by several visionary researchers.

When, in the 1960's, former Harvard University psychologist Timothy Leary proclaimed his misunderstood slogan, 'Turn on, tune in, drop out,' he used the analogy of communicative electronics in urging a shift in the pervading social philosophy and myth. LSD was only one vehicle of change; the counter-culture movement itself was another.

Albert Hofmann, the Swiss pharmaceutical chemist who accidentally discovered the psychedelic properies of LSD and isolated psilocybin from mushrooms, has formulated a transmitter-receiver concept, but it is admittedly dualistic and provides only one-way communication.[52] Furthermore, he explains that the metaphor is not a metaphysical model and has no basis, its existence solely an intellectual contrivance and tool.

In his scheme, the familiar reality of objects in space and of matter as determined by scientific instruments constitutes the transmitter of 'outer space', and the ego-directed psychological realities, which are as numerous as human beings (and other organisms of consciousness-mind), act as receivers of 'inner space'. The antennae are our basic five sense organs (Buddhist schools describe eight; the other senses are organs of conscious-ness related to the coordination and intergration of the usual five, to ego, and to memory-influenced activity). Our psychological operations translate and transform these exterior signals into individualistic sounds, sights, smells, tastes, and feelings. Music, art, architecture, and literature are cultural 'symbols of spirit'. Noting that the continuing process of reception and decoding creates an ever-changing human reality, Hofmann concludes, 'Every human being is the creator of a world of his [or her] own.' Transcendence of the dual-component system comes first from recognizing the common origin and evolution of the duality and second, while putting the brain in the category of transmitter, from giving its plan and development under the direction of the spiritual receiver. Hofmann does not comment on the illogic of a receiver that influences the transmitter. Perhaps that is why he does not take his model seriously.

Sheldrake also discusses the radio in his hypothesis of morphic resonance.[53] If we were ignorant of the broadcast of electromagnetic waves from a distant studio and tower, we would attempt to explain the function of a radio solely by its component parts, and regard the produced sounds as an emergent property of complex interactions of the transistors, capacitors, and so forth. We would be confident of this hypothesis because any damaged part would alter the quality of sound or prevent it altogether. Also reassuring would be, after thorough analysis of the wiring arrangement in the radio, the assembly of a copy that issued the same sorts of sounds. If the type of sound changed (from the baroque of J.S. Bach to the clash of heavy metal rock), or if the stereo sound suddenly became monophonic, we would suspect the fault of the radio when actually the inducer was the broadcasting studio.

While Sheldrake concentrated on the tuning in (resonance) of different morphogenetic fields by the physically developing organism, we can appreciate the application of the radio model to the physical brain as a biological receiver of the external, nonemergent information source, consciousness-mind, which is primarily responsible for effecting certain body activities. This concept has been traced to Hippocrates, the great Greek physician of 400 B.C.E., who distinguished the brain as the interpreter or messenger of consciousness.[54] Thus, by this frame of reference, the brain is not the source of consciouness-mind, and a damaged brain will distort or fail to give the message. Acknowledging the usefulness of the analogy, we, nevertheless, should not build our philosophy on it; the details can get in the way.

I find it odd that Hofmann, Sheldrake, Dossey, and others did not convert the radio receiver to a transceiver, since the hypothesis of morphogenetic fields, like Whitehead's process metaphysics, requires present circumstances to be incorporated into the ever-present past to guide the activities of the next moment. The duality of brain and consciousness-mind, which these thinkers express, glosses over the scientific evidence that the neuroendocrinoimmunological network (brain, etc.) affects consciousness-mind. This is not the case of confusing faulty parts with a faulty message, as in the radio model. Mutations, disease, and dis-ease not only alter the reading of the message, but the flux in body systems also write the message. The biological components are awareness-mind, and therefore are united with consciousness-mind in a two-way flow of relational processes.

Duality, an opportunistic tyrant, will creep even into treatises, such as this one and those cited above, that attempt to convey the 'oneness' of all and the identification of the whole as mind/consciousness. Alas, to say *one* implies *two* and to regard a *whole* creates its *parts*. Knowledge and speech depend on categories (to a certain extent, discovering a component simultaneously creates and names it) but we should also be aware of not-one, not-two, although we can not discuss it.

Dogen knew this problem very well.[2]

Mind itself is buddha:
    Practice is difficult. Explanation is not difficult.
Mindless-mind, non-buddha buddha:
    Explanation is difficult. Practice is not difficult.

How does you practice mindless-mind? Just do it! You already understand.

From the restricted perspective of consciousness-mind, we can dismiss the uniqueness of ego as an empty construction, but still wonder about the separation or individualization of consciousness-mind among organisms. Unique experiences leading to unique brain pathways, memories, thoughts, and behavior seem to keep us apart, although biology and sociology limit the deviations to variations on a human theme.

However, the subconsciousness and perhaps the awareness-mind of individuals may be in close communication.

We already have the case of identical twins. Except for self-sufficient hermits, humans are units of a society and certainly of a species. This higher order influences us covertly, affecting physiology, reproduction, and probably social attitudes in times of socio-ecological stress. Specific or at least enhanced mutation may also occur through such collective direction and environment I described earlier in the case of bacteria facing a nutritional crisis. But the subconsciousness network may also extend to other vertebrates. Both the amazing travels over hundreds, even thousands of miles of abandoned pet dogs and cats, seeking their owners, and the equally uncanny connections of people on land with distant unseen dolphins and other marine life, which seem to signal their presence, indicate the union of consciousness-mind among individuals.[12,13] Such communication is called telepathy, but it may be a form of remote viewing or precognition, or all may be attributes of another unconventional system of information processing. We will continue the discussion of these strange doings in the next chapter.

I close here as I began, once more with words of Dogen.[2]

A snowy heron
on the snowfield,
where winter grass is unseen,
hides itself
in its own figure.

Chapter 12

A MOON-POINTING FINGER

Parapsychology/Conclusion

Sell your cleverness and buy bewilderment.
Cleverness leads to mere opinion,
bewilderment to intuition.
                    Jalal-uddin Rumi

I don't express myself in my painting.
I express my not-self.
                    Mark Rothko

Normally, the last chapter of scientific monographs or the last section of similar reviews in journals, particularly the stuffy academic sort, is dedicated to three formal structures. The author is obliged to at least a half-hearted devil's advocacy by which chief alternative views opposing or glancing off the thesis are duly mentioned. These divergent interpretations are given so as not to ruffle any peer ego-feathers. The second component is a not-too-bizarre speculation (modest, to avoid any risk of credibility), which is shaped to implant seeds of heterodoxy that may nudge the establishment toward the author's opinion. The final element is a grand conclusion with an eye to the future (the future of civilization and, between the lines, the future of the author). I have often been guilty of this traditional practice myself. In this, the last chapter of the book, I will not disappoint the reader wedded to this admittedly logical organization, but conservatism will not dictate the content.

First, I need not present the positivist dogma. It has reigned for over 150 years, you learned it in school, and it is continually reinforced by the unwitting propaganda of newspaper articles and television programs. Also, any variants of the unitary mind-only concept (which should not be confused with the idealism of George Berkeley) are perfectly reasonable. I have no quarrels with them, since they, like mine, like those of the 1300-year-old Hua-Yen school, are only interpretations and inferences, maps of different styles, maps of what can not be expressed anyway. Hence, if one believes that mind exists or existed in a form other than my descriptions of matter-mind, awarenessness-mind, and consciousness-mind, who is to prove otherwise? If another sees the universe as having a direction or a final goal, or being governed by a collective consciousness-mind, why should I protest? There is no scientific fact here, no concept that can be validated at all, probably not even to oneself. However reasonable, these are only beliefs or guesses and, foremost, they are play.

Nevertheless, I do oppose dualistic concepts even though they may be disguised by a holistic veneer. For me, mind is indistinguishable from cosmos. As far as he went, Sir Arthur Eddington, a physicist, also supported this concept: The stuff of the world is mind-stuff....The mind-stuff is not spread in space and time....The physical world is entirely abstract and without 'actuality' apart from its linkage to consciousness.[1] However, George Wald, a biologist, does not: '[M]ind, rather than being a very late development in the evolution of living things, restricted to organisms with the most complex nervous systems..., instead has been there always, and...this universe is life-breeding because the pervasive presence of mind had guided it to be so....[W]hen I speak of mind pervading the universe, of mind as a creative principle perhaps primary to matter, any Hindu will acquiesce, will think, yes, of course, he is speaking of Brahman.'[2] But a Buddhist might object.

Gregory Bateson, an anthropologist among the pioneers of cybernetics and related communications and systems theory, understood mind as processes of pattern interactions.[3] His approach was based on six key points. Top of his list was that mind is an aggregate of interacting parts or components, which themselves could be mental if, in turn, composed of interacting parts. He excluded machines and galaxies unless they interact with a life form, in which case they form parts of a higher system. For him, these interactions are due to time-related differences whose relationships are outside space-time. He referred to interactive ideas of physical features, not the physical event. Mental process, he said, require collateral energy and are circular in cause-effect determination. Lastly, information is coded and read through logical hierarchies in metacommunication. Bateson's principles are similar to my own conclusions, although I am significantly more liberal in scope.

Erich Jantsch, a systems scientist, and I also share some ideas of process metaphysics, for he stated, 'Mind is self-organization dynamics proper,' but he compromised that stand with 'An equilibrium structure [here meaning static] has no mind.'[4] Perhaps he meant to say is not mind. (I wonder how we could detect such a structure, if it existed!) He further fell into duality with 'Mind and matter are complementary aspects in the same self-organization dynamics, mind as dissipative and matter as conservative principle.'

I differ in that mind is not *in* matter, not *in* the universe, not *in* the dynamics of structures; rather, matter *is* mind, as awareness is mind. There are no separations of mind. Matter-mind, awareness-mind, and consciousness-mind obviously are not complementary, but they are concepts and categories of pattern interactions. The awareness-mind of a bacterium is not distinct from the awareness-mind of a neuron, although their patterns of activities or behaviors clearly differ.

Still, I make a poor advocate for the loyal opposition to the positivist party in power. Rather I am a scientist, albeit a mystic, who readily gives plausibility to what many regard as nonsense, but who, nevertheless, is cautious before ajudging fact. While we must accept an individual's cultural impressions of a psychological phenomenon, we should challenge any label of it being a noumenon, a form independent of our awareness-mind and especially consciousness-mind.

The next portion is the speculation. Yes, the entire book is a speculation, but the wild side, those aspects of any discipline typically relegated to the pale at the back of a textbook, takes us deeper into the paranormal, abilities that are actually quite normal and are considered so in many non-Western cultures. Biologists, physicians, and physicists, such as Lyles Watson, Larry Dossey, Russel Targ, and Robert Jahn and Brenda Dunne, have described their encounters and examinations of psi.[5-8] They are part of a long series of researchers, some Nobel laureates—if that matters—who have been amazed and intrigued by these stunning occurrences.[9] In contrast, Bateson, who espoused metacommunication, hypocritically and prejudicially dismissed these phenomena as superstition, dreams, hallucinations, and fiction.[10] He ignored the advice John Hunter gave to Edward Jenner—now a fundamental of science: 'I think your solution is just; but why think? Why not try the experiment?'[11]

The key to recognizing our own powers, although they may be weak, is to mentally exhale, to let go of the burden of concepts, including the existence of psi. According to Targ, self-proclaimed semi-professional 'psychics' are least able to perform remote viewing, probably because their egos and reputations are at risk. This temporary casting-off is not easily accomplished; meditation has proven effective for me, but any means will do.

Precognition is perhaps the most commonly experienced psi event.[12] It is the only one that I have personally validated and can effect. For me, it happens spontaneously and, occasionally, in dramatic fashion, such as the horrific dream about being laid-off at work that was realized the next morning nearly word-for-word. Another example is, after arising from sleep, my blurting out of the phrase, 'Napa Labor Temple', which was of no significance until three weeks later when, immediately after an exhilarating hot-air balloon ride, I spotted these words on a pretentious sign affixed to a small bland dwelling in the city of Napa. In another dream I met certain unknown Caucasian men in an unfamiliar underground train station, people I would not encounter until five months later in a visit to Tokyo. Of course, there was the common experience of receiving a long-distance telephone call from a nearly forgotten friend, in this instance, after I had meditated and, to my surprise during a subsequent brisk walk, projected his appearance on a passer-by of only coarse resemblance. (Did you find all the common threads?) If you are typical, you have had similar happenings.

I can also put this form of psi to the test. Like the famous Rhine test of anticipating the patterns of a series of cards (star, square, and so forth), humorously depicted in the movie

Ghostbusters, and exactly like the pioneering parapsychological work of physiologist and immunologist Charles Richet, I have been able to predict successfully characteristics of the playing card that would appear after shuffling and cutting. It is not a matter of guessing. Through meditation and visualization, as employed in Targ's and Jahn and Dunne's studies, I would occasionally see the card with confidence about its number or face and color and sometimes suit. If there was no strong mental image, I would not attempt a guess, since it would not be meaningful. Failure is thereby reduced in frequency and is associated with fatigue. In one such trial involving a successful series of four precognitive identifications, the random odds were about 1:1,800,000, but, of course, the selections were not at random. In monitored tests, I have been likewise correct in anticipating features and their positions on unseen photographs or the essential forms of hidden objects. In these instances, the image and feeling are, in the artistic sense, impressionistic and cubist rather than photographic and, therefore, easier to achieve. My father can do it, my neighbor can do it, and you probably can do it, too.

But are we discussing precognition or postcognition? Much of the controversy on precognition focuses on the problem of information going backwards in time-space contrary to thermodynamics, physics, and common sense. Precognition would seem to require a thorough overhaul of current science and metaphysics. There are several ways to consider the phenomenon that would not necessitate much of a shift.

A 'simultaneous' radio and television broadcast from a distant site is sometimes received a second or so apart, one being dependent on satellite relay, the other on telephone lines, and neither precisely instantaneous with the event. Likewise, the neural awareness-mind processes involved in consciousness-mind are time-dependent, occurring in less than one-tenth of a second. As described previously, an event rising and falling well within this time, such as a flashed image or word, is not recognized by our attentive consciousness, although subconscious-mind and awareness-mind are stimulated. *Thus, our cognitive processes lag behind acquired or inherent reflexes;* our hand jumps from an accidentally touched hot or very cold surface before we determine the reasons why. Unless we are fully attentive, lightning flashes seem to strike downward. If alert, we discover that they flash upward, the photon discharge following back up a track of ionization that a moment before formed downward.

Could we then be cognizant of a supposed future event that has already taken place? Limiting the 'future' to fractions of a second, Benjamin Libet, a research neurophysiologist at the University of California at San Francisco, has already established the principle.[13,14] He compared the subjective onset of an electrical stimulus applied to the skin of an arm or hand and to various regions of the brain (felt as tingling on the body), as reported by patients. The two stimuli were triggered simultaneously or in different order. When patients described the stimulus to the skin as preceding the impulse to the cortex of the brain, it, in fact, had occurred afterwards. *Libet's subjects were turning back the clock of experience.*

A train of electrical pulses (30 to 120 per second) sent to the brain by implanted electrodes that lasted less than 200 to 500 milliseconds (depending on pulse frequency and electrical current) was not consciously sensed. This site- and time-dependent insensitivity contrasts stimulation of the skin, where only 15 milliseconds were required for the impulse to travel the nerve network between the skin and the cortex. In the study, a single pulse was never sensed, except when it was applied to the skin.

Understanding that awareness- or subconsciousness-mind and consciousness-mind are segregated by time, Libet then considered the philosophical question of free will.[14,15] Which comes first: the intention to act or measurable cerebral activity? He knew from the research of Hans Kornhuber and Luder Deecke at the University of Ulm that a voltage spike (the 'event related potential') occurs 800 to 1000 milliseconds before a required movement of the hand. In a new experiment in which subjects indicated the moment of their willful intention to perform a given yet voluntary act, Libet found a spike 550 milliseconds *prior* to their own measured response, which is 350 milliseconds *after* the readiness potential. Their consciousness to act, which preceeded muscle activation by 150 to 200 milliseconds, apparently was recognition of intent already as awareness-mind (perhaps the -800 millisecond spike) and the subconscious-mind (perhaps the -350 millisecond spike). *Libet found that free will is not a decision to act, but a conscious decision not to act,* because subjects could elect to accept or to veto the urge within the last 200 milliseconds.

These studies demonstrate that awareness-mind is the karma zone in which consciousness-mind and its processes have only a feedback role in impulse generation. (Meditators can observe these karmic bubbles and cascades.) Libet's research team now has determined that events occurring below the threshold of consciousness-mind can be detected and constructively responded to in awareness-mind.[14] In choosing one of two buttons that was correlated with a stimulus of various pulse frequencies, patients were allowed also to record their level of confidence. Beating the 50/50 odds, the subjects made correct 'guesses' when stimuli were not sensed. *Rapid decision-making, hence, may occur without full consciousness.*

Libet's investigations, however, concern time intervals below one second. I long have had the peculiar feeling that my consciously attentive life is actually unfolding, that it is a retracing, or in terms of modern communications, that it is on tape-delay. It is a feeling of fulfilled potentiality that far exceeds millisecond delays. Perhaps you also have had such a deep feeling. This is not strict determinism, since we do have some capacity for conscious volition. However, this regulatory loop may be of minor impact. The underlying impulses and controls seem vast. Picture yourself as running like some caged hamster along the inside surface of a rotating flexible wheel in the form of a Möbius strip. There is no inside to a Möbius strip! The way out of the bind, to see that the path, our life path, is a twisted loop, is to pull back to a more distant vista or to jump into a higher dimension.

Lama Govinda likewise regarded time as internalized, subjectifed space—through remembrance and feeling of duration—and space as externalized, objectified time.[16] Hence, time and space are the inside and outside of the same reality, time-space, that goes beyond such opposites.

Mind is empty of objective reality. Within matter-mind, where resonating whirls of a continuum are completely free of time's cruel arrow, forward and backward processes occur equally without consequence. Positron or electron, proton, photon, or pi-meson, they are all different attributes of the same flux. Matter-mind is of no space and time until it influences or is 'perceived' by processes of awareness-mind, the activities we call chemistry, and it is consciousness—mind that calls it such. Our language indicates this relationship: the words *material* and *matter* have the same Indo-European root as *measure* and *meter*, as well as *maya* and *mother*, which is to say that the material world prankishly arises from measurement. Time is thereby given a set direction, but not a constant rate, since we know that physically measured time, biological time, and perceived time do not match.[17]

These different aspects of time are equally valid for their respective form of mind. Since consciousness has no location (that is to say, it does not occupy space even if you regard it as an emergent tranformation of neurophysicochemical patterns), it lacks the shackles of rigid physical time. Instead, consciousness-mind processes take place in flexible psychobiological time. Unfortunately, the labor of urban workers is regulated by the mechanical clock more appropriate for the examination of matter-mind. *Thus, matter-mind is timeless and spaceless; awareness-mind creates space-time and is regulated by it; and consciousness-mind is again spaceless but quasi-timeless.* Mind (Tao) can not be defined according to space-time; it can not be satisfactorily defined at all.

Consciousness-mind has various levels, as described in the previous chapter. Subconsciousness-mind is the most free, the most open to nonattentive stimuli, which may include a network of inter-organismal subconsciousness. If ego is the commander, this structure is the noncommissioned officer, who keeps the organism drilled and efficient. Parapsychological processes probably occur here. The subconsciousness-mind is to ego-chained consciousness as a Cray ultra high-speed, ultra dense capacity computer is to my obsolete plodding 64K CP/M personal computer.

In one scheme of precognition, while thinking- consciousness cranks through the information of self-environment interactions, the subconsciousness has already acted, from moments perhaps up to six months ahead. However, because precognition is rarely precise in all details, and, in some circumstances, the subject can avoid the event (such as an airplane crash), it is unlikely that the visualized future event actually has occurred. What is interacting are ghost-like karmic forces, gestaltic packages of potentia, or some other aspect of mind activity. (Choose your favorite concept and nomenclature.) However, the notion of the potential and the actual as both real, both interdependent operative forces— whereby the actual creates the conditions and limits for the potential, which in turn influences actualization—is appealing and consistent with strange feedback loops. Quantum theory involves such probabilities.

Hence, information does not go backwards in time; con— sciousness receives from subconsciousness-mind the impression or best projection of potentia. Highly dramatic and meaningful incidents will have the sharpest, flag-waving probabilities. Such feeds from subconsciousness-mind are surely continuous, but attentive consciousness-mind must be receptive to this resource. Achieving that quality of attentiveness is thus far an art, not a science.

How the model of quantum physics can be used in pre- cognition has been described by several researchers. In his interpretation of quantum probabilities, Ninian Marshall, a psychiatrist, described how a perturbed electron enters a vir- tual transition state at the various quantum energy levels, trying them out as it were before actualizing at one of them.[12] As a biologist, I can visualize this process as an amoeba prob- ing multiple channels with its many pseudopodia before draw- ing itself into one. Recognizing that firing thresholds of neu- rons follow such quantum indeterminism, Marshall proposed that a number of neural quantum events can act in concert, forming a pattern that is amplified through resonances in brain circuitry. His scheme depends on a proclivity among the virtual transitions to organize their noise into a harmonic pattern, as a seed induces an orderly crystal within a chaotic supersaturated solution. Consciousness would then tune into these peak probabilities in the form of visual or word patterns.

Electrical superconductivity and lasers work in much the same way. In the first instance, all the atoms in certain metals at cold temperatures act as one, with consistent electron energy levels, and photon waves in lasers likewise become ``rently in phase. A similar model, involving probability waves and tunneling, has been formulated by Jahn and Dunne.[8]

Neurological evidence may be at hand. Waiting additional confirmatory studies is Wolf Singer and Charles Grey's observation and interpretation that distant neurons processing sensory information are coordinated by a synchronous oscillation of firings at 40 hertz.[18]

Details of other notions that utilize tachyons (hypothetical particles moving faster than light), wormholes and superimposed parallel universes, and the possible holographic nature of mind, including matter and consciousness, will take us too far afield. What matters is that all of these conjectures feature wave-forms and their resonances in a universe where causality is not locally restricted.

Earlier I related that the electroencephlogram traces of twins are alike, and that twins are somewhat telepathic. Jacobo Gringberg-Zylberbaum and Julieta Ramos at the National Autonomous University of Mexico and the attached National Institute for the Study of Consciousness discovered synchrony of EEG waves between unrelated adults trying to communicate without visual, tactile, or auditory contact.[19]

Sitting apart inside a sound-proof, electrically insulated Faraday cage, a pair of subjects (13 sets were examined) signaled each other mentally during a 15-minute test period. Both hemispheres of each subject were monitored by EEG with 320 correlations performed electronically every 82 seconds. As each session progressed, the extent of correlation of EEG patterns increased. The traces at the beginning and end of the trial, when contact was not attempted, were clearly dissimilar, but during the signaling period the EEG patterns became increasingly alike. Seven of ten independent judges were able to match the EEG traces of three pairs in contact from a series of 15 randomly mixed EEG charts. EEG patterns of the best empathetic pair while in contact were nearly congruent. While delighted, excited, but not surprised, I reserve final judgment until these results are confirmed independently and expanded using similar methods.

Carl G. Jung was the father of Western mystical psychology, offering such seminal concepts as synchronicity and archetypes within a collective consciousness. The classic story of his encounter with an insect was a watershed in developing his views of the paranormal and the deep-seated, inherited, semi-Platonic ideal forms within the subconsciousness, and although it is rather tame by the today's standards, it bears repeating.

While Jung was with one of his patients in Switzerland, the woman told him about the dream she had had the previous night in which someone presented her a golden scarab, a symbol of Egypt.[12,20] As she was relating the dream, an incessant tapping at his office window occurred. He went to the window and opened it. An insect flew in, which he caught in his hand; it was a rose chafer, a scarabaeid beetle. Jung recognized that this synchronous meaningful event was related to precognition and telepathy and that it challenged convential ideas about causality. He sought a new perspective that could provide some general explanation for these psychological phenomena.

The biological foundation of his concept was evolution, in which the patterns of emotions, behavior, and consciousness of our animal and primate ancestors persist in us as the initially developed arrangement of brain neurons. We are born with a starter kit of built-in memories or references, not of individual activities, but of inherited quasi experiences. These he called *archetypes* after St. Augustine's first description of cultural essences.[21] Archetypes are emotion-linked fundamental images and structures common to the myths of all cultures as symbols and metaphors, and include, for instance, the circular mandala (reasonable since our optic image is a disc), a spiral maze or any kind of labyrinth, and a cross or swastika. There may be an innate repulsion to spiders, snakes, and certain crawling insects. Perhaps a collective memory of poisoning may be its source; also, twin studies suggest that some complex phobias are genetic.

We can find archetypes in dreams. The details, of course, will vary with culture and era, but many of us have dreamt at least once about anxiously searching in corridors, streets, or other endless branching channels for something, perhaps misplaced keys, a parked car, or the room for a school examination decades after having completed schooling. Feelings of weightlessness, experienced by us as fetuses, may figure in a dream or occasionally while attentively alert. Jung called the collection of these core patterns, which unite all humanity, the *collective unconscious*.[21] Jung believed that synchronicity/ precognition and telepathy are somehow related to resonances between individuals of a 'transpsychic reality' manifested through common archetypes.

Searching as well for a physical foundation, he and nuclear physicist Wolfgang Pauli collaborated in 1952 on an opinion supporting an acausal, spaceless and timeless cosmos, in which matter and mind [meaning matter-mind/awareness-mind and consciousness-mind] are complementary attributes arising from each other.[22] They modeled this interpenetrative arrangement on the particle/wave duality of quantum entities.

Pauli's reputation is among the highest tiers of the scientific pantheon. As brilliant and logical as Bohr and as mystical and skeptical as Einstein, he also understood the quest of all mystical scientists and scientific mystics who are unpersuaded and dissatisfied by both narrow, bland positivistic rationalism and equally intransigent religious nihilism. He declared, 'I consider the ambition of overcoming opposites, including also a synthesis embracing both rational understanding and the mystical experience of unity, to be the mythos, spoken or unspoken, of our present day and age.'[23] Pauli died in 1958. As we pause on the brink of a new millennium, the need for this synthesis in our global culture is especially acute, but, as if destined on the scales of Fate, the opportunities are great and perfectly timed. I am optimistic.

Perhaps it is wishful thinking. The acceleration of creative social and technological events in this century is astonishing. Where before, hundreds of years or longer comprised historical eras, we now attempt to group them by decades. A middle-aged witness and performer in the passing parade, I see on balance a sociocultural movement toward a more humanistic ideal.

In 1969, gazing down from my ivory tower research laboratory or assisting in the crude clinical laboratory of a church basement free clinic diagnosing gonorrhea and other infections of the sexually incautious, I laughed at the naive utopian hippie dreams of an Age of Aquarius. The subsequent anti-Vietnam War rebellion with the viscious constitutionally abusive counteraction of local, state, and federal governments and, later, the forgetful and jaded 1970s and 1980s seemed to collapse that happy posit. The hippie ideal, as any romantic fairy tale world, can not occur, but I no longer mock the prediction of a new epoch, another turn of the dharma wheel.

Professional historians will shake their heads at the simplicity. However, there are periods of internationally experienced internal strife, such as the revolutionary era that peaked in Europe in 1848, which seem to pervade the globe as some harmonic miasma. In our own time and for various separate reasons and politics, the social spirit for dissent and change came to a head in 1968 and was felt in Beijing as well as Paris, Prague, and Provo Park. More recently, the humanistic democratic changes and drives that have gripped the world does hold portent. The dispelling of the fearful and dehumanizing mind-frame that took us through 'duck-and-cover', underground home bomb shelters, and the Cuban Missile Crisis to the recognition of Gaia and the global village by the leaders of the great powers, however tardy, however insuffient, indicates a pendulum swing toward cooperation and mutualism.

As part of this movement, the commensal relationship and synthesis of mystic and scientific philosophy, similar to the accommodation and blend of Western and Eastern industrial practices, is more than a possibility. Neither science nor religion as institutions can convey the experience of unity in which nothing is united and in which there is no experiencer. This transcendence is an event of individuals, not societies. Nevertheless, both approaches can promote and include the event in their lore. Such an evolution is the stuff of creative insight, if not fusion. Therefore, neuroscience and transpersonal psychology must conjoin, and the normal paranormal must be scientifically probed to separate the actual from the imagined and the self-deception. As the problem of blackbody radiation would not go away and the placebo effect could not be ignored, scientists are obliged to deal forthrightly with the siddhis.

Psi exists, but its principles and mechanisms are undetermined. There may be, as I expect, only one metaphysical principle with various manifestations dependent on circumstances, including 'out of body' experiences, clairvoyance, telepathy, precognition, and remote viewing. I take no position on the question of consciousness-mind directed influences on healing and growth of [apparently] external life forms and of the existence of psychokinesis, other than development and editing of neuropathways. While favoring the model of resonance, I still appreciate that all these expressions are empty words, representations useful only for the sake of communication.

We have come to the final traditional sections, the summation and conclusion, but I shall provide them through a discussion of a new yet related topic.

The end of a book is metaphorically the end of life. Any question of self must lead to this ultimate mystery. One year I investigated the microbial ecology of AIDS patients and of patients who yet asymptomatically carry that brutal virus.[24] At the time of the study, these people were facing or undergoing a slow death of severe emaciation, recurrent fungal and bacterial opportunistic infections, and, for some, cancer and dementia. They were the most informed patients about their condition and treatments a medical specialist could encounter. Their attitude towards life and death was edifying. Condemned, and having passed through the typical steps of anger and denial, they embraced life fully, almost stoically. One man, who dramatically altered his stressful and hurried lifestyle and mental disposition to one of carefully planned nutrition, regular noncompetitive exercise, and meditation, was the healthiest; he told me that he had never felt better. He was relaxed, energetic, and free. Yet he had very few helper lymphocytes. A letting-go to achieve nonattachment and acceptance can develop with traditional faith, a deep personal philosophy, or the absence of choice, the impossibility of escape. It can lead to transcendence.

How does life and death fit into the presented scheme of mind and its manifestations? It is traditional in the Far East for a dying sage to write a death poem, a final statement on existence. Zen Master Ta-Kuan (1573-1645) at first refused the request by his students. At the last moment he brushed the character for dream.[25] Basho also refused when his turn had come, declaring that since every moment of life is the last, every poem is a death poem. Simultaneously, I must add, every moment of life is the first. Thus, every moment exists as if it were a frame of a holographic movie passing across the laser light of memory.

The problem is reduced to this: Because ego self—image is a mirage, what is it that supposedly dies? I can hear you tensing your larynx. Squashing a mosquito on your arm kills the mosquito, you decry as a modern day Samuel Johnson, who kicked a rock and then claimed objective reality of matter. Yes, that mosquito will not fly again, will nevermore feast on blood. But go back one step and define life precisely. Having been defeated by that impossible task, you then may fall back to declaring that it is intuitively obvious. However, you would be wrong. A mystic's intuition is different than most, and what is alive for such an individual will seem ludicrous to others.

An oceanic wave crashes on the beach: Did the water die? The water of the wave danced a vertical two-step while the impulse passed horizontally. Did the impulse die? The energy of the wave continued as a displacement of the sand. *Within ceaseless transformations we arbitrarily create partititons.* What was the source of the wave? Remember the story of Ananda and the bell. *Singular causality is a delusion.*

Still, some things do cease. Take individual memory accretion, for example. It is memory that informs us that we live and exist for more than one quantum fluctuation, but event memory is utilized one at a time and muscle coordinative memory is enfolded in each moment. If we lived truly moment to moment, whereby no comparisons were made to previous events or for projections of possible forthcoming happenings, we would not know that we were alive! Thus, death is memory death, and without memory there can be no ego-sense, no self-awareness, no consciousness-mind at all. Are, then, those patients in mental limbo—such as the encephalitis victims described by Oliver Sacks[26] and, even more extreme, individuals in coma—alive or dead? Awareness-mind persists in these people, but even the enzyme hydrolysis of a sugar within a test tube is an example of awareness-mind. We as observers proclaim the coma victim as alive, but this conclusion is a result of our thinking and conception.

Recall that everything about us is in flux, is dying or regenerating, decaying or being synthesized, and undergoing removal or replacement. Molecules and cells come and go, tissues change their constituents, organs atrophy, neurological links are formed, lost, and altered, and we learn and forget. Nothing remains constant, except change and a consciously created abstraction of identity. Furthermore, we are not separate individuals. Every pattern interpenetrates and is interdependent. We are a community of organisms. We are connected with our bacteria, our environment, our society and species, our planet, and our sun. Our past is within our present and our present dictates and limits our future, whose potentia may be perceived. Our deeds continue as influences on others, and although becoming increasingly dilute with each generation, they contribute to the commonwealth.

In transcendence there is no separation between life and death, indeed, as given in the Heart Sutra, there is 'no old age and death and also no extinction of them...no origination, no stopping, no path, no cognition; also no attainment with nothing to attain.' In classical Greece, Apollonius of Tyana said much the same: 'There is no death or birth of anyone except by appearance. The change from being to becoming seems to be birth as the change from becoming to being appears to be death. Actually, no one is ever born, no one ever dies.'[25] The concept of life simultaneously creates the notion of death, as form arises with emptiness.

Asked to comment on death, Einstein expanded the concept to wholeness: 'I feel such a sense of solidarity with all living things that it does not matter to me where the individual begins and ends.'[27] He said, *where*, not *when!* The mystic views a realm of no beginning, no end, no self, no other. I, too, am in solidarity—with the living rock of the noble Sierra Nevada and the living cloud gently entering San Francisco Bay, as well as with the dead peach tree blossoming in splendor and the dead horse galloping in the fields for its own pleasure.

To be separate is to be an *idiot*. The word, akin to idiotype, is derived from the Greek for a private or peculiar person. And person, as you know, is the mask we wear, perceived by our audience. And we the actors are also the audience of our acts, which create the script for the next scene in the continuing performance. And, as in Hamlet, the play is a play within a play. And, as in Indra's net, the play is included in every other play, as all plays exist in ours. Some of you may have once watched a very intelligent British television series called *The Prisoner*, developed by and starring Patrick McGoohan, which is a twisted Kafkaesque Alice-in-Wonderland offshoot of his popular *Secret Agent* series. Each mythical episode begins with McGoohan at a table facing the director of The Village. The director, who is replaced from time to time, is 'Number 2'. McGoohan asks, 'Who is Number 1?' The director curtly responds, 'You are Number 6.' Timing and inflection in speaking this sentence is crucial, and in the last episode it is distinctly altered as McGoohan's character finally transcends the commonly perceived situation. Through guided life retrospection by Number 2, he discovers and finally discloses the long unspecified 'information' that he was obliged to convey, thus, freeing himself from bondage. (He resigned to seek peace of mind, for he knew too much—a premise based on Taoist teaching.) The exchange was not original. The monk Hui-Chao asked Master Fa-Ye (885-958), 'What is Buddha?' Fa-Yen answered, 'You are Hui-Chao.'

We have heard about 'reincarnation' in Hindu thought and especially in Tibetan Buddhism, where certain young boys are sought in particular localities (precognized before their birth by a dying lama) and tested as the bearers (tulkus) of some aspects of the deceased lama's consciousness-mind. Ian Stevenson, a researcher at the University of Virginia, has extensively and carefully examined the question of childhood memory of a previous life, and thus far has amassed over 150 detailed cases.[28] Such occurrences are usually reported in cultures that accept the possibility, including—besides those of Southeast Asia—certain Shiite Moslems, East and West Africans, northwest Native Americans, and central Australian tribes. I suppose that this sounds like a variation of the Vulcan mind-meld known to all fans of the *Star Trek* science-fiction series. We must reject the transfer of any soul or substance in our metaphysic, which spurns an objective self, but *reincarnation* is a Western term with unfortunate connotations. We are born out of the universe and on death we are resorbed, as different chunks of water (in the form of ice), arising from and floating in water, eventually melt back into itself. There are other reports that do provide additional plausibility: children with accurate memories of events they could not have witnessed, and especially the fluency in unusual foreign languages in a few children and people with multipersonality disorders, who had no opportunity to master them.[5,29,30] Stevenson also reported a case of xenoglossy in a Jewish woman from Odessa who, only when hypnotized, could converse in an obscure, nearly extinct Scandanavian dialect.[31] This said, I still am mildly skeptical about tulkus.

However, we could speak instead of a karmic or mental impulse persisting as ripples passing through water long after a thrown rock disappears. Since the universe seems to be largely a system of interpenetrative waves and of interacting complementary, resonant, and harmonious waves, the idea of karmic informational waves induced by consciousness-mind is not that outlandish. This impulse could find a harmonic or resonant embodiment of awareness- and consciousness-mind. Ananda Coomaraswamy used the simile of billiard balls in close contact; a ball hitting the mass stops (dies) but its momentum is transferred to the last ball in series, which then moves out (lives). What is the form of this karma unit, and how would it fit into the receiver-transmitter scheme of the brain? For that matter, what is energy? We do not know, perhaps can not know. We, nevertheless, can examine its effects and transformations, which, in fact, is one of the roles of science.

Again, all of this thinking and interpretation should not be taken as truth. Natsume Soseki (1865-1915) understood this as he sat writing:

Butterfly! These words
From my brush are not flowers,
Only their shadows.

A Japanese lord asked Zen Master Hakuin (1686-1769) about the different events occurring to enlightened and unenlightened men upon their death. Haukin replied, 'Why ask me?' 'Because you are a Zen Master!' the nobleman retorted. 'Yes,' nodded the Master, 'but not a dead one!'25 This is why a monk sometimes sits in meditation in a graveyard; it is not to ask the dead, but to confront and penetrate directly the nature of death.

In this probe of life and death we encountered layers of paradox. Self exists as a name given to a set of activities or dynamic patterns called here matter-mind, awareness-mind, and consciousness-mind. Self, therefore, is a streaming within a cosmic ocean of emptiness. It does not exist from moment to moment, except through implicit momentum. Self is not localized in space-time, nor is it timeless and spaceless. Self-identity is mutually created by organisms through their behaviors and feedbacks. When a perceived unit organism dies, its identity goes with it, but the organism, being insepa-rable from all else, neither lives nor dies. In other words, *self is real as an illusion; it is not an illusion of reality.*

We discover life and death and no-life, no-death; inside and outside and not-in, not-out; self and other and not-one, not-two. In the *Hsinhsinming,* a synopsis written by the third Chinese patriarch of Zen, we find the strange loop: 'Things are things because of mind; mind is mind because of things.'32 Of course, the things in the two sections differ as phenomenon and noumenon.

As a youngster in the 1950's, I read an allegory in the form of a science-fiction short story, whose composition fore-shadowed my adult career and deepest interests. [May the author forgive my liberties; alas, I am depending on a decrepit 30-year-old memory.] The tale concerned two computer ex-perts, who had learned that some Tibetan lamas were engaged in a continuing, already centuries-old quest of recording all the names of dieties used throughout the universe. Bringing along their computer, the scientists arrived at the monastery by evening, and told the lamas that their device would easily and quickly supply a list of the names (and a lot of mean-ingless words) simply by permutations of the alphabet. The program was entered, and soon the lamas gathered around the rising stack of printout paper. They were astonished and pleased to see the hundreds of thousands of names the scien-tists had already found. 'By the way,' asked one of the technologists, 'what is the purpose of this collection?' The abbot replied that they had assumed the search to be an endless task and that if they somehow did reach the goal, then the universe would come to an end. [Among Zen Buddhism's Four Great Vows is 'The teachings are infinite; we vow to master them all.'] 'What superstition!' muttered one of the scientists.Then the other noticed that the stars were disappearing.

Science will not complete the picture of existence; organized religion and its tenets will also fail. The Tao Te Ching of Lao Tzu begins with the admonition that the Tao can not be fixed by naming, that it can not be expressed, but, nevertheless, goes on for many pages trying to convey its essence and properties to the reader. The numerous volumes of Buddhist teachings and motivational examples are equally incapable. This book has engaged in the same folly. These chapters of selected scientific evidence and principles are sutras on the dharmas in disguise. I hope that the presented notions of self and mind have been worthy of pondering and of self-exploration.

Indeed, by now you may intellectually accept the congruent realms of form and formlessness, of self and no-other-than self, of separation and seamless unity. However, with acceptance and analysis there yet remains doubt, the same great doubt faced by Zen monks. Thinking has its limits, and interpretations should not be trusted, because intellect, a soft veneer, is subject to the power of argument. Logic can not overcome the paradoxical relationships of reality, nor can we smash the doubt by belief. We must trandscend it.

Zen Master Wu-Men Hui-K'ai (1183-1260), who compiled one of the major collections of koans, *The Gateless-Gate,* wrote[33]

> If you understand 'it', all things are one;
> If you do not, they are different and separate.
> If you do not understand 'it', all things are one;
> If you do, they are different and separate.

Do you understand his poem? Did you 'feel' a shift with the change in perspective? If not, KATZ!

How, then, can we incorporate these primary principles into our marrow? How do we acquire the freedom to quantum jump the realms? Mere philosophy is shallow and easy to ignore or compromise in the diverse relationships and activities of daily life. After all, it is how we live our short lives and how we function in society—applications and ethics—that ultimately matters.

A peculiar sudden attainment, psychologically related to but spiritually deeper and more extensive than *Aha!* and *Eureka!*, is the wisdom sword that cuts a passage through the thicket of doubt and other dissatisfactions and suffering. Some call it enlightenment, some speak of realization, awakening, or satori. It is the aim of the Seeker, but consciously grasping for it is a sure way to prevent it. Enlightment is a concept, as any other, and hence it is an anchor. We must let go of both our scientific and religious teachings and question all authority, including the final authority, ourselves. One of the koans included in Master Wu-Men's collection has this concern as one of its themes:[33]

Each morning Zen teacher Jui-yen (ninth century) called, 'Master!' and answered himself, 'Yes?' He continued, 'Be awake!', affirming, 'Yes!' 'Do not be deceived by others anytime, anywhere,' he warned. 'I will not be deceived,' he replied.

Here is Jui-yen in two minds talking to himself. Who is the Master? Which is Jui-yen?

Since scientific data may be sufficiently instrumental for only a rare few, I have included koans as above to help forge that transcending blade. Koans are not riddles and do not have single solutions, but, rather, are historical examples of Zen in action and of the initiation of enlightenment. I have provided a clue or tactic to the penetration, deciphering, and attainment of some koans in the discussions of the ubiquitous self-referential feedback loops we find in nature. You probably have read the koans scattered throughout the book without any attempt to grasp the Zen. Now is a good time to seize them and provide a demonstration of their context.

Koans are but one method. For those who do not routinely practice meditation, I urge your discovery of this important noetic tool of creativity and auto-experimentation. Meditation

Bibel '92

WHERE WORDS FAIL

can take place as formal sitting on cushions following your breath, repeating a meaningful word or phrase, simply concentrating on a visual image or soundscape, or examining koans, or it can be accomplished with long silent and attentive hikes alone in a wilderness. Even Tai Chi Chuan and dance involve aspects of meditation. The many approaches each include a variety of mental devices for concentration. May you develop your own philosophy as reflected by the mirrors of external and internal scientific experiments, your personal explorations and introspectional experience. For the benefit of all, may you attain clear moment-to-moment mind for correct grasping of each situation, relationship, and action. How? Casting off the chains of analysis, just do it!

During the T'ang dynasty, Nan-Ch'uan was a great, highly respected Zen Master. Lu-Hsuan, a governmental official, speaking metaphorically asked the Master, 'A man had kept a goose in a bottle, but as the bird grew larger it could no longer leave the bottle. The man sought to remove the goose without injuring it, but he also wanted to avoid breaking the bottle. How would you extract the goose?'

Nan-Ch'uan cried out, 'Honorable sir!'

'Yes?' replied the official.

'There, it is out!' smiled the Master.[34]

What is this goose? How was it released? Do not explain. This book is already filled with dead philosophical words. Instead, demonstrate your attainment with a live expression that cuts to the marrow. If you still do not know what live words are, ask a four-year-old child!

What is Zen? You already understand. Black lines on white paper.

* * *

'I can't explain myself, I'm afraid, sir,' said Alice, 'because I'm not my self, you see.' 'I don't see,' said the Caterpillar.

* * *

Shadow of the pen
drifting with the setting sun—
words lost in darkness.

THE ZEN HELIX
Based on Zen Master Seung Sahn's Circle Diagram

0 °	90 °	180 °	270 °	360 °
$1 + 1 = 3$ $1 + 0 = 1$	$1 = 0$ $0 = 1$	$1 \times 0 = 0$ $100 \times 0 = 0$	$3 \times 3 = 9$ $3 \times 3 = 100$	$1 + 2 = 3$ $1 + 0 = 0 + 1$
Form only form	Form: emptiness	No form	Form : any form	Form: form
Emptiness: only emptiness	Emptiness: form	No emptiness	Emptiness: form/emptiness	Emptiness: emptiness
Everyday consciousness	Karma consciousness	No-thing	Freedom/magic	Love
Relative existence	Existence/nonexistence	True emptiness	Aboute existence	The Absolute
Attachment: name & form	Attachment: thinking	Attachment: emptiness	Attachment: freedom	Nonattachment thinking
Passive acceptance	Conceptualization	Pure perception	Creativity	Compassion
Illusion	Delusion	Idle awareness	Imagination	Correct function
Only like this: Black lines, white paper		Without like this: Silence Become-one like this: Katz!		Just like this: Just do it!
'You already understand'	'Dog chases the bone'	'Only don't know'	'Head is a dragon, tail is a snake'	'When hungry, eat!'

REFERENCES

Preface
1. Jacob F. The Statue Within. An autobiography. Basic Books, New York, 1988.
2. Ziman J. An Introduction to Science Studies. The philosophical and social aspects of science and technology. Cambridge University Press, Cambridge, 1984.
3. Bibel DJ. Milestones in Immunology. A historical exploration. Science Tech/Springer-Verlag, Madison, WI, 1988.
4. Medawar PB. Advice to a Young Scientist. Harper & Row, New York, 1979.

Chapter 1: Into the abyss
1. Hoover T. The Zen Experience. New American Library, New York, 1980.
2. Begley S, Murr A, Springen K, Gordon J, Harrison J. All about twins. Newsweek (November 23):58-69 (1987).
3. Rose NR., Mackay IR (eds). The Autoimmune Diseases. Academic Press, Orlando, 1985.
4. Hurley TJ III. Multiple personality mirrors of a new model of mind? Investigations, Institute of Noetic Sciences. 1(3/4):1-23 (1985).
5. Black S., Humphrey JH, Niven JSF. Inhibition of Mantoux reaction by direct suggestion under hypnosis. British Medical Journal 1:1649-52 (1965).
6. Beer AE, Billingham RE. The Immunobiology of Mammalian Reproduction. Prentice-Hall, Englewood Cliffs, NJ. 1976.
7. Lovelock JE. Gaia. A new look at life on Earth. Oxford University Press, Oxford, 1979.
8. Lovelock J. The Ages of Gaia. A biography of our living Earth. Norton, New York, 1988.
9. Gleick J. Chaos. Making a new science. Viking, New York. 1987.
10. Capra F. The Tao of Physics. An exploration of the parallels between modern physics and Eastern mysticism. 2nd ed. Shambhala, Boulder, 1983.
11. Watson I. Lifetide. Simon & Schuster, New York, 1979.
12. Jantsch E. The Self-Organizing Universe. Scientific and human implications of the emerging paradigm of evolution. Pergamon Press, Oxford, 1980.
13. Crew FA. The meaning of death. In: The Humanist Outlook (Ayer AJ, ed). Pemberton, London, 1968.
14. Vallery-Radot R. The Life of Pasteur. Archibald Constable, London, 1902.
15. Kuhn TS. The Structure of Scientific Revolutions. 2nd ed. University of Chicago Press, Chicago, 1970.
16. Kitchener RF (ed). The World View of Contemporary Physics. Does it need a new metaphysics? State University of New York Press, Albany, 1988.
17. Wallace BA. Choosing Reality. A contemplative view of physics and the mind. Shambhala, Boston, 1989.

18. Einstein A. Ideas and Opinions (Seelig C, ed; Bargmann C, transl). Crown, New York, 1985.
19. Griffin DR (ed). The Reenchantment of Science. Postmodern proposals. State University of New York Press, Albany, 1988.
20. Davies P. God and the New Physics. Simon & Schuster, New York, 1983.
21. Wilber K (ed). Quantum Questions. Mystical writings of the world's great physicists. Shambhala, Boulder, 1984.
22. Heisenberg W. Physics and Philosophy. The revolution in modern science. Harper, New York, 1958.
23. Campbell J. The Masks of God. Oriental Mythology. Penguin Books, New York, 1962.
24. Lipsey R. An Art of Our Own. The spiritual in twentieth- century art. Shambhala, Boston, 1988.
25. Coward H. Jung and Eastern Thought. State University of New York Press, Albany, 1985.
26. Goleman D, Thurman RAF, ed. MindScience. An East-West dialogue. Wisdom, Boston, 1991.
27. Dossey L. Recovering the Soul. A scientific and spiritual search. Bantam, New York, 1989.
28. Hofstadter DR. Godel, Escher, Bach: an eternal golden braid. Basic Books, New York, 1979.
29. Eccles J, Sperry R, Prigogine I, Josephson B. Nobel Prize Conversations. Saybrook, San Francisco, 1985.
30. Dyson FJ. Energy in the Universe. Scientific American 225(3)50-59 (1971).
31. Kelley KW. The Home Planet. Addison-Wesley, Reading, MA and Mir, Moscow, 1988.

Chapter 2: There be dragons here

1. Heisenberg W. Physics and Philosophy. The revolution in modern science. Harper, New York, 1958.
2. Russell B. Wisdom of the West. Crescent Books, New York, 1959.
3. MacCallum M. The breakdown of physics? Nature 257:363 (1975).
4. Jeans J. The Mysterious Universe. Macmillan, New York, 1930.
5. Davis PJ, Hersh R. The Mathematical Experience. Houghton Mifflin, Boston, 1981.
6. Sheldrake R. Cause and effect in science: a fresh look. Noetic Sciences Review, No. 11:8-16 (Summer 1989).
7. Wallace BA. Choosing Reality. A contemplative view of physics and the mind. Shambhala, Boston, 1989.
8. Tweney RD, Doherty ME, Mynatt CR (eds). On Scientific Thinking. Columbia University Press, New York, 1981.
9. Hayward JW. Shifting Worlds, Changing Minds. Shambhala, Boston, 1987.
10. Robinson AL. Quantum jumps seen in a single ion. Science 234:24-25 (1986).
11. Wall JS, Hainfeld JF, Bittner JW. Preliminary measurements of uranium atom motion on carbon films at low temperatures. Ultramicroscopy 3:81-86 (1978).

12. Monson KL, Wall JS, Hainfeld JF. Visibility and stability of a 12-tungsten atom complex in the scanning transmission electron microscope. Ultramicroscopy 21:147-156 (1987).
13. Crewe AV. A high-resolution scanning electron microsope. Scientific American 224(4):26-35 (1971).
14. Cricenti A, Selci S, Felici AC, Generosi R, Gori E, Djaczenko W, Chiarotti G. Molecular structure of DNA by scanning tunneling microscopy. Science 245:1226-1227 (1989).
15. Dehmelt H. Experiments on the structure of an individual elementary particle. Science 247:539-545 (1990).
16. Price AF, Wong M-L, transl. The Diamond Sutra and the Sutra of Hui Neng. Shambhala, Boston, 1985.
17. Pool R. Quantum pot watching. Science 246:888 (1987).
18. Herbert N. Quantum Reality. Beyond the new physics. Anchor Press, Garden City, NY, 1985.
19. Robinson AL. Demonstrating single photon interference. Science 231:671-672 (1986).
20. Flam F. Making waves with interfering atoms. Science 252:921-922 (1991); Pool R. Optics' new focus: beams of atoms. Science 255:1513 (1992).
21. Davies PCW. God and the New Physics. Simon and Schuster, New York, 1983.
22. Davies PCW, Brown JR. The Ghost in the Atom. Cambridge University Press, Cambridge, 1986.
23. Pagels HR. The Cosmic Code. Quantum physics as the language of nature. Simon and Schuster, New York, 1982.
24. Abbott L. The mystery of the cosmological constant. Scientific American 258(5):106-113 (1988).
25. Chang G CC. The Buddhist Teaching of Totality. The philosophy of Hwa Yen Buddhism. Pennsylvania State University Press, University Park, PA, 1971.
26. Sheldrake R. A New Science of Life. The hypothesis of formative causation. Tarcher, Los Angeles, 1981.
27. Becker RO, Selden G. The Body Electric. Electromagnetism and the foundation of life. Morrow, New York, 1985. p. 268.
28. Cha Y, Murray CJ, Klinman JP. Hydrogen tunneling in enzyme reactions. Science 243:1325-1330 (1989).
29. Krueger AP, Reed EJ. Biological impact of small air ions. Science 193:1209-1213 (1976).
30. Soyka F, Edmonds A. The Ion Effect. Bantam, New York, 1978.
31. Pool R. Seeing chaos in a simple system. Science 241:787-788 (1988).
32. Pool R. Quantum chaos: enigma wrapped in a mystery. Science 243:893-895 (1989).
33. Simons G. Are Computers Alive? Evolution and new life forms. Birkhauser, Boston, 1983.
34. Buckminster Fuller R. Critical Path. St. Martin's Press, New York, 1981.
35. Whitehead AN. Science and the Modern World. Cambridge University Press, London, 1926.
36. Luk C (Lu K'uan Yu). Ch'an and Zen Teaching. First series. Shambhala, Berkeley, 1970.

37. Shibayama Z. Zen Comments on the Mumonkan (Kudo S, transl).
   Harper & Row, San Francisco, 1984.
38. Wilber K (ed). Quantum Questions. Mystical writings of the world's
   great physicists. Shambhala, Boulder, 1984.

Chapter 3: And 'mid these dancing rocks

1. Bendiner, E. The passions and perils of Pauling. Hospital Practice
   April:210-243 (1983).
2. Maugh TH II. Chemicals: how many are there? Science 199:162 (1978).
3. Rebek J Jr. Model studies in molecular recognition. Science
   235:1478-1484 (1987).
4. Koshland DE Jr. Protein shape and biological control. Scientific
   American 229(4):52-64 (1973).
5. Gund P, Andose JD, Rhodes JB, Smith GM. Three-dimensional
   molecular modeling and drug design. Science 208:1425-1431 (1980).
6. Alper J. The microchip microbe hunters. Science 247:904-806 (1990).
7. Shibayama Z. Zen Comments on the Mumonkan. Harper & Row, San
   Francisco, 1984.
8. Gleick J. Chaos. Making a new science. Viking, New York. 1987.
9. Pool R. Is it healthy to be chaotic? Science 243:604-607 (1989).
10. Steen LA. The science of patterns. Science 240:611-616 (1988).
11. DeLucas LJ et al. Protein crystal growth in microgravity. Science
    246:651-654 (1989).
12. Anfinsen CG. Principles that govern the folding of protein chains.
    Science 181:223-230 (1973).
13. Stryer L. Biochemistry. 3rd ed. Freeman, New York, 1988.
14. Lehninger AL. Biochemistry. Worth Publishers, New York, 1970.
15. Bowie JU, Reidhaar-Olson JF, Lim WA, Sauer RT. Deciphering the
    message in protein sequences: tolerance to amino acid substitutions. Science
    247:1306-1310 (1990).
16. Hoffman M. Straightening out the protein folding puzzle. Science
    254:1357-1358 (1991).
17. Skolnick J, Kolinski A. Simulations of the folding of a globular protein.
    Science 250:1121-1125 (1990).
18. Oparin AI. The Origin of Life on the Earth. Oliver and Boyd,
    Edinburgh, 1957.
19. Holden A, Singer P. Crystals and Crystal Growing. Heinemann, London,
    1961.
20. Waddington CH. The Strategy of Genes. Allen and Unwin, London 1957.
21. Odin S. Process Metaphysics and Hua-Yen Buddhism. A critical study
    of cumulative penetration vs. interpenetration. State University of New
    York Press, Albany, 1982.
22. Chang GCC. The Buddhist Teaching of Totality. The philosophy of
    Hwa Yen Buddism. Pennsylvania State University Press, University Park,
    1971.
23. Whitehead AN. Process and Reality. (Griffin DR, Sherburne DW, eds)
    Corrected ed. Macmillan, New York, 1978.
24. Wilber K (ed). The Holographic Paradigm and Other Paradoxes.
    Shambhala, Boulder, 1982.

25. Cleary T. Entry into the Inconceivable. An introduction to Hua-Yen Buddhism. University of Hawaii Press, Honolulu, 1983.
26. Sheldrake R. A New Science of Life. The hypothesis of formative causation. Tarcher, Los Angeles, 1981.
27. Govinda AB. Creative Meditation and Multi-Dimensional Consciousness. Quest, Wheaton, IL, 1976.
28. Herbert N. Quantum Reality. Beyond the new physics. Anchor Press, Garden City, NY, 1985.
29. Beebe TP Jr, Wilson TE, Ogletree F, Katz JE, Balhorn R, Salmerson MB, Siekhaus WJ. Direct observation of native DNA structures with the scanning tunneling microscope. Science 243:370-373 (1989).
30. Drake B, Prater CB, Weisenhorn AL, Gould SAC, Albrech KTR, Quate KCF, Cannell DA, Hansma HG, Hansma PK. Imaging crystals, polymers, and processes in water with the atomic force microscope. Science 243:1586-1598 (1989).
31. Wiberg KB, Hadad CM, Breneman CM, Laidig KE, Murcko MA, LePage TJ. The response of electrons to structural changes. Science 252:1266-1272 (1991).

Chapter 4: 2,000 light-years from home

1. Campbell J. The Inner Reaches of Outer Space. Alfred van der Marck, New York, 1986.
2. Fraser JT, Lawrence N, Haber FC (eds). Time, Science, and Society in China and the West. University of Massachusetts Press, Amherst, 1986.
3. Smith DH. The Wisdom of the Taoists. New Directions, New York, 1980.
4. Collingwood RG. The Idea of Nature. Oxford University Press, New York, 1960.
5. Jeans J. The Mysterious Universe. Macmillan, New York, 1930.
6. Blandford RD, Kochanek CS, Kovner I, Narayan R. Gravitational lens optics. Science 245:824-830 (1989).
7. Zukav G. The Dancing Wu Li Masters. An overview of the new physics. Morrow, New York, 1979.
8. Brush SG. Prediction and theory evaluation: the case of light bending. Science 246:1124-1129 (1989).
9. Hawking SW. A Brief History of Time. From the Big Bang to black holes. Bantam, New York, 1988.
10. Flam F. COBE finds the bumps in the Big Bang. Science 256:612 (1992).
11. Waldrop MM. Dark matter, structure, and strings. Science 233:1386-1388 (1986).
12. Waldrop MM. Seeing the Unseeable. Science 248:1189 (1990).
13. Waldrop MM. Brown dwarf candidates abound. Science 245:29-30 (1989).
14. Waldrop MM. The quantum wave function of the universe. Science 242:1248-1250 (1988).
15. Flam F. A long, hard look at the Virgo cluster. Science 253:1389 (1991).
16. Arnold E. Indian Minatures. Editions du Sud, Paris, 1968.
17. Kerr RA. Does Chaos permeate the solar system? Science 244:144-145 (1989).
18. Gleick J. Chaos. Making a new science. Viking, New York. 1987.

19. Palga J. A surprise near Virgo. Science 245:933 (1989).
20. Waldrop MM. Seeing all there is to see in the universe. Science 241:418-419 (1988).
21. Waldrop MM. A window looking out on Creation. Science 250:32 (1990).
22. Geller MJ, Huchra JP. Mapping the universe. Science 246:897-903 (1989).
23. Bibel DJ, Lawson JW. Morphology and viability of large bodies of streptococcal L-forms. Infection and Immunity 12:919-930 (1975).
24. Cline MJ. The White Cell. Harvard University Press, Cambridge, MA, 1975.
25. Porter KR, Tucker JB. The ground substance of the living cell. Scientific American 244(3):57-67 (1981).
26. Marx JL. Organizing the cytoplasm. Science 222:1109-1110 (1983).
27. Waldrop MM. Are we all in the grip of a great attractor? Science 237:1296-1297 (1987).
28. Woosley SE, Phillips MM. Supernova 1987A! Science 240:750-9 (1988).
29. Waldrop MM. Supernova 1987A on center stage. Science 238:1038-1041 (1987).
30. Goddard D. Self-Realization of Noble Wisdom. The Lankavatara Sutra. Dawn Horse Press, Clearlake, CA, 1983.
31. Cleary T. Entry into the Inconceivable. An introduction to Hua-Yen Buddhism. University of Hawaii Press, Honolulu, 1983.
32. Hoffmann Y. Radical Zen. The sayings of Joshu. Autumn Press, Brookline, MA, 1978.

Chapter 5: Shadows in the flame

1. Hoyle F. Wickramasinghe NC. Prebiotic molecules and interstellar grain clumps. Nature 266:241-243 (1977).
2. Hoyle F. Wickramasinghe NC. Origin and nature of carbonaceous material in the galaxy. Nature 270:701-703 (1977).
3. Imshenetsky AA, Lysenko SV, Kazakov. Upper boundary of the biosphere. Applied and Environmental Microbiology 35:1-5 (1978).
4. Crichton M. The Andromeda Strain. Knopf, New York, 1969.
5. Hoyle F, Wickramasinghe NC. Diseases from Space. J.M. Dent, London, 1979.
6. Chyba CF, Thomas PJ, Brookshaw L, Sagan C. Cometary delivery of organic molecules to the early Earth. Science 249:366-373 (1990).
7. Taylor GR. Space microbiology. Annual Review of Microbiology 28:121-137 (1974).
8. Klein HP. Microbiology on Mars? ASM News 42:207-214 (1976).
9. Fox JL. Martian life: another look. ASM News 55:409-410 (1989).
10. Jannasch HW. The microbial basis of life at deep-sea hydrothermal vents. ASM News 55:413-416 (1989).
11. Lovelock J. The Ages of Gaia. A biography of our living Earth. Norton, New York, 1988.
12. Wright IP, Grady MM, Pillinger CT. Organic materials in a Martian meteorite. Nature 340:220-222 (1989).
13. Woese CR. Archaebacteria. Scientific American 244(6):98-122 (1981).

14. Shibayama Z. Zen Comments on the Mumonkan (Kudo S, transl). Harper & Row, San Francisco, 1984.
15. Dickerson RE. Chemical evolution and the origin of life. Scientific American 239(3):70-86 (1978).
16. Roll-hansen N. Experimental method and spontaneous generation: The controversy between Pasteur and Pouchet, 1859- 1864. Journal of the History of Medicine 34:273-292 (1979).
17. Watson JD, Hopkins NH, Roberts JW, Steitz JA, Weiner AM. Molecular Biology of the Gene. 4th ed. Benjamin/Cummings, Menlo Park, CA, 1987.
18. Holliday R. A different kind of inheritance. Scientific American 260(6):60-73 (1989).
19. Cairns JJ, Overbaugh J, Miller S. The origin of mutants. Nature 335:142-145 (1988).
20. Shaprio JA. Bacteria as multicellular organisms. Scientific American 258(6):82-89 (1988).
21. Plomin R. The role of inheritance in behavior. Science 248:1838 (1990).
22. Burnet FM. Virus as Organism. Evolutionary and ecological aspects of some human virus diseases. Harvard University Press, Cambridge, MA, 1945.
23. Marshall E. The scourge of computer viruses. Science 240:133-4 (1988).
24. McAfee J, Haynes C. Computer Viruses, Worms, Data Diddlers, Killer Programs, and Other Threats to Your System. St. Martin's Press, New York, 1989.
25. Simons G. Are Computers Alive? Evolution and new life forms. Birkhauser, Boston, 1983.
26. Schrödinger E. What is Life? The physical aspect of the living cell; Mind and Matter. Cambridge University Press, Cambridge, 1967.
27. Jantsch E. The Self-Organizing Universe. Scientific and human implications of the emerging paradigm of evolution. Pergamon Press, Oxford, 1980.
28. Madore BF, Freedman WL. Computer simulations of the Belousov-Zhabotinsky reaction. Science 222:np (1983).
29. Huxley, A. The Perennial Philosophy. Harper & Row, New York, 1970.
30. Barrett W. Zen Buddhism: Selected Writings of D.T. Suzuki. Doubleday, Garden City, NY, 1956.
31. Lipsey R. An Art of Our Own. The spiritual in twentieth- century art. Shambhala, Boston, 1988.
32. Luk C. The Vimalakirti Nirdesa Sutra. Shambhala, Boston, 1990.
33. Latour B. Science in Action. Harvard University Press, Cambridge, MA, 1987.
34. Wallace BA. Choosing Reality. A contemplative view of physics and the mind. Shambhala, Boston, 1989.
35. Kottler DB. Louis Pasteur and molecular dissymmetry, 1844- 1864. Studies in the History of Biology. Vol 2. Johns Hopkins University Press, Baltimore, 1978. pp 57-98.
36. Corrigan JJ. D-Amino acids in animals. Science 164:142-149 (1969).
37. Dubos R. Pasteur's dilemma. The road not taken. ASM News 40:703-709 (1974).
38. Kondepudi DK, Kaufman RJ, Singh N. Chiral symmetry breaking in sodium chlorate crystallization. Science 250:975-976 (1990).

39. Hegstrom RA, Kondepudi DK. The handedness of the universe. Scientific American 262(1):108-115 (1990).
40. Man EH, Sandhouse ME, Burg J, Fisher GH. Accumulation of D-aspartic acid with age in the human brain. Science 220:1407-1408 (1983).
41. Marshall E. Racemization dating: great expectations. Science 247:799 (1990).
42. Fox SW, Dose K. Molecular Evolution and the Origin of Life. W.H. Freeman, San Francisco, 1972.
43. Pool R. Closing the gap between proteins and DNA. Science 248:1609 (1990).
44. Waldrop MM. The golden crystal of life. Science 250:1080 (1990).
45. Waldrop MM. Goodbye to the warm little pond? Science 250:1078-1080 (1990).

Chapter 6: Tracks in the ocean foam

1. Olby R. The Path to the Double Helix. Macmillan, London, 1974.
2. Judson HF. The Eighth Day of Creation. Makers of the revolution in biology. Simon and Schuster, New York, 1979.
3. Varlea F, Maturana HR, Uribe R. Autopoiesis: the organization of living systems, its characterization and a model. Biosystems 5:187-196 (1974).
4. Watson JD, Hopkins NH, Roberts JW, Steitz JA, Weiner AM. Molecular Biology of the Gene. 4th ed. Benjamin/Cummings, Menlo Park, CA, 1987.
5. Bauer W, Crick FHC, White JH. Supercoiled DNA. Scientific American 243(1):118-133 (1980).
6. Eigen M, Gardiner G, Schuster P, Winkler-Oswatitsch R. The origin of genetic information. Scientific American 244(4):88-118 (1981).
7. Waldrop MM. Did life really start out in an RNA world? Science 246:1248-1249 (1989).
8. Lewis R. RNA can be a catalyst. Science 218:872-874 (1982).
9. Waldrop MM. Catalytic RNA wins chemistry Nobel. Science 246:325 (1989).
10. Rich A, Kim SH. The tree-dimensional structure of transfer RNA. Scientific American 238(1):52-62 (1978).
11. Leszczynski JF, Rose GD. Loops in globular proteins: a novel category of secondary structure. Science 234:849-855 (1986).
12. Yutang L. The Wisdom of Laotse. Modern Library, New York, 1976.
13. Lake JA. The ribosome. Scientific American 245(2):84-97 (1981).
14. Stern S, Powers T, Changschlien L-M, Noller HF. RNA-protein interctions in 30S ribosomal subunits: folding and function of 16S rRNA. Science 244:783-790 (1989).
15. Dawkins R. The Selfish Gene. Oxford Univesity Press, New York, 1976.
16. Holmes SW. Horioka C. Zen Art for Meditation. Tuttle, Rutland, VT, 1986.
17. Steitz JA. Snurps. Scientific American 258(6):56-63 (1988).
18. Barinaga M. Introns pop up in new places—What does it mean? Science 250:1512 (1990).
19. Xu M-Q, Kathe SD, Goodrich-Blair H, Nierzwicki-Bauer SA, Shub DA. Bacterial origin of a chloroplast intron: conserved self-splicing Group I introns in cyanobacteria. Science 250:1566-1570 (1990).

20. Kuhsel MG, Strickland R, Palmer JD. An ancient group I intron shared by eubacteria and chloroplasts. Science 250:1570-1573 (1990).
21. Lewin R. Biggest challenge since the double helix. Science 212:28-32 (1981).
22. French DL, Laskov R, Scharff MD. The role of somatic hypermutation in the generation of antibody diversity. Science 244:1152-1157 (1989).
23. Marx JL. A parent's sex may affect gene expression. Science 239:352-353 (1988).
24. Holliday R. A different kind of inheritance. Scientific American 260(6):60-73 (1989).
25. Hayflick L. The cell biology of human aging. New England Journal of Medicine 295:1302-1308 (1976).
26. Marx JL. Aging research (I): cellular theories of senescence. Science 186:1105-1107 (1974).
27. Marx JL. Aging research (II): pacemakers for aging? Science 186:1196-1197 (1974).
28. Radman M, Wagner R. The high fidelity of DNA duplication. Scientific American 259(2):40-46 (1988).
29. Ames BN.. Identifying environmental chemicals causing mutations and cancer. Science 204:587-593 (1979).
30. Commoner B, Vithayathil AJ, Dolara P, Nair S, Madyastha P, Cuca GC. Formation of mutagens in beef and beef extract during cooking. Science 201:913-916 (1978).
31. Hayes W. The Genetics of Bacteria and Their Viruses. Studies in basic genetics and molecular biology. 2nd ed. Wiley, New York, 1968.
32. Brock TD. The Emergence of Bacterial Genetics. Cold Spring Harbor Laboratory Press, Cold Spring Harbor, NY, 1990.
33. Cairns J, Stent GS, Watson JD. Phage and the Origins of Molecular Biology. Cold Spring Harbor Laboratory of Quantitative Biology, Cold Spring Harbor, NY, 1966.
34. Varmus HE. Form and function of retroviral proviruses. Science 216:812-820 (1982).
35. Novick RP. Plasmids Scientific American 243(6):103-127 (1980).
36. Bibel DJ, Smiljanic RJ. Interactions of Trichophyton mentagrophytes and micrococci on skin culture. Journal of Investigative Dermatology 72:133-137 (1979).
37. McCarty M. The Transforming Principle. Discovering that genes are made of DNA. Norton, New York, 1985.
38. Diener TO. Viroids: structure and function. Science 205:859-866 (1979).
39. Prusiner SB. Novel proteinaceous infectious particles cause scrapie. Science 216:136-144 (1982).
40. Lewin R. DNA fingerprints in health and disease. Science 233:521-522 (1986).
41. Lewin R. DNA typing on the witness stand. Science 244:1033-1035 (1989).
42. Hoover T. The Zen Experience. New American Library, New York, 1980.
43. Izutsu T. Toward a Philosophy of Zen Buddhism. Prajna, Boulder, 1982.

Chapter 7: Across the Great Divide

1. Margulis L. Kingdom Animalia. The zoological malaise from a microbial perspective. American Zoologist 30:861-875 (1990).
2. Schwartz RM, Dayhoff MO. Origins of prokaryotes, eukaryotes, mitchondria, and chloroplasts. Science 199:395-403 (1978).
3. Goodenough UW, Levine RP. The genetic activity of mitochondria and chloroplasts. Scientific American 223(5):22-29 (1970).
4. Schope JW, Oehler DZ. How old are the eukaryotes? Science 193:47-49 (1976).
5. Madoff S. (ed). Mycoplasma and the L Forms of Bacteria. Gordon and Breach, New York, 1971.
6. Bibel DJ, Lawson. Morphology and viability of large bodies of streptococcal L-forms. Infection and Immunity 12:919-930 (1975).
7. Raff RA, Mahler HR. The non-symbiotic origin of mitochondria. Science 177:575-582 (1972).
8. Uzzeli T, Spolsky C. and Raff RA, Mahler HR. Origin of mitochondria. Science 180:516-517 (1973).
9. Lewin R. No genome barriers to promiscuous DNA. Science 224:970-971 (1984).
10. Cann RL, Stoneking M, Wilson AC. Mitochondrial DNA and human evolution. Nature 325:31-36 (1987).
11. Margulis L. Symbiosis and evolution. Scientific American 225(2):48-57 (1971); Marriage of convenience. The Sciences. Sep/Oct:31-36 (1990).
12. Whitman W. Leaves of Grass. Penguin, New York, 1981.
13. Gould SJ. Darwinism and the expansion of evolutionary theory. Science 216:380-287 (1982).
14. Cairns J, Overbaugh J, Miller S. The origin of mutants. Nature 335:142-145 (1988).
15. Hall BG. Adaptive evolution that requires multiple spontaneous mutations. I. Mutations involving an insertion sequence. Genetics 120:887-897 (1988).
16. Hall BG. Increased rates of advantageous mutations in response to environmental challenges. ASM News 57:82-86 (1991).
17. Koestler A. Janus. A summing up. Vintage, New York, 1979.
18. Jantsch E. The Self-Organizing Universe. Scientific and human implications of the emerging paradigm of evolution. Pergamon Press, Oxford, 1980.
19. Hofstadter DR. Godel, Escher, Bach: an eternal golden braid. Basic Books, New York, 1979.
20. Jahn RG, Dunne BJ. Margins of Reality. The role of consciousness in the physical world. Harcourt Brace Jovanovich, San Diego, 1987.
21. Watson L. Beyond Supernature. Bantam, Toronto, 1988.
22. LaBerge S. Lucid Dreaming. Ballantine, New York, 1986.
23. Metzner R (ed). The resonating universe: explorations of an integrative metaphor. ReVISION 10(1):3-56 (1987).
24. Suzuki DT. Manual of Zen Buddhism. Grove, New York, 1982.
25. Lipsey R. An Art of Our Own. The spiritual in twentieth-century art. Shambhala, Boston, 1988.

26. Moore-Ede MC, Sulzman FM, Fuller CA. The Clocks That Time Us. Physiology of the circadian timing system. Harvard University Press, Cambridge, MA, 1982.
27. Becker RO, Selden G. The Body Electric. Electromagnetism and the foundation of life. Quill, New York, 1985.
28. Natalini JJ. Circadian rhythms: considerations in the laboratory. American Laboratory June 1979:97-102 (1979).
29. Hilts P. The clock within. Science 80(12):61-67 (1980).
30. Rama S, Ballentine R, Hymes A. Science of Breath. A practical guide. Himalayan International Institute of Yoga Science and Philosophy, Honesdale, PA, 1979.
31. Czeisler CA, Allan JS, Strogatz SH, et al. Bright light resets the human circadian pacemaker independent of the timing of the sleep-wake cycle. Science 233:667-671 (1986).
32. Lewy AJ, Sack RL, Miller LS, Hoban TM. Antidepressant and circadian phase-shifting effects of light. Science 235:352-354 (1987).
33. Takahashi JS, Zatz M. Regulation of circadian rhythmicity. Science 217:1104-1111 (1982).
34. Kolata G. Finding biological clocks in fetuses. Science 230:929-930 (1985).
35. Ralph MR, Foster RG, Davis FC, Menaker M. Transplanted suprachiasmatic nucleus determines circadian period. Science 247:975-978 (1990).
36. Kolata G. Genes and biological clocks. Science 230:1151-1152 (1985).
37. Edelman GM. Topobiology. Scientific American 260(5):76-88 (1989).
38. Hall ET. The Dance of Life. Doubleday, New York, 1983.
39. Pool R. Is it healthy to be chaotic? Science 243:604-607 (1989).
40. Peterson I. Ribbons of chaos. Science News 139:60-61 (1991).
41. Langreth R. Engineering dogma gives way to chaos. Science 252:776-778 (1991).
42. Berendt J-E. Nada Brahma: The World is Sound. Destiny, Rochester, VT, 1987.

Chapter 8: All for one, one for all

1. Gibran K. The Prophet. Knopf, New York, 1966.
2. Coleman W. Biology in the Nineteenth Century: Problems of form, function, and transformation. Wiley, New York, 1971.
3. Giere A. hydra as a model for the development of biological form. Scientific American 231(6):44-54 (1974).
4. Lewin R. Why is development so illogical? Science 224:1327-1329 (1984).
5. Mlot C. A well-rounded worm. Science 252:1619-1620 (1991).
6. Waldrop MM. Spontaneous order, evolution, and life. Science 1543-1545 (1990).
7. Shapiro JA. Bacteria as multicellular organisms. Scientific American 258(6):82-89 (1988).
8. Shapiro JA. Multicellular behavior of bacteria. ASM News 57:247-253 (1991).
9. Binet A. The Psychic Life of Microorganisms: a study in experimental psychology. McCormack T (transl). Open Court, Chicago, 1889.

10. Koshland DE Jr. Bacterial Chemotaxis as a Model Behavioral System. Raven Press, New York, 1980.
11. Berg HC. How bacteria swim. Scientific American 233(2):36-44 (1975).
12. Adler J. The sensing of chemicals by bacteria. Scientific American 234(4):40-47 (1976).
13. Tsang N, Macnab R, Koshland DE Jr. Common mechanism for repellents and attractants in bacterial chemotaxis. Science 181:680-683 (1973).
14. Adler J, Tso W-W. EDecision'-making in bacteria. Chemotactic response of Escherichia coli to conflicting stimuli. Science 184:1292-1294 (1974).
15. Bibel DJ, Smiljanic RJ. Interactions of Triphophyton mentagrophytes and micrococci on skin culture. Journal of Investigative Dermatology 72:133-137 (1979).
16. Shibayama Z. Zen Comments on the Mumonkan (Kudo S, transl). Harper & Row, San Francisco, 1984.
17. Wireman JW, Dworkin M. Morphogenesis and developmental interactions in Myxobacteria. Science 189:516-523 (1975).
18. Kim SK, Kaiser D. Cell alignment required in differentiation of Myxococcus xanthus. Science 249:926-928 (1990).
19. Devreotes P. Dictyostelium discoideum:; a model system for cell-cell interactions in development. Science 245:1054-1058 (1989).
20. Epstein IR. Spiral waves in chemistry and biology. Science 252:67 (1991).
21. Dawkins R. The Selfish Gene. Oxford Univesity Press, New York, 1976.
22. Sheldrake AR. The ageing, growth and death of cells. Nature 250:381-385 (1974).
23. Hoover T. The Zen Experience. New American Library, New York, 1980.
24. Morris SC. Burgess Shale faunas and the Cambrian explosion. Science 246:339-346 (1989).
25. Gould SJ. Wonderful Life. The Burges Shale and the nature of history. Norton, New York, 1989.
26. Pool R. Pushing the envelope of life. Science 247:158-160 (1990).
27. Otte D, Endler JA (eds). Speciation and Its Consequences. Sinauer, Sunderland, MA, 1989.
28. Becker RO, Selden G. The Body Electric. Electromagnetism and the foundation of life. Morrow, New York, 1985.
29. Edleman GM. CAMs and Igs: Cell adhesion and the evolutionary origins of immunity. Immunological Reviews 100:11-45 (1987).
30. Edelman GM. Topobiology. Scientific American 260(5):76-78 (1989).
31. Bibel DJ, Aly R, Bayles C, Strauss WG, Shinefield HR, Maibach HI. Competitive adherence as a mechanism of bacterial interference. Canadian Journal of Microbiology 29:700-703 (1983).
32. Beachey EH (ed). Bacterial Adherence. Chapman & Hall, London, 1980.
33. Rodriguez-Boulan E, Nelson WJ. Morphogenesis of the polarized epithelial cell phenotype. Science 245:718-725 (1989).
34. Singer SJ, Nicolson GL. The fluid mosaic model of the structure of cell membranes. Science 175-720-731 (1972).
35. Rothman JE, Lenard J. Membrane asymmetry. Science 195:743-753 (1977).

36. Mandelkow E, Mandelkow E-M, Hotani H, Hess B, Muller SC. Spatial patterns from oscillating microtubules. Science 246:1291-1293 (1989).
37. Yutang L. The Wisdom of Laotse. Modern Library, New York, 1976.

Chapter 9: Forming a more perfect union

1. Marples MJ. The Ecology of Human Skin. Charles C Thomas, Springfield, IL, 1965.
2. Lovelock JE. Gaia. A new look at life on Earth. Oxford University Press, Oxford, 1979.
3. Fuller RB. Critical Path. St. Martin's Press, New York, 1981.
4. Capra F. The Turning Point. Simon and Schuster, New York, 1982.
5. Storer JH. The Web of Life. New American Library, 1956.
6. Carson R. Silent Spring. Houghton Mifflin, Boston, 1962.
7. De Bell G (ed). The Environmental Handbook. Ballantine, New York, 1970.
8. Dubos R. Celebrations of Life. McGraw-Hill, New York, 1982.
9. Rosebury T. Microorganisms Indigenous to Man. McGraw-Hill, New York, 1962.
10. Dobell C. Antony van Leeuwenhoek and His Little Animals. Harcourt, Brace and Co., New York, 1932.,
11. Schierbeek A. Measuring the Invisible World. Abelard- Schuman, London, 1959.
12. Bibel DJ. The discovery of the oral flora—a 300-year retrospective. Journal of the American Dental Association 107:569-570 (1983).
13. Alexander M. Microbial Ecology, Wiley, New York, 1971.
14. Listgarten MA, Mayo H. Amsterdam M. Ultrastructure of the attachment device between coccal and filamentous microorganism in 'corn cob' formations of dental plaque. Archives of Oral Biology 18:651-656 (1973).
15. Jones SJ. A special relationship between spherical and filamentous microorganisms in mature human dental plaque. Archives of Oral Biology 17:613-616 (1972).
16. Aly R, Shinefield HR. Bacterial Interference. CRC Press, Boca Raton, FL, 1982.
17. Bibel DJ, Aly R, Bayles C, Strauss WG, Shinefield HR, Maibach HI. Competititve adherence as a mechanism of bacterial interference. Canadian Journal of Microbiology 29:700-703 (1983).
18. Postgate J. Microbes and Man. Penguin, Middlesex, 1975.
19. Dixon B. Invisible Allies. Temple Smith, London, 1976.
20. Luckey TD. Germfree Life and Gnotobiology. Academic Press, New York, 1963.
21. Williamson AP (ed). A special report: four-year study of a boy with combined immune deficiency maintained in reverse isolation from birth. Pediatric Research 11:63-89 (1977).
22 Suzuki DT. Zen Buddhism (Barrett W, ed). Doubleday, Garden City, New York, 1956.
23. Crease R. Biomagnetism attracts diverse crowd. Science 245:1041-1043 (1989).

24. Becker RO, Selden G. The Body Electric. Electromagnetism and the foundation of life. Morrow, New York, 1985.
25. Noble WC. Microbiology of the Skin. 2nd ed, Lloyd-Luke, London, 1981.
26. Andrews MLA. The Life that Lives on Man. Faber, London, 1976.
27. Aly R, Shirley C, Cunico B, Maibach HI. Effect of prolonged occlusion on the microbial flora, pH, carbon dioxide, and transepidermal water loss on human skin. Journal of Investigative Dermatology 71:378-381 (1978).
28. Taylor GR. Space microbiology. Annual Review of Microbiology 28:121-137 (1974).
29. Bibel DJ, Aly R, Shinefield HR. Antimicrobial Activity of Sphingosines. Journal of Investigative Dermatology 98:269-270 (1992).
30. Marsh P. Oral Microbiology. Aspects of Microbiology 1. American Society for Microbiology, Washington, DC, 1983.
31. Skinner FA, Carr JG. The Normal Microbial Flora of Man. Academic Press, London, 1974.
32. Drasar BS, Barrow PA. Intestinal Microbiology. Aspects of Microbiology 10. American Society for Microbiology, Washington, DC, 1985.
33. Drasar BS, Hill MJ. Human Intestinal Flora. Academic Press, London, 1974.
34. Bibel DJ, Aly R, Lahti L, Shinefield HR, Maibach HI. Microbial adherence to vulvar epithelial cells. Journal of Medical Microbiology 23:75-82 (1987).
35. Smith JM. Models in Ecology. Cambridge University Press, Cambridge, 1974.
36. Pool R. Ecologists flirt with chaos. Science 243:310-313 (1989).
37. Holmes SW. Horiokka C. Zen Art for Meditation. Tuttle, Rutland, VT, 1973.
38. Bibel DJ, Aly R, Shinefield HR, Maibach HI, Strauss WG. Importance of the keratinized epithelial cell in bacterial adherence. Journal of Investigative Dermatology 79:250-254 (1982).
39. Aly R, Shinefield (ed). Bacterial Interference. CRC Press, Boca Raton, FL, 1982.
40. Macdonald A, Smith G. (ed). The Staphylococci. Proceedings of the Alexander Ogston Centennial Conference. Aberdeen University Press, Aberdeen, Scotland, 1981.
41. Finegold SM. Interaction of antimicrobial therapy and intestinal flora. American Journal of Clinical Nutrition 23:1466-1471 (1970).
42. Hanelman SI, Hawes RR. The effect of long-term systemic antibiotic administration on the numbers of salivary organisms. Archives of Oral Biology 10:353-360 (1965).
43. Marples RR, Kligman AM. Ecological effects of oral antibiotics on the microbial flora of human skin. Archives of Dermatology 103:148-153 (1971).
44. Aly R, Maibach HI. Effect of antimicrobial soap containing chlorhexidine on the microbial flora of skin. Applied and Environmental Microbiology 31:931-935 (1976).
45. Bibel DJ. Ecologic effects of a deodorant and a plain soap upon human skin bacteria. Journal of Hygiene (Camb.) 78:1-10 (1977).
46. Bibel DJ, Lovell DJ. Skin flora maps: a tool in the study of cutaneous ecology. Journal of Investigative Dermatology 67:265-269 (1976).

Chapter 10: A sense of the whole

1. Bibel, DJ. Milestones in Immunology. A historical exploration. Science Tech/Springer Verlag, Madison, WI, 1988.
2. Silverstein. A History of Immunology. Academic Press, San Diego, 1989.
3. Needham J. China and the origins of immunology. Eastern Horizon 19(1):6-12 (1980).
4. Chernyak L, Tauber AI. Metchnikoff and the Origins of Immunology. From metaphor to theory. Oxford University Press, New York, 1991.
5. Chernyak L, Tauber AI. The birth of immunology: Metchnikoff, the embryologist. Cellular Immunology 117:218-233 (1988).
6. Loeb L. The Biological Basis of Individuality. Charles C Thomas, Springfield, IL, 1945.
7. Hamburger J. Discovering the Individual. Norton, New York, 1978.
8. Medawar PB. The Uniqueness of the Individual. Methuen, London, 1957.
9. Cooper EL (ed). Contemporary Topics in Immunobiology. Vol. 4. Invertebrate Immunology. Plenum, New York, 1974.
10. Manning MJ, Turner RJ. Comparative Immunobiology. Blackie, Glasgow, 1976.
11. Bretscher P, Cohn. A theroy of self-nonself discrimination. Science 169:1042-1049 (1970).
12. Klein J. Immunology. The science of self-nonself discrimination. Wiley, New York, 1982.
13. Langman RE. The Immune System. Evolutionary principles guide our understanding of this complex biological defense system. Academic Press, San Diego, 1989.
14. Burnet FM, Fenner F. The Production of Antibodies. 2nd ed. Macmillan, Melbourne, 1949.
15. Edleman GM. CAMs and Igs: Cell adhesion and the evolutionary origins of Immunity. Immunological Reviews 100:11-45 (1987).
16. Cunningham AJ. Gestalt immunology': a less reductionist approach to the subject. IN: Theoretical Immunology (Bell GI, Perelson AS, Pimbley GH Jr, ed). Marcel Dekker, New York, 1978. pp 45-61.
17. Cunningham AJ. Mind, body and immune response. IN: Psychoneuroimmunology (Ader R, ed). Academic Press, New York, 1981. pp 609-617.
18. Burnet M. Forward. IN: The Autoimmune Diseases (Rose NR, Mackay IR, ed). Academic Press, Orlando, 1985. pp xvii-xxii.
19. Varela FJ, Coutinho A, Dupire B, Vaz NN. Cognitive networks: immune, neural, and otherwise. IN: Theoretical Immunology, Part 2 (Perelson AS, ed). Santa Fe Institute Studies in the Sciences of Complexity, Addison-Wesley, Reading, MA, 1988. pp 359-375.
20. Perelson AS. Toward a realistic model of the immune system. IN: Theoretical Immunology, Part 2 (Perelson AS, ed). Santa Fe Institute Studies in the Sciences of Complexity, Addison-Wesley, Reading, MA, 1988. pp 377-401.
21. Shaw GB. The Doctor's Dilemma. Penguin, Baltimore, 1965.
22. Darden KAG, Streilein JW. Can a mammalian species with monomorphic class I MHC molecules succeed? IN: Paradoxes in Immunology (Hoffman GW, Levy JG, Nepom GT, ed). CRC Press, Boca Raton, FL, 1986. pp 9-26.

23. Hoffman GW. The smell of H-2. IN: Paradoxes in Immunology (Hoffman GW, Levy JG, Nepom GT, ed). CRC Press, Boca Raton, FL, 1986. pp 111-114.
24. Marx JL. Structure of MHC protein solved. Science 238:613-614 (1987).
25. Barinaga M. How the nose knows: olfactory receptor cloned. Science 252:209-210 (1991).
26. Bona Ca. Regulatory Idiotopes. Wiley, New York, 1987.
27. Chang C-Y, Kohler H. A novel chimeric antibody with circular network characteristics: autobody. Annals of the New York Academy of Science 475:114-122 (1986).
28. Marx JL. Making antibodies work like enzymes. Science 34:1497-1498 (1986).
29. Lerner RA, Benkovic SJ, Schultz PG. At the crossroads of chemistry and immunology catalytic antibodies Science 252:659-667 (1991).
30. Lefevre G, Tran D, Hoebeke J, Josso N,. Anti-idiotypic antibodies to a monoclonal antibody raised against anti-mullerian hormone exhibits anti-mullerian biological activity. Molecular and Cellular Endocrinology 62:125-133 (1989).
31. Marx JL. Making antibodies without the antigens. Science 228:162-165 (1985).
32. Kennedy RC, Eichberg JW, Lanford RE, Dreesman GR. Anti-idiotypic antibody vaccine for type B viral hepatitits in chimpanzees. Science 232:220-223 (1990).
33. Levey RH. Immunological tolerance and enhancement: a common mechanism. Transplantation Proceedings 3(1):41-48 (1971).
34. Nossal GJV. Immunologic Tolerance: collaboration between antigen and lymphokines. Science 245:147-153 (1989).
35. Linsk R, Gottesman M, Pernis B. Are tissues a patch quilt of ectopic gene expression? Science 246:261 (1989).
36. Roitt IM, Brostoff J, Male DK. Immunology. Mosby, St. Louis, 1985.
37. Beer AE, Billingham RE. The Immunobiology of Mammalian Reproduction. Prentice-Hall, Englewood Cliffs, NJ, 1976.
38. Zimmerman DR. Rh. The intimate history of a disease and its conquest. Macmillan, new York, 1973.
39. Moulin AM. The immune system: a key concept for the history of immunology. History and Philosophy of the Life Sciences 11:221-236 (1989).
40. Ader R (ed). Psychoneuroimmunology. Academic Press, New York, 1985.
41. Locke S, Ader R, Besedovsky H, Hall N, Solomon G, Strom T (ed). Foundations of Psychoneuroimmunology. Aldine, New York, 1985.
42. Bernton EW, Beach JE, Holaday JW, Smallridge RC, Fein HG. Release of multiple hormones by a direct action of itnerleukin-1 on pituitary cells. Science 238:519-521 (1987).
43. Besedovsky H, de Rey A, Sorkin E, Dinarello CA. Immunoregulatory feedback between interleukin-1 and glucocorticoid hormones. Science 233:652-654 (1986).
44. Grossman CJ. Interactions between the gonadal steroids and the immune system. Science 227:257-261 (1985).
45. Smith EM, Harbour-McMenamin D, Blalock JE. Lymphocyte production of endorphins and endorphin-mediated immunoregulary activity. Journal of Immunology 135(2/Suppl):779s-782s (1985).

46. Felten DL, Felten SY, Carlson SL, Olschowka JA, Livnat S. Noradrenergic and peptidergic innervation of lymphoid tissue. Journal of Immunology 135(2/Suppl):755s-765s (1985).
47. Gurney ME, Apatoff BR, Spear GT, Baumel MJ, Antel JP, Bania MB, Reder AT. Neuroleukin: a lymphokine product of lectin- stimulated T cells. Science 234:574-581 (1986).
48. Wechsler R. A new prescription: mind over malady. Discover (Feb):50-61 (1987).
49. Dixon R. Dangerous thoughts. Science 86 (Apr):63-66 (1986).
50. Marx JL. The immune system belongs in the body . Science 227:1190-1192 (1985).
51. Metalnikov S. Role du Systeme Nerveux et des Facteurs Biologiques et Psychiques. Masson, Paris, 1934.
52. Black S, Humphrey JH, Niven JSF. Inhibition of Mantoux reaction by direct suggestion under hypnosis. British Medical Journal i:1649-1652 (1965).
53. Good RA. Foreward: Interactions of the body's major networks. IN: Psychoneuroimmunology (Ader R, ed). Academic Press, New York, 1985.
54. Hurley TJ III. Multiple personality mirrors of a new model of mind? Investigations. Institute of Noetic Sciences 1(3/4):1-23 (1985).
55. Braun BG. Psychophysiologic phenomena in multiple personality and hypnosis. American Journal of Clinical Hypnosis 26(2):124-137 (1983).
56. Smith GR, et al. Psychological modulation of the human immune response to Varicella zoster. Archives of Internal Medicine 145:2110-2112 (1985).
57. Ghanta VK, Hiramoto RN, Solvason HB, Herbert Spector N. Neural and environmental influences on neoplasia and conditioning of NK activity. Journal of Immunology 135 2/Suppl):848s-852s (1985).
58. MacQueen G, Marshall J, Perdue M, Siegel S, Bienenstock J. Pavlovian conditioning of rat mucosal mast cells to secrete rat mast cells Protease II. Science 243:83-85 (1989).
59. O'Regan B, Hurley TJ III. Placebo The hidden asset in healing. Investigations. Institute of Noetic Sciences 2(1):1-32 (1985).
60. Mu Soen Sunim. Thousand Peaks. Korean Zen tradition and teachers. Parallax Press, Berkeley, 1987.
61. Laudenslager ML, Ryan SM, Drugan RC, Hyson RL, Maier SF. Coping and immunosuppresion: inescapable but not escapable shock suppresses lymphocyte proliferation. Science 221:568-570 (1983).
62. Liang Z, Ji L. Mastering the Art of War (Cleary T, transl). Shambhala, Boston, 1989.
63. Pert CB, Ruff MR, Weber RJ, Herkenham M. Neuropeptides and their receptors: a psychosomatic network. Journal of Immunology 135 (2/Suppl):820s-826s (1985).
64. Pert C. Neuropeptides: the emotions and bodymind. Noetic Sciences Review 2:13-18 (Spring 1987).
65. Roth J, LeRoith D, Collier ES, Weaver NR, Watkinson A, Cleland CF, Glick SM. Evolutionary origins of neuropeptides, hormones, and receptors: possible applications to immunology. Journal of Immunology 135 (2/Suppl):816s-826s (1985).

66. Chang GCC. The Buddhist Teaching of Totality. The philosophy of Hwa Yen Buddhism. Pennsylvania State University Press, University Park, PA, 1971.

Chapter 11: Singing the body electric

1. Kasulis TP. Zen Action, Zen Person. University of Hawaii Press, Honolulu, 1985.
2. Tanahashi K (ed). Moon in a Dewdrop. Writings of Zen Master Dogen. North Point Press, San Francisco, 1985.
3. Stent G. Limits to the scientific understanding of man. Science 187:1052-1057 (1975).
4. Medawar P. The Limits of Science. Oxford University Press, Oxford, 1987.
5. Metzner R (ed). Psychedelics Revisited. ReVISION 10(4):1-72 (1988).
6. Holden C. Twins reunited. Science 80 November:55-59 (1980).
7. Holden C. The genetics of personality. Science 237:598-601 (1987).
8. Begley S, Murr A, Springen K, Gordon J, Harrison J. All about twins. Newsweek (November 23):58-69 (1987).
9. Farger SL. Identical Twins Reared Apart. A reanalysis. Basic Books, New York, 1981.
10. Bouchard TJ Jr, Lykken DT, McGue M, Segal NL, Tellegen A. Sources of human psychological differences: The Minnesota study of twins reared apart. Science 250:223-228.
11. Schave B, Ciriello J:. Identity and Intimacy in Twins. Praeger, New York, 1983.
12. Holroyd S. Psi and the Consciousness Explosion. Taplinger, New York, 1977.
13. Watson L. Beyond Supernature. Bantam, New York, 1988.
14. Targ R, Harary K. The Mind Race. Understanding and using psychic abilities. Villard, New York, 1984.
15. Jahn RG, Dunne BJ. Margins of Reality. The role of consciousness in the physical world. Harcourt Brace Jovanovich, San Diego, 1987.
16. Lichenstein H. The Dilemma of Human Identity. Jason Aronson, New York, 1977.
17. Wilber K (ed). Quantum Questions. Mystical writings of the world's great physicists. Shambhala, Boulder, 1984.
18. Assagioli R. Self-realization and psychological disturbances. ReVISION 8:21-31 (1986).
19. Hofstadter DR. Godel, Escher, Bach: an eternal golden braid. Basic Books, New York, 1979.
20. Stevens CF. The neuron. Scientific American 241(3):55-65 (1979).
21. Becker RO, Selden G. The Body Electric. Electromagnetism and the Foundation of Life. Morrow, New York, 1985.
22. Cornell-Bell AH, Finkbeiner SM, Cooper MS, Smith SJ. Glutamate induces calcium waves in cultured astrocytes: long-range glial signaling. Science 247:470-473 (1990).
23. Barinaga M. Is nitric oxide the Eretrograde messenger? Science 54:1296-1297 (1991).

24. Deyo RA, Straube KT, Disterhoft JF. Nimodipine facilitates associative learning in aging rabbits. Science 243:809-811 (1989).

25. Needham J. Science in Traditional China. A comparative perspective. Harvard University Press, Cambridge MA, 1981.

26. Aoki C, Siekevitz P. Plasticity in brain development. Scientific American 259(6):56-64.

27. Miller KD, Keller JB, Stryker MP. Ocular dominance column development analysis and simulation. Science 245:605-615 (1989).

28. Cowan WM, Fawcett JW, O'Leary DDM, Stanfield BB. Regressive events in neurogenesis. Science 225:1258-1265 (1984).

29. Dodd J, Jessell TM. Axon guidance and the patterning of neuronal projections in vertebrates. Scinece 242:692-699 (1988).

30. Meister M, Wong ROL, Baylor DA, Shatz CJ Synchronous bursts of action potentials in ganglion cells of the developing mammalian retina. Science 252:939-943 (1991).

31. Cotman CW, Nieto-Sampedro M. Cell biology of synaptic plasticity. Science 225:1287-1294 (1984).

32. Purves D, Voyvodic JT, Magrassi L, Yawo H. Nerve terminal remodeling visualized in living mice by repeated examination of the same neuron. Science 238:1122-1126 (1987).

33. Palca J. Famous monkeys provide surprising results. Science 252:1789; 1857-1860 (1991).

34. von der Heydt R, Peterhans E, Baumgartner G. Illusory contours and cortical neuron responses. Science 224:1260-1262 (1984).

35. Winckelgren I. How the brain 'sees' borders where there are none. Science 256:1520-1521 (1992).

36. Wise SP, Desimone R. Behavioral neurophysiology: insights into seeing and grasping. Science 242:736-741 (1988).

37. Begley S, Carey J, Sawhill R. How the brain works. Newsweek (February 7):40-47 (1983).

38. Squire LR, Mechanisms of memory. Science 232:1612-1619 (1986).

39. Zola-Morgan SM, Squire LR. The primate hippocampal formation: evidence for a time-limited role in memory storage. Science 250:288-290 (1990).

40. Sperry R. Some effects of disconnecting the cerebral hemispheres. Science 217:1223-1226 (1982).

41. Hamilton CR, Vermeire BA. Complementary hemisphere specialization in monkeys. Science 242:1691-1694 (1988).

42. Gazzaniga MS. Organization of the human brain. Science 245:947-952 (1989).

43. Kosslyn SM. Aspects of a cognitive neuroscience of mental imagery. Science 240:1621-1626 (1988).

44. Hall ET. Beyond Culture. Anchor Press/Doubleday, Garden City, 1977.

45. Posner MI, Petersen SE, Fox PT, Raichle ME. Localization of cognitive operations in the human brain. Science 240:1627-1631 (1988).

46. Kihlstrom JF. The cognitive unconscious. Science 237:1445-1452 (1987).

47. LaBerge, S. Lucid Dreaming. Ballantine, New York, 1986.

48. Suzuki S. Zen Mind, Beginner's Mind. Weatherhill, New York, 1970.

49. Bankei. The Unborn. The life and teaching of Zen Master Bankei 1622-1693 (Waddell N, transl). North Point Press, San Francisco, 1984.

324 ■ REFERENCES

50. Wilber K (ed). The Holographic Paradigm and Other Paradoxes. Shambhala, Boulder, 1982.
51. Hubel DH. The brain. Scientific American 241(3):45-53 (1979).
52. Hofmann A. The transmitter-receiver concept of reality. ReVISION 10(4):5-11 (1988).
53. Sheldrake R. A New Science of Life. The hypothesis of formative causation. Tarcher, Los Angeles, 1981.
54. Hippocrates. The Sacred Disease. Hippocrates. Vol 2 (Jones WHS, transl). Harvard University Press, Cambridge, MA, 1952.

Chapter 12: A moon-pointing finger

1. Eddington A. Nature of the Physical World. Cambridge University Press, Cambridge, 1928.
2. Wald G. The cosmology of life and mind. Noetic Sciences Review, Spring 1989:10-15 (1989).
3. Bateson G. Mind and Nature. A necessary unity. Bantam, Toronto, 1980.
4. Jantsch E. The Self-Organizing Universe. Scientific and human implications of the emerging paradigm of evolution. Pergamon Press, Oxford,, 1980.
5. Watson L. Beyond Supernature. Bantam, New York, 1988.
6. Dossey L. Recovering the Soul. A scientific and spiritual search. Bantam, New York, 1989.
7. Targ R, Harary K. The Mind Race. Understanding and using psychic abilities. Villard, New York, 1984.
8. Jahn RG, Dunne BJ. Margins of Reality. The role of consciousness in the physical world. Harcourt Brace Jovanovich, San Diego, 1987.
9. Holroyd S. Psi and the Consciousness Explosion. Taplinger, New York, 1977.
10. Bateson G, Bateson MC. Angels Fear. Towards an epistemology of the sacred. Macmillan, New York, 1987.
11. Fisk D. Dr.Jenner of Berkeley. Heinemann, London, 1959.
12. Zohar D. Through the Time Barrier. A study of precognition and modern physics. Paladin, London, 1983.
13. Libet B, Wright EW Jr, Feinstein B, Pearl DK. Subjective referral of the timing for a conscious sensory experience. A functional role for the somatosensory specific projection system in man. Brain 102:193-224 (1979).
14. Libet B. Conscious subjective experience vs unconscious mental functions: a theory of the cerebral processes involved. IN: Models of Brain Function (Cotterill RMJ, ed). Cambridge University Press, Cambridge, 1989. pp 35-49.
15. Libet B. Neural destiny. Does the brain have a will of its own? The Sciences 29:32-35 (Mar-Apr 1989); 29:10-11 (Sep-Oct 1989).
16. Govinda A. Creative Meditation and Multi-Dimensional Consciousness. Quest, Wheaton, IL, 1976.
17. Shallis M. On Time. An investigation into scientific knowledge and human experience. Schocken, New York, 1982.
18. Barinaga M. The mind revealed? Science 249:856-858 (1990).

19. Grinberg-Zylberbaum J, Ramos J. Patterns of interhemispheric correlation during human communication. International Journal of Neruoscience 36:41-53 (1987).
20. Jung CG. Synchronicity. An acausal connecting principle (Hull RFC, transl). Princeton University Press, Princeton, NJ, 1973.
21. Jung CG. The Archetypes and the Collective Unconscious. Vol 9, Part 1. The Collected Works of C.G. Jung (Read H, Fordham M, Adler G, ed). Princeton University Press, Princeton, NJ, 1968.
22. Pauli W. The influence of archetypal ideas on the scientific theories of Kepler (Silz P, transl). IN: The interpretation of Nature and the Psyche. Bollingen Foundation, New York, 1955.
23. Wilber K (ed). Quantum Questions. Mystical writings of the world's great physicists. Shambhala, Boulder, 1984.
24. Bibel DJ, Aly R, Conant MA, Shinefield HR. From HIV infection to AIDS: changes in the microbial ecology of skin and nose. Microbial Ecology in Health and Disease 4:9-17 (1991).
25. Kapleau P (ed). The Wheel of Death. Harper & Row, New York, 1971.
26. Sacks O. Awakenings. Dutton, New York, 1983.
27. Born M. The Born-Einstein Letters. Walker, New York, 1971.
28. Stevenson I. Children Who Remember Previous Lives. A question of reincarnation. University Press of Virginia, Charlottesville, 1987.
29. Stevenson I. Unlearned Language. New studies in xenoglossy. University Press of Virginia, Charlottesville, 1984.
30. Keyes N. The Minds of Billy Milligan. Random House, New York, 1981.
31. Stevenson I. Xenoglossy: a review and report of a case. Proceedings of the American Society for Psychical Research 31(2):1-268 (1974).
32. Blyth RH. Zen and Zen Classics. Vol 1. Hokuseido Press, Tokyo, 1982.
33. Shibayama Z. Zen Comments on the Mumonkan (Kudo S, transl). Harper & Row, San Francisco, 1984.
34. Chung-Yuan C. (ed). Original Teachings of Ch'an Buddhism. Grove Press, New York, 1982.